BOOF
AROUND IN
ES

1

BOOEY
AROUND IN CIRCLES

By ERIC BOOCOCK

With Martin Neal

First published in English in August 2006 by
Retro Speedway
Tel: 01708 734 502
www.retro-speedway.com

©Copyright Retro Speedway & Eric Boocock

Printed by Biddles Ltd, King's Lynn, Norfolk

Distributed by Retro Speedway
103 Douglas Road, Hornchurch, Essex, RM11 1AW, England
Email: editorial@retro-speedway.com

Set in Times Roman

ISBN 0-9551176-6-4

Cover photography by Mike Patrick & R. S. Oliver

The views expressed in this book are those of Eric Boocock
and not necessarily those of the publisher.

This book is dedicated to my wife Diane,
my son Ritchie and my daughter Sallie.

Contents

Acknowledgements

As well as my family, I'd also like to say a huge thank you to Terry Warren whose research has been invaluable, to Martin Neal for all his hard work, to Elf Oils and Lewis Leathers for their sponsorship during my racing days, to Gary Barlow of GB Fencing and not forgetting all the promoters who let me ride on their tracks!

Many of the photographs used in the book were kindly given to me, many moons ago, by those doyen of speedway snappers, the late Wright Wood (his collection now courtesy of John Somerville) and R.S. Oliver, who were very much a part of the Northern scene in particular – in fact, Wright covered my riding career in pictures from beginning to end.

My publisher and I would also like to thank others for their excellent work behind the camera lens: Alf Weedon, Mike Patrick, Ken Carpenter, John Hipkiss, Martin King (Australia), Trevor Meeks (courtesy of John Somerville), Ray Liddy, the late Don Ringrow, Halifax Courier and Bradford Telegraph & Argus, Dave Fairbrother and Graham Platten, plus any other photographers or agencies whose pics we may have used and which we have not been able to credit individually.

Two sides of the fence . . . Eric and Peter Collins as rivals (above) before the 1974 British Final at Coventry.
Below: Manager and No.1 enjoying happy times at Belle Vue.

Foreword
By Peter Collins MBE

IT is impossible to over-emphasise the massive influence Eric Boocock had on my career and I felt honoured when asked to contribute this foreword to his book.

Eric was my boss and team manager at Belle Vue for seven years, and later he and Ian Thomas managed England to its only World Championship grand slam, so we've seen a lot of each other over the years and are still good mates today.

We had some great times together with both Belle Vue and England but Eric was also a tremendous help to me on an individual, one-to-one basis too.

I've read the chapters from this book that relate to the help he gave me at both the 1976 and 1977 World Finals and, take it from me, he has very much underplayed his own role in my achievements. Modesty has obviously forbidden him from telling just how much work he did behind the scenes in the pits at Katowice on what was the biggest day in my speedway career.

Apart from respecting Eric for what he had done himself as a top rider for Halifax and England over a very long period, I also trusted him implicitly. Later on in the book, Eric says that the work he did on my clutch between my five rides in Poland made little difference to me becoming World Champion, but I can assure you it did. With all due respect to my mechanics, who were very good, I fully trusted Eric and when he said he would take the clutch plates out after each of my rides, clean them and re-assemble them again, I was happy to let him get on with it. The clutch was better for the work he'd done on it and with him looking after my interests in the pits, it meant that all I had to do between heats was relax and focus on the next race. I was happy for Eric to have the final word on any mechanical issues at the 1976 World Final.

What most people won't know is that Eric also shielded me from potential worries in the Katowice pits that afternoon. The Poles, clearly trying to throw a spanner in the works, had put in a protest, questioning the fuel I was using in my Weslake. They even took a sample away for analysis. As it happened, I got my fuel from the same communal drum that all the other riders used that day, so there was never a chance that I'd done anything illegally.

But it's to Eric's credit I wasn't even aware of any protest going in about me until after the meeting, because he'd kept all that nonsense away from me, he'd protected me from the situation. The first I knew of it was when an FIM official came up to me at the end of the final and gave me a test tube containing a sample of my fuel – and then told me I was in the clear! Booey did me proud in Poland.

Eric was with me all the way again the following year, when my defence of the title was effectively wrecked by that drain cover which crashed against my shin at Hyde Road just six days before the World Final in Gothenburg. He got on to Sir Charles Forte, the boss of Belle Vue owners Trust House Forte, and arranged for the use of his private jet to fly myself, my wife Angela, Eric and Jack Fearnley out to Sweden at the last possible moment.

He arranged for a Swedish doctor to come and examine me on our arrival at the hotel in Gothenburg – I had some 250 stitches in my leg – and, although I'd missed the previous day's official practice, Eric took me to the Ullevi Stadium the next morning so that I could get a look at the track. He found an old stretcher on a trolley and wheeled me round the circuit so that I could check it out – I lent forward and poked the track surface with one of my crutches!

It didn't quite work out for me on a very, very wet night but we had a good go at it and, again, I had a lot to thank Eric for in helping me to at least finish second to Ivan Mauger.

The first I knew of Eric was in my days as a young fan of Belle Vue in the 60s, when he was the undisputed No.1 at Halifax and one of the top English riders along with his brother, Nigel, Ray Wilson, Martin Ashby and Terry Betts. My dad always took me to home meetings at Hyde Road but I'd go with my mates and their fathers to the away matches on northern tracks, like Sheffield and Halifax, which were closest to us. I guess I must have been cheering for Aces stars like Soren Sjosten and Cyril Maidment to beat Booey but they never seemed to get the better of him round that awesome, banked track and I can't remember ever seeing Belle Vue win at The Shay when I was a young supporter. Chris Pusey came on the scene in the late 60s and he used to complain about the Halifax track, but it wasn't until I rode there myself in the early 70s that I realised what a good track it was to race on. In fact, one of my first maximums in the British League, after moving up from Rochdale to Belle Vue, was at Halifax . . . and I managed to beat Eric twice to score a maximum! I don't remember him making any funny or sarcastic comments to me – knowing him, he would have taken those defeats like a man.

It was an honour to be asked by Eric to ride in his testimonial meeting in 1974 – we all gladly rode for nothing in recognition of the very loyal service he'd given Halifax in particular and the sport in general. The Shay was heaving that day, you couldn't have got another supporter in the place. He was the first British rider ever to be awarded a testimonial meeting and it set a trend that a number of us have since gratefully benefited from.

When England became a major force again from 1973 onwards, I was part of a very successful new era when Eric's own riding career was coming to an end – but he still had a massive part to play in my development. In fact, he provided the final piece in the jigsaw that, I believe, turned me into the rider I became in the mid-70s when I reached my peak.

I can't remember the exact details of the meeting – it may have been a Test match or a league fixture for Belle Vue – but I was riding at Ipswich one Thursday night and then at Hackney the following evening. To avoid having to drive all the way back to Manchester, Eric, my mechanic Steve and I stayed overnight in a bed and breakfast in Ipswich. After the meeting at Foxhall Heath, we went for a Chinese meal before retiring to our B&B – the three of us all crammed into one room.

We were just chatting away, as you do, late at night and Eric was his usual self – a laugh-a minute – when we suddenly got talking about speedway in more serious term. What Eric said to me that night had a profound effect on me and my career from that point onwards.

He impressed on me the importance of hard work and thorough preparation of my machinery in the workshop. He explained, in detail, how to strip down everything on the bike and how to clean and maintain certain parts of the engine properly.

I must admit, I'd been a bit hit and miss in that respect until our chat, believing that pure riding ability would win through, but everything he said made good sense. I learned a lot just by listening to him and took everything he said on board.

Although I had no influence on Eric joining Belle Vue as manager in 1975, I was delighted that he did because it suited me perfectly. His experience and knowledge guaranteed him the respect of all the riders and we were a very happy team with him around. His arrival was certainly one of the best things to ever happen to me. Apart from the advice he'd give the riders, Eric would always carry a set of overalls with him, so he could help out mechanically too if required. He was never afraid to get his hands dirty for the cause.

He was a fantastic team manager and very unfortunate not to win the BL championship during his time at Hyde Road. He treated everybody the same and always said to us: "We win as a team and we lose as a team." He would never have a go at riders and he got the best out of all of us, but in a nice way. He didn't call team meetings – I don't remember us ever having one – but it was enough for him to simply say to us that we were representing the biggest and best speedway club in the world. He didn't get heavy with any riders, or issue ultimatums like: 'Win this one or you'll be out on your ear', as some modern-day managers seem to do.

Eric would also occasionally get involved with his riders socially and I've enjoyed some great days with him riding our trials bikes on Mick Grant's farm. Eric's got speedway and motorcycles in his blood, although we shouldn't forget that behind every great man there's a great woman – and I know how much Eric must appreciate all the support he's had from Diane and their children, Ritchie – who was our mascot at Belle Vue – and Sallie. I've regretted not seeing more of Eric and his lovely family and I intend to put that right in the future.

I expect this book to reflect Eric's approach to life in calling a spade a spade – he's in that mould of forthright sporting heroes from Yorkshire who include Harvey Smith, Geoff Boycott and Brian Close. But Eric coming from the opposite side of the Pennines to me has never been a problem – I'm not a racist!

After all, I know just how much Eric Boocock did to help make me the rider I was.

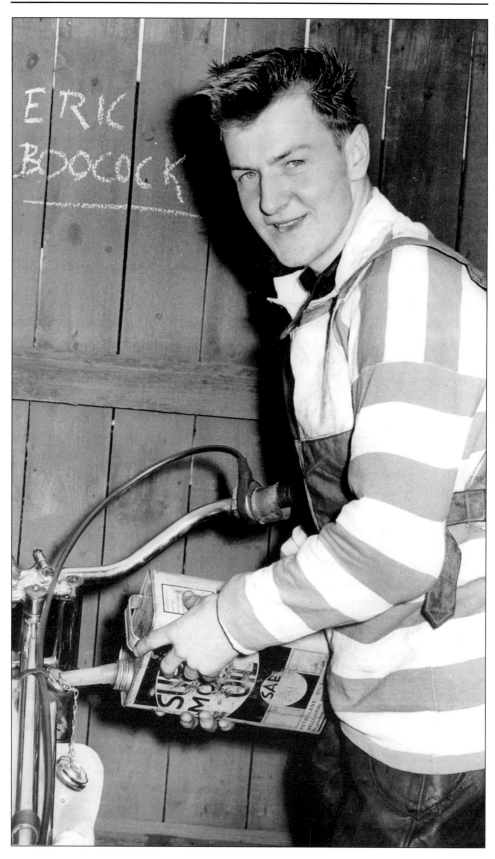

1

ACTING THE GOAT

FOR 45 years the sport of speedway has been my life. I've beaten – and been beaten by – the best of them, ridden all over the world and taken England to the very top of the tree as a manager. I'm still as passionate about it today as I was as a kid and if someone transported me back to when I was 16, I'd do it all over again.

But after an exciting and mischievous childhood which was jam-packed full of action and adventure, I suppose my love affair with a thrill-a-minute sport like speedway was inevitable. I had an unbelievably great time as a kid and I'm certain that the capers we got up to back then shaped the way I lived my adult life. So before I start telling the story of Eric Boocock the speedway rider, I'd like to give a little insight into Eric Boocock the schoolboy.

I grew up in a tiny village called Coxley, near Wakefield in West Yorkshire. It was a dead end into the village and at the bottom there was a footpath through the woods to the textiles mill where my dad was manager. There were only 18 houses in the village and there were only four lads my age, and I don't think there were any girls. So if anything went wrong, we got the blame.

We were buggeroos – all of us! We weren't ever guilty of any wilful damage. We wouldn't ever smash anyone's windows or anything like that, we'd just be larking around like kids do. But we were full of tricks and if anything went wrong in the village, it would be one of us who had done it.

This was in the days before electric street lights had reached our neck of the woods and there was only one gas lamp in the whole village, so on mischief night we'd play pranks like jumping out at people from the dark with a blanket over our heads. Sometimes we would even pee down people's chimneys too! But we had to make our own fun. There were no televisions in the village then and the only time I'd ever seen TV was round at my aunty's house for the coronation. There were about 30 of us crammed into her living room to watch it. So, you see, we had to make our own entertainment in those days.

At the bottom of the village, just past the mill where my father worked, there was a big wood and in the school holidays our parents would have to come and get us to bring us in every night for the whole six weeks. We used to have great fun rebuilding the mill dam and then we would swim in it. We used to build underground dens and make fires to cook the trout we had caught in the stream.

I always loved pushbikes and, during the summer, I used to cycle the 70 miles over to my auntie's in Scarborough and have a week's holiday there. There was an old pushbike shop in the next village, Horbury Bridge, where my mates and I would go to get an old frame for a kids' bike and attach two wheels and handlebars, although there would be no crank in it and no chain. We used to carry these bikes up to Netherton Primary School and hide them in a garden, because it was downhill all the way back through the woods. We used to come down there on the bikes and see who could go the fastest. Once, we got reported for nearly killing a coalminer as we raced down the hill! He was a cantankerous old bugger and he complained that we were dangerous . . . which, to be fair, was right because we had no brakes so we couldn't stop! In our defence, we used to shout at him to shift but he was a bit deaf so he couldn't hear us, but we had some near misses before the school banned the bikes – well, our type of bike anyway!

One winter, I think it was 1957, we had really bad snow. It was over our heads. There were snowdrifts everywhere. So we built a sledging track and built a ramp to go up over the wall. One of the lads was called Ian Rose and his uncle was in charge of all the lighting in the local pit, which is now the National Coalmining Museum for England. The lamps were in a battery pack and the miners used to clip them to their helmets, but we had our own way of using them. Ian's uncle used to bring six battery packs and six lamps home from work and we would place them down the sledging track because there were no other lights. Sometimes we would fasten three or four sledges together and have a big chain. It was a really great laugh and we used to do it night after night until the snow melted.

We had an absolutely enormous amount of fun. I didn't want to go to school because I had so much fun doing other things, although I never bunked off because my mother would have killed me. She was very strict, my mother, but great fun. Daisy was her name. If she said you had to be home by 11 o'clock, she didn't mean five past! And I'm talking when I was 17 or 18!

My father's name was Carl and he lived for the mill where he worked. The mill made industrial cleaning cloths to supply Vickers Armstrong in Barrow-in-Furness who would order 200 gross a month. When I was a kid I used to help out there, and my dad used to infuriate me. He would say: "After dinner you could just do to do this or that." That was his phrase – you could just do to do it. I used to say: "Dad, haven't you got any more staff in this bloody place? Why me?" He would tell me: "Because you're the floater – the jack of all trades." But he never ever got cross, my dad. If I told him I wasn't doing it, he's say: "Don't do it then". And guess who would be doing it after dinner? That's right – my dad. My dad lived for the mill. Even when he retired he did another 13 years. He couldn't keep away. He would come up for his tea and then say: "I've just got to finish a little job," and my mother would say: "Go on then, bugger off!"

I was the youngest of four children – I was a mistake, my mother used to tell me. Nina was the eldest and I have another sister called Elaine. In between them, Nigel was born. I think you've probably heard of him!

While I was at primary school, I passed my 11-plus so I went to Ossett Grammar School, which I really didn't like. Nigel had been there too – and I remember the first time I got into trouble I was sent to the headmaster and he said: "Oh no, not another Boocock!"

My interest in motorised fun can be traced to my grandfather, Henry, who had the first motorcycle and sidecar in Wakefield. He had one even before the local police force did, and my father and him used to do a lot of motorcycle trials. Everyone knew my grandad. He was a right character. My father must have inherited some of those genes because he used to enter motorcycle trials and there were always bikes around the place – many in various states of repair, or disrepair in a lot of cases.

But it was my Uncle Ernest who got Nigel started in speedway – Ernest Whitwam. He wasn't actually an uncle at all but that's what we used to call him because he was so close to the family. We didn't own a car, but he had a Riley 9 sportscar and used to take Nigel to speedway.

Where we grew up in Coxley we had a smallholding of about three acres. You could pick up a bike for about £3 in those days and there weren't the problems there are these days with noise and neighbours, so we could ride out there virtually morning, noon and night until we'd run out of petrol and had no money to put any more in the tank.

Then the coal board outcropped the land, along with the adjoining 12 acres and, while they were at it, they built us a speedway track for us to play on. This was 1956 and Nigel hadn't long got started in the sport, but it wasn't for him to practice on – it was a place for us to enjoy ourselves. We were surrounded by junk and motorcycles so we used to use old bikes and put speedway tyres on to get more grip.

It was through Nigel that I became interested in speedway, although I'm not entirely sure how it evolved. I remember that after the outcrop had gone we built another track down by the stream. If any of us got into any trouble, we ended up in the water! The top half of the field was quite rough but it had two fantastic corners. Along with my friend John Dews – who also went on to become a speedway rider – I sourced a couple of bikes, spending two quid here and three quid there to build them up.

"Once we got reported for nearly killing a coalminer as we raced down the hill. He was a cantankerous old bugger and complained that we were dangerous"

I could go faster going left than right. I was only 14 or 15, Nigel had just started riding and I remember thinking: "This is alright turning these corners. I like this." You could lean the bike right over because it was tacky and sticky, and my dad used to lend us a stopwatch so we could time each other and see who would go the quickest.

We were acting the goat, that's all we were doing. But Nigel was riding by then so when it came to the school holidays I would go to loads of meetings. He used to take me all over the country and he got to the World Final as reserve in 1956 even though he hadn't been riding all that long. Needless to say, we were all there for that one, making our way to London on a chartered Speedway Special train which left from Bradford.

I remember going to Southampton in a VW Beetle with Nigel and Arthur Forrest. We stopped in the New Forest in a bed and breakfast. We saw all these shoes outside the doors and Nigel and Arthur mixed them all up for a laugh! I'd never seen that – I didn't know you left your shoes outside your door to be cleaned before morning. I was 14 so it was a different world for me as a youngster.

Nigel would use me as a decoy so he could go and see his girlfriends. He was twice as bad as me – a complete buggeroo. To be kind to him, you would class him now as a wild child. When he started riding and doing well, he was a good-looking young lad who attracted plenty of girlfriends. He used to tell me we going to Bradford for something or the other and we would go there all right, but not to see who he'd told my mother! So he used to say I could go to the next meeting with him if I didn't say anything. It was good fun for me too because I was part of the plot against my mum.

I didn't have any particular speedway heroes but there were some good riders in those days – Briggo, Ove Fundin, Peter Craven, Ron How and Geoff Mardon. They were at the top of the tree back then and, believe me, they were hard lads. They had to be because the league matches in those days were really tough. The riders used to knock shit out of one another! That said, it wasn't as dangerous as it was today because they weren't going as fast. The difference was that in those days the riders were getting grip. There was shale on the tracks, whereas these days they are as slick as a board and the engines rev twice as fast as the old JAPs, and certainly much easier to ride.

There was an eight-year age difference between Nigel and me, which is quite a lot when you're that age. He was a man and I was still a boy, but at that time we had a good relationship. I can't ever remember a date when I thought: "I want to be a speedway rider" though. It just evolved.

Although I used to travel around with Nigel, he had his own spanner man, Roy Adams, helping him right from when he joined Coventry. But I had a little pair of overalls and I would help out Jack Young, the legendary Australian rider who twice won the World Championship. When I say help out, it was a bit of fuel, a bit of oil and cleaning goggles, nothing more. Before he went out for a race he would light a fag and balance it on the edge of his toolbox. When he came back into the pits he could just get two more draws out of it. One piece of advice he gave me was: "The idea is to get to the finishing flag first – not how fast you can get there." He was quite right too – as I later discovered, you could win races without busting a gut to go fast. If someone is a fair way behind, you can give your engines a breather and not work yourself as hard, yet still get the same points. He was a lovely bloke and when I went to Australia I used to stay at his house.

With Nigel doing well, I decided I wanted a piece of the action too. Nigel and my dad built a bike out of bits – a 'bitsa' we called it – but it was a proper speedway bike and I would take it out on the track we'd made at the bottom of the field. After the bikes we'd had before, this one was bloody quick! It was a 500cc single JAP and I felt mighty proud of it.

Around this time, Frank Varey, who was the promoter at Sheffield, used to call in at my mum and dad's because they made dishcloths and mop heads at the mill. He would bring jars of jam and honey and we had a bit of an exchange. I asked him if

I could have a practice at Owlerton. He said: "If you can get to the stadium in the mornings before I get there to do the track, you can practise." So my dad, who had a little Ford van by then, used to take me and John Dews over to Sheffield on a Friday and we had to leave at six in the morning. We needed my dad to do the honours because neither John nor I was allowed to drive, although in truth I'd driven millions of miles by then. Sometimes when I'd gone to meetings with Nigel, he'd say: "You can drive back if you like." I was only 15 – but I didn't refuse!

When we arrived at Owlerton, we would snap the lock on the big pit gate, which is still the pit gate today. We knew we could pull the lock really hard and get in because Frank had told us! We would let ourselves in, park on the centre green and would roll round the track at 6.30 in the morning. Even though it was so early, no-one ever complained.

Frank was an absolute fanatic about his track. It was his baby and he would arrive at the stadium at about ten-past seven. He would watch for a bit and talk to my dad. He'd say: "Four more laps and that's it." We would say: "Go on, Frank just four more." He would let us do another four and then we'd ask him again. He would say: "Oh, go on then," and we would be off again. When we finally had to leave we'd head off and go straight to work – already looking forward to the following Friday morning and our next ride around Sheffield.

I was working in the mill by this time, although I went to college in the evenings and qualified as a textiles engineer. I'd left grammar school at 15 because I hated it. There was too much other stuff going on around me. Nigel was doing really well and he went to Sweden to ride one year. It's just a hop on a plane these days, but back then you had to look on the map to see where he'd been. It was a lot more glamorous than being at grammar school. I didn't stay at school long enough to find out how I had done and I didn't sit any exams.

I hated grammar school, probably because it was too regimented. As soon as you

With the great Frank Varey, who literally opened the door to my career at Sheffield on Friday mornings.

stepped out onto the drive leading up to the school, you had to wear your school cap. If you were caught not wearing it, you got detention. You had to wear your blazer and have it fastened, bring all your books and have a satchel. Even at that age I didn't like that stuck-up authority.

The first week I was there I was put in detention – and there wasn't one week, in the entire time I was there from the age of 11 to 15, that I wasn't kept back for detention. But it was never for anything serious, just for things like being late for a class or being caught jumping over the school wall to get a bag of chips at dinner time.

One teacher I remember had a great party piece – he could draw two horses, completely symmetrical – on the blackboard at the same time with a piece of chalk in each hand. He threw a rubber at me in one lesson – I threw it back, so that was another detention. Another time I got detention when some friends and I got caught after finding our way into one of the three big air-raid shelters that were in the grounds. They hadn't been open since the end of the war but we were in there every lunchtime running around with some flashlights and tin hats we had found in there – until we got caught. I couldn't wait to leave school, and on my last day there I staged my final act of defiance. You were supposed to push your bikes on the way out until you had gone through the gates, but I rode mine down the full length of the school drive with my hands off the handlebars and my cap on backwards. When I got to the end I stopped, took my cap off and hung it on the gates.

Looking back, I realise that school was important and that I should have got some qualifications in case it all went pear-shaped. But, although I wasn't a particularly good pupil, I did well at sports, metalwork and woodwork. I also appreciate now that a grammar school education stood me in good stead – my general knowledge, spelling and letter-writing skills certainly stem from it.

At the age of 15, I was working 48 hours a week at the mill and I used to bring home ten shillings – 50p in today's money. My mum used to keep half and give me half back. With that money I used to go out to the Mecca Ballroom dancing every Sunday night. I went there on my motorbike which was a 650cc Matchless which cost me the princely sum of £10, and, if it was wet I used to put polythene bags over my shoes so I wouldn't get splattered up. Petrol was 1s 11d a gallon, which is less than 10p, so I could last all week on five shillings.

I had my first ride on a speedway track under the lights at Coventry after their last meeting of the 1960 season. Our Nigel always used to call me Young Un and I always called him Young Un, even though he was older than me – I've really no idea why! So, after my big moment, he came up to me and said: "Young Un, you we flying, you were unbelievable." I was really pleased until he added: "But I'm going faster when I'm going up to the starting tapes!" I thought one day, I'll show you.

As my birthday is in February, I knew I would be old enough to ride at the start of the next season. With a bike and a pair of two-piece leathers – complete with three-inch wide braces to hold the trousers up – and kitted out with a speedway bike of my own, I was on my way . . .

2

I THINK WE'D BETTER SIGN YOUR BROTHER

S TARTING my speedway career at Middlesbrough was the best thing I could have done – if you could cope with the bumps at Cleveland Park, you could ride anywhere.

I joined the Bears, who were members of the Provincial League at that time, in 1961 and stayed there until I joined Halifax at the start of 1965. It all began when I turned 16 and I had a couple of second halves at Middlesbrough. Maurice Morley was the Boro team manager and he and Nigel had a business together repossessing HP cars, so I got to know him through my brother.

These days you can get from Wakefield to Middlesbrough in about 45 minutes, but back then, before the motorways were built, it was a two-and-a-half-hour trek all round the houses, but Maurice was a very good driver. The first time he picked me up and took me to Cleveland Park, we went up on spec and he said he would get me my first ride that night. We got there and, although I had put the bitsa bike in the boot, I didn't have my leathers. I forgot those, the scatterbrain I was in those days. I borrowed a bike from Vic Lonsdale – or 'Wild Man Vic' as they called him. His heart was in the right place, but he just couldn't ride! May 4, 1961 that was, and I found myself lining up for the second heat of the reserves' scurry in the second half of the Middlesbrough v Plymouth match – and I won it!

To be honest, I really don't remember it now. I know I won it, and that I reached the final, but I couldn't tell you who else was in that race. What I do know is that I would have been really chuffed and I know I would have been nervous. In fact, I was nervous right until the very last race of my whole career. Nigel was worse still and could be physically sick before a meeting. Even now when I ride trials, which is pure fun at an amateur level, I still get so nervous you wouldn't believe it. It takes me about an hour to settle down.

That night was the start of a 14-year relationship with Reg Fearman because I didn't ever ride for anyone else. Reg was the promoter at Cleveland Park, along with Mike Parker. He saw me ride and said to Nigel: "I think we'd better sign your brother on a contract." Well, I didn't know what a contract was! But Nigel told me it would be a good idea so I signed for Middlesbrough.

I wasn't in the team, but I was on their books. I had been asking Frank Varey at Sheffield if I could have a ride there, but he kept telling me he didn't think I was ready. Then one week he told me he finally thought I was ready to have a ride – so I said: "I think you'd better ask Mr Fearman because I've signed a contract with

Middlesbrough." Frank flipped! He went mad and actually banned me from the stadium. "Don't come back," he told me, he was that cross. But I was only a kid and I was very timid. I told him I had been asking for a while but he couldn't give me a ride, so I went to Middlesbrough instead.

The following Thursday night I wasn't riding at Middlesbrough, which gave me the chance to watch Sheffield, as I did regularly in those days. Frank saw me paying to get in – and gave me another roasting. I daren't try and get in through the back way after what he'd said to me a week earlier, but he told me: "Don't you ever pay to get into this stadium again!" So that was it – we had made up, which was lovely.

As it turned out, my mate John Dews ended up signing for Sheffield. It was a shame in a way because we had gone to the same junior school and grown up together. We practiced together and our families were good friends. My sister even ended up marrying his brother. But we both signed for Thursday night tracks, which meant we couldn't go to meetings with each other.

I lived to regret borrowing a bike from Vic Lonsdale on that first night, though. Later on that season we were up at Newcastle. The riders were on two minutes and he couldn't get his bike to start. He asked if he could borrow mine, as I owed him a favour. I let him borrow it, of course, but I said to him: "Just don't bend it. Don't crash."

You can guess what happened. First corner – straight into the fence and he bent it quite badly. But that was a valuable lesson – don't borrow, don't lend.

I can't recall ever having had high hopes of being World Champion or anything like that, but what I do remember was my first ever cheque in speedway and my overwhelming ambition to beat Our Kid. It was about £3.50 in today's money. At that time I was working all week in the mill to earn that much, yet I got the same for one night's racing. Just two races, in fact, because the going rate was 10 shillings a point, plus travel expenses. In those days the banks used to return all your cheques once you had cashed them, and I kept that one for a long while afterwards. I looked

That's me, in 1961, chasing Newcastle's Vic Lonsdale, who taught me an expensive lesson in the early days.

Middlesbrough Bears, 1961. Left to right: Bob Webb, Clive Hitch, Kev Torpie, myself, promoter Reg Fearman, Brian McKeown and Johnnie Fitzpatrick. On bike: Eric Boothroyd.

at that cheque and thought: "This is not only fun, but it's better than working." I knew that if I got better at speedway, I wouldn't have to spend as much time in the mill. That really made my mind up what I wanted to do.

It didn't even cross my mind that it might be safer working in the mill. I can honestly and truthfully say that I never, ever, thought speedway was dangerous. Look at the facts – you had four people, some of them of a higher standard than the others, all riding a speedway bike, all going the same way and all knowing what they were doing. I didn't underestimate the risks and I had a few crashes over the years and came home thinking "that was lucky" but crossing the road is a lot more dangerous – especially when you are in a group of four! Even when I smashed my arm up in 1973, I just considered it part and parcel of the sport.

Even after an injury as bad as that, which I'll come to in more detail later in the book, I wanted to ride again. I don't know what the definition of 'dangerous' is in the dictionary, but it never put me off riding.

After that first night at Middlesbrough, I began to get regular rides, and Maurice Morley was a great help. He would get me from A to B and he was involved with Reg Fearman and Mike Parker of Northern Speedway Limited, or the 'Quality Street Gang', as I used to call them. You had to be in with them because they controlled so many tracks. Maurice was the gold-wrapped Quality Street! Without him I could not have got to the tracks I was riding at, and he would never charge me a penny for taking me.

My bike always went in the car boot and I remember coming home from

Middlesbrough one night and discovering that I hadn't put the thing in properly. We got home and realised that, somewhere on the journey, we had lost the front wheel! It was about one o'clock in the morning and pitch black but he went back to look for it, although he never found it. Today I could get a front wheel delivered in the morning from about five suppliers, but in those days everything you did was a problem. I look at photographs of my bike in those days and I had made the seat, made the oil tank, made the chain guard, made the air cleaner. You had to in those days – Alec Jackson was the only person you could get bits from and his business was based in Tottenham, north London.

One of the tracks the Quality Street Gang controlled was Newcastle and that's where I made my Provincial League debut on May 22 of that year… in the colours of Wolverhampton! Wolves were riding at Brough Park and arrived short-handed. I was there as usual and was asked to make up the numbers. Although I scored only one point from three rides, it was a great thrill.

My first experience as a member of the Bears team was on June 5, 1961 when I scored three points from two rides in a Northern League fixture at Cleveland Park. I got a big round zero on my Provincial League debut at Rayleigh on June 30, but I soon began to settle down. Mind you, Cleveland Park was a demanding track to ride. When it was high tide on the North Sea, the water used to come from the nearby River Tees, up the drains and flood the track. If you had a wet Wednesday, the track would have time to dry out in time for the following night's meeting – but only if you didn't have a high tide on Thursday!

The top dressing on the track was black ash from the power station and we didn't have tear-offs in those days, so you can imagine how difficult it was to see through. Another problem was that the track must have been based on cobblestones. When the surface of the track used to break away, you could see them as you came out of turn two, except there were two or three missing.

We were on JAPs, which didn't rev anywhere near as hard as the bikes of today, and had big, wide Dunlop tyres. So if you got it wrong there, you were in trouble – the bike used to stand straight up. On one occasion my bike ended up with the forks over the fence and I landed on the dog track! It was a good speedway track, but an awkward one. Sometimes it wasn't terribly well prepared and that made it doubly difficult. But I reckoned that if you could ride at Middlesbrough, you could ride anywhere – and it was my home track so it was great for me. All I needed to do when I went anywhere else was ride a lot quicker.

Starting out at Middlesbrough did me a world of good. I always said that the best thing I ever did in my career was start at Middlesbrough. That first year I scored more points away from home than I did at Cleveland Park, which proved I was learning something. I say to the young riders today – don't ever sign for a big track, because all you'll be doing is going flat out in circles. Ride at somewhere like Newcastle where there are long straights and tight corners. How many Aussies do you see who have been good the first year they have come over here to ride? It takes them a season to adapt from the big, flat out tracks they have over there to places like Rye House or Arena Essex.

Above: They're off! A home clash with Edinburgh from 1963 shows (left to right) Dud McKean, myself, Wayne Briggs and Eric Boothroyd heading for the first turn at Cleveland Park.
Below: I'm first away this time on the inside, with Kev Torpie for company.

Nevertheless, Middlesbrough was a good track and there were many ways you could get round it. You could go wide if you wanted, flat out round the bottom of the fence, or you could go round the inside or through the middle. Although it was a smallish track, it was a good one because there were so many different racing lines and, because it was so patchy, there were some good meetings there.

I was only 16 when I started riding and that was unheard of in speedway back then. Kids are riding in the Conference League at 15 now, but in those days it was a rarity to see a rider so young. I was riding against people who were in their late 40s and

They were a friendly bunch of supporters at Middlesbrough – and some interesting fashions from the early 60s too! Speedway has always been a wonderful family sport and the picture above illustrates that perfectly.

early 50s! Some of them had been brought out of retirement just to fill a team place, but they were all decent old codgers, if that's the right expression. They were all helpful – maybe that's because they knew I was Nigel's brother, I don't know but I'm sure it must have helped.

My first big score came in early July, when I recorded nine points in the Cleveland Best Pairs, and I followed that up with seven points from four rides in a challenge match at Edinburgh. Now I was starting to make progress and putting some good scores together. That was partly due to the fact we were on sliding scale points money. We were paid the equivalent of 50p a point if we got between one and four points, 75p if we scored between five and eight, and £1 for anything above that. So if you were on seven points with one ride to go, it was worth trying that bit harder to get a second place finish.

There was a kid called Bob Webb who rode at Middlesbrough at the time. Nigel and Maurice Morley had let him have a Vauxhall Wyvern but he didn't keep up the payments on it. It was a car they had repossessed. Maurice had arranged for it to come back from Middlesbrough – they were repossessing it a second time. Now I wasn't even 17 but I got the job of bringing it back. I went up to Cleveland Park to ride and Maurice told me: "You're driving that Vauxhall home?" It was a long way then – you had to go down the old A1, through Boroughbridge and Ferrybridge, about a two-hour journey. I'll never forget coming into Thirsk, where I went the wrong way down a one-way street. I had no licence because I wasn't old enough, and no-one to accompany me either. I didn't say a word to my mum and dad about that, though. You could never get away with it today because there is so much traffic, but although it was quiet, it was also pitch black on that journey, which made me feel pretty nervous all the way.

> "It didn't even cross my mind that it might be safer working in the mill. I can honestly say that I've never thought speedway was dangerous"

I finished that year with an average of 5.04 from 23 meetings – pretty good for my first season in the sport, I thought. Little did I know, however, that I would be crossing my fingers desperately hoping to be fit for the start of the 1962 season. Well, I would have been crossing them if I'd been able to. One of my friends was Derek Bedford whose father was the caretaker of a big mill just down the road. They made expensive wool but suffered from a series of burglaries, so he bought a retired police dog to use as a guard dog. He had it on a chain, which must have been at least 150 yards long, to enable it to run up and down the yard where the stock was kept.

Derek, John Dews and I used to go there on a Sunday morning, particularly in winter, let ourselves in and wash the vans parked in the yard. They had a couple of big Yorkshire boilers, which were always lit, so we would bring the cars into the boiler house where it was warm. It was a lovely dog and we used to let it off its lead and let it roam about the yard. One day the dog came into the boiler house and I was stroking its head when it got hold of my hand. The natural reaction was to try and get my hand away, but it got hold of the other one too so it had both my hands in its mouth. Eventually I managed to get free and I ran up a ladder in between the two

Above: April 1963 and me and Clive Hitch look like we've spent the night down a coal mine rather than a meeting at Cleveland Park.
Below: Oops, nearly off! I'm just about managing to hold on to my JAP around Middlesbrough in our home match against Wolverhampton, while my partner Dave Younghusband and Wolves' Cyril Francis lead the chase.

boilers and onto the steam cock valve up at the top. I looked behind me and the dog was coming up the ladder! Normally a dog won't climb a ladder, but it was a police dog so it had been taught how to do it.

There I was, up in the roof of the boiler house and still the dog was coming at me, so I climbed on to one of the big oak beams and jumped in the coal below. I scrambled away and just got through the big sliding doors at the entrance before it could get me again. I looked at my hands and they were covered in blood, so John took me to hospital in Wakefield. He was driving a Bond Mini three-wheeler at the time and I'm sure we went round at least one corner on two wheels!

You could see right through both hands where the dog had bitten me. I needed eight stitches and I lost nine fingernails – it had chomped that hard. I still went to the Mecca Ballroom that Sunday night, though! Before I left the hospital I heard a nurse say "not another dog bite?" and it was Derek! He'd gone to get the dog to put it on its lead and the dog had put four gorgeous teeth marks in each side of his arm. Eventually the dog got hold of Derek's dad too and put him in hospital.

The owners decided they had had enough and called out the vet to put it down by feeding it poisoned meat. The vet said he'd given it so much it should have flattened an elephant, but it was still chewing away . . . at the oak table leg in the mill office. Eventually it dropped dead and, when they did the autopsy, they discovered it had cancer of the liver, which explained why it had been behaving that way. Another lesson learned – don't play with big dogs!

They did some extensive work on the Cleveland Park track over the winter.... allegedly. To be honest, I couldn't tell any difference at all. They certainly changed the top surface to a different colour and we didn't have any more trouble with those cobblestones, although they were certainly still there.

I bought a bike from Nigel over the winter and from the early weeks of the 1962 season, I was wearing the No.2 racejacket, which meant my riding partner was Eric Boothroyd. Eric was the Bears' No.1 and captain, and was the top rider in the Provincial League. He was king of the kids that year and our partnership was rated as one of the best in the league. He was a good bloke to ride with and he had been a mate of Nigel's for years, so in the school holidays I had done a few trips with him as well.

It certainly didn't do me any harm being paired with him and I scored 42 bonus points that season. Eric got the credit for that because of his team-riding skills, but I can't remember much team-riding going on, to be honest. I can't ever remember him dropping back to look after me if I was leading a race, although he probably did lots of times. We were fairly good gaters and we just happened to be first and second. But it was a good partnership and I enjoyed riding with him.

In April of that season we rode against Bradford and in the opening heat Eric lowered the track record by almost two seconds. Tommy Roper was second and I was third and he also finished inside the old record. But was it just a quick watch? It's the same these days – we are in the 21st century and the majority of tracks are still timing races on a stopwatch. They have had photo finishes in dog racing ever since I have been going to speedway so, if the technology is there to do that, surely they can time speedway races more accurately. So when anyone breaks a track

Boro Bears, 1963. Left to right: Kev Torpie, myself, Eric Boothroyd, Johnny Fitzpatrick, Fred Greenwell, Dave Younghusband and Clive Hitch.

record I don't pay too much attention to it. If a rider takes a tenth of a second off the lap record, that could simply be down to the fact the timekeeper has pressed the button a little later than he should have done.

My progress continued during 1962 and, as well as raising my league average to 6.51, I reached my first big night – the Provincial League Riders' Championship at Belle Vue in September. Len Silver, now promoter at Rye House, was riding for Exeter at the time and won the title. Although I scored only two points, it was an amazing experience to ride in front of 20,000 people at Hyde Road. The atmosphere at Belle Vue was like Wembley and, of course, I was the promoter there for eight years, which I will come to later in the book.

I also recorded my first maximum that season – the record books show it was against Edinburgh on September 13, although in truth I really don't remember the occasion now, but I know I would have been thrilled to bits at the time.

What I do vividly remember, however, is our journey to Neath a few weeks before that – it was a nightmare! Trevor Redmond ran the show there and 1962 was their one and only season in operation. We had to go there the night after we had ridden a Provincial League meeting at Plymouth. We set off, in convoy, from Devon in what we thought was plenty of time and arrived at the Aust ferry to take us into South Wales, only to find it had gone. We then had to drive all the way up to Bristol to cross the River Avon, before heading back again and through the mountains to Neath. It was August, so you can imagine the amount of holiday traffic on the roads.

 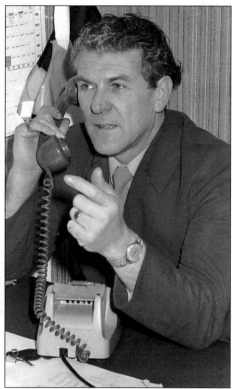

Left: Silver Sash match-race winner at Middlesbrough in 1963.
Right: Maurice Morley, my first team manager and a great help in my early days.

We stopped by the side of the Clifton Suspension Bridge in Bristol and I was busting for a pee, so I jumped over the railings… and disappeared down the other side. I ended up about 20 feet down a hell of a steep slope on the other side of the railings and the others had to get a tow rope to pull me back up. When I eventually got back over the railings we rang Trevor Redmond to tell him we had been held up, so he ran the second half first, while he waited for us to arrive.

The convoy set off again to Neath where, unfortunately, he had no floodlights. The track was set in a big bowl so, because it was getting dark towards the end of the meeting, he asked everyone who had parked their cars around the track to turn their headlights on, to ensure we finished all 13 heats.

I'll also remember that season as being the first in which I was able to drive myself to meetings. I became the proud owner of a provisional licence at the start of the year and my mum and dad bought me a second hand Morris 1000 van. I promised I would repay my parents not only for that, but also for all the other financial help they had given me to get me started and, later that summer, I went to the bank and withdrew £300 to repay my 'loan'. I presented them with the cash, although what I didn't tell them was that the remaining balance of £9 was all the money I had left in the world. Still, it was an incentive to score a few extra points.

My mother was co-pilot for the majority of meetings as nobody else was free to come with me to the midweek fixtures because they were all working. We had a Provincial League fixture at Cradley Heath that June but unfortunately she wasn't available and I couldn't get anyone to come with me – so I decided to go on my own! There wasn't as much traffic on the roads in those days and there were no motorways, so I decided to give it a go. My mother wanted me to take my L-plates off, but I wouldn't. My reasoning was that, if I got stopped, I could only get done for one offence. Driving without a qualified driver next to me was an offence, all right, but I couldn't have been done for having no L-plates!

All went well until I was quite close to Dudley, where the stadium was, and I was pulled over by a police car. The copper saw the L-plates and wanted to know who was learning. I told him it was me. He wanted to know why I wasn't accompanied, so I explained that I lived near Leeds – it was no good saying Wakefield in those days – and that I was a contracted professional speedway rider, that I was riding at Cradley Heath that evening but that I couldn't get anyone to come with me. The copper had a look at my bike in the back, and noticed it had my name on it. "Are you any relation to that Nigel Boocock?" he asked, "I've seen him ride at Cradley and he's good." I explained that he was my brother – so he wished me a safe journey, told me to be careful and sent me on my way!

That wasn't the only time I was stopped by the police on my way to a meeting either. On another occasion I had stopped at Ole Olsen's house on the way to an open meeting and we were late leaving. We were driving like lunatics trying to get there in time and, sure enough, both Ole and I were flagged down and given tickets for speeding. When we arrived at the stadium we discovered that the lord mayor and the local police had been invited along as special guests.

We got there late because we had been stopped and were furious. We made our way into the dressing rooms, and the next thing we knew, the two coppers who had

stopped us walked in. They came over to us, asked for the tickets back and tore them up! They said their super was in the area so they had to issue tickets to keep him happy, but by the end of the meeting everyone had got to hear that Ole and I had been done for speeding.

Then, at the post-meeting get-together, who should I be introduced to but the main policeman! "I hear you've had a bit of trouble with our lads tonight," he said. I explained, without giving too much away, that we were running a bit late and that it was nothing serious. "Have you got a ticket?" he asked me. I didn't know what to say. Not wishing to land the other two policemen in hot water after they had ripped our tickets up, I said: "Yes, I suppose I have."

Off duty and a 'little fish' with big ideas . . .

He told me to go and fetch the ticket from my van and he would rip it up. Obviously, I couldn't do that because it had already been destroyed. Instead, I walked out of the bar, down to my van and went straight home – I never heard another thing about it.

By this time I was starting to get noticed and I began the 1963 season in good form. But, as far as everyone was concerned, I was still Nigel's brother. I was still a little fish in a little pond. People like Briggo and Ove Fundin – they were the big fish in the big pond and we were worlds apart.

We had a lot of injury problems that season which meant more responsibility for me and Dave Younghusband. Dave was, and indeed still is, a very good friend and we were particularly close when we raced together at Halifax, so I'll talk about him

With Boro Bears team-mate Eric Boothroyd and Wolverhampton's Graham Warren.

more in the next chapter. At this stage we were young riders coming through, but we didn't feel any extra weight on our shoulders due to riders like Eric Boothroyd, Brian McKeown and Johnny Fitzpatrick being out injured. We knew we were weak-handed but that was the promoters' problem, not ours. We were just part of a team doing our job. We felt we were progressing at a nice, steady rate and doing our best with the limited ability we had at the time.

"He was a hard rider and I remember him and Ivan Mauger having to be parted from the changing room floor at Cradley because they were fighting"

I was Middlesbrough's top points scorer that year. I did 45 matches, which is more than I had ever done before. I improved on my previous year's performance in the Provincial League Riders' Championship by scoring seven points and I also beat Colin Pratt to win the Silver Sash and more individual honours came my way when I won the Battle of Britain individual meeting at Cleveland Park. I was accused at the time of knocking off Cradley's Ivor Brown in the run-off decider and, when he didn't appear for the re-run, the trophy was awarded to me. All I can say is that, if I did knock him off, he deserved it!

Ivor was a hard rider and I remember him and Ivan Mauger having to be parted from the changing room floor at Cradley Heath one night because they were fighting. They hated each other. I got on all right with Ivor, but he was a dirty bugger! He had more craft than he had ability. He was a very good gater and, once

Receiving some friendly advice from brother Nigel.

he was in front, he would zig-zag all over the place so you couldn't get past him. So I really couldn't care less whether I knocked him off or not, although I would never have done it deliberately. It would have been an accident but I probably got the nod from the referee because of Ivor's reputation.

That season wasn't without its low points, though, and I was riding at Meadowbank the night that Peter Craven got killed. He had won the World Championship in 1962 and was riding for Belle Vue in a challenge match against Edinburgh shortly after the 1963 final at Wembley.

Because Edinburgh were in the Provincial League (second division) and Belle Vue were in the National League (first division), the Aces riders had to start each race on big steel plates, which were then whipped away by the track staff, to try and even things up by giving the Edinburgh riders an advantage at the start. I had taken a guest booking to ride for the Monarchs so I saw the crash.

It was a freak accident – the sort of thing you see hundreds of times, but without such terrible consequences. George Hunter went into the first bend and either lost a chain or his bike seized up. He finished up on his backside and the bike was spinning round on the clutch, as it does. Peter was behind him and went to go round him. Meadowbank was a lovely track, always nicely prepared, and there was plenty of room for him.

But, as he went to go round him, George's bike spun and his back wheel hit Peter's front wheel and shot him right, straight into the solid wood fence they had there. He banged his head and was carted off in the ambulance. We knew it was serious, but we didn't know it was life-threatening. It was a few days later when he died. Unfortunately helmets were cheap and cheerful in those days. They were the best available at the time and, remember, when speedway started in 1928, they were using leather helmets. All the same, they were crap.

The loss of Peter Craven was a massive blow to British speedway and came at a time when the sport was already in turmoil. Mike Parker was at loggerheads with the other Provincial League promoters after he signed Rick France from National Leaguers Leicester and was eventually kicked out of the promoters' association. The Speedway Star described 1963 as a "season of disaster" and it got even worse in the winter when Southampton closed down, leaving the NL with just six tracks. At one point the situation became so desparete that George Allan, the Speedway Control Board chairman, suggested a team of riders from the Swedish League should ride in the senior league of Britain . . . and call themselves "Sweden."

Crowds had dropped in the National League and so had the pay. Things got so bad that in 1964 we ran 'black'. Every single Provincial League rider was banned sine die by the SCB. They wanted us to amalgamate with the National League but we wouldn't – so we were banned.

Ken Sharples was the boss at Belle Vue at the time and he offered me a good contract to ride for them in the top flight. It was around £600, which was a lot of money back then, and in fact I rode in their opening two matches of the season – one at Hyde Road and the other at Norwich. Nigel was adamant that I should join the Aces, but I pointed out to him that his league had only six teams in it. There were

14 in ours, so by staying in the Provincial League I would get that many more chances of earning my living, plus all the experience that went with it. I told him I would be far better off doing that than going to Coventry or Wimbledon five times a year. In any case, because there were only six teams in the National League, they were all so strong that every one of them would have at least two World Finalists – what chance would I have of beating them at 19-years-old? All I would do was demoralise myself.

He tried to convince me that I would never be allowed to ride again if I rode black, but I said: "Of course I'll ride again! It won't come to that – after next winter something will happen." So I stopped where I was and, in the winter of 1965, amalgamation between the two leagues took place. Despite what Nigel had tried to tell me, I was still riding then, although the ban was never, ever officially lifted. If you get banned sine die, it means for life or until the suspension is lifted – but it never was lifted.

Throughout my four years at Middlesbrough I managed to maintain a steady progress, although, at the end of my final season there, my Provincial League average had dipped slightly from 8.51 to 8.35. Taking other matches into account, though, I had improved and my average for all matches at the end of 1964 was 8.52, compared to 8.22 a year earlier. I did an interview with the Speedway Star at the time in which I admitted my progress over the previous season had not been as great as I had hoped. I'm not sure why that was. So many times you see a young whiz kid come out of nowhere and then get to a certain level – and once they get to that level, it determines whether they are going to go up or down. You might stay at that level for a while but, if you are going to make it, you'll start going up again. Also you have to remember that I was a heat leader by then, so I was involved in much harder races and gained more tactical substitute rides.

It was only the top riders in the National League who were a lot better than our top lads in the Provincial. The very best were outstanding and that gap was enormous. But I remember Nigel saying to me at the end of 1964: "We'll see how good people like you and the likes of Charlie Monk, George Hunter and Ivan Mauger are. You'll find out what it's like when you're up against National League riders."

But I told him: "No – it's you who will get the shock."

For a few years after the amalgamation we had 19 tracks in one big British League and it was fantastic. That was when speedway took off again and there was variety again. It was also when the "little fish", as Nigel had called us, started growing a bit bigger. People like Ivan, who had sparkled in our league, started sparkling against the big, big fish. And what a big fish he turned out to be!

It was rough and ready in those days. There were hardly any professionals because everyone had a job. Eric Boothroyd had two greengrocers' shops but still rode speedway. It had an amateur feel to it, right down to track preparation and safety features. The goggles we wore were ones which had been used in the war – gas goggles they were called, and soldiers used to wear them when they were shooting at tank units in the desert. We all bought them from Alf Weedon. You had to turn the corner up or they would steam up, which meant if it was dry, dust would get in and

Above: Going into the third turn at Cradley Heath.
Below: Receiving congratulations from Councillor Fred Moore after winning the Battle of Britain trophy at Middlesbrough in 1963, with Reg Fearman in the background.

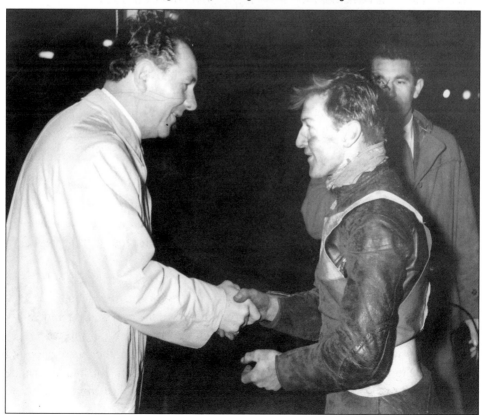

Acting the goat with Edinburgh's George Hunter.

if it was wet, all the muck would get in. There were no dirt deflectors or tear-offs in those days! You can ride in some really bad weather these days but back then we used to often get totally wiped out on the first turn.

The equipment was rough and ready too, but I always took pride in mine. There were some rough bikes and there were no machine examiners – whatever you turned up with, you rode. You see kids now who aren't even in a Conference League team but they have got better and more equipment than I had when I retired. But that is just the way it was then and you would never see me riding a dirty bike or in dirty leathers. You didn't have any world-renowned tuners like Otto Lantenhammer and Hans Zierk in those days, so you did everything yourself.

It amazes me today that there are kids who have been riding for years but they wouldn't even know how to set a set of tappets. Maybe you don't need to, but my argument is that if you are a speedway rider and you have only got two meetings a week, what are you going to do for the rest of the week? Why don't you spend time learning? All a speedway bike is is a pushbike with an engine in it. It's the most basic thing in the world. It doesn't resemble any other motorbike in the world, it's a one-off, but how simple is it to learn how it works?

I spent a lot of time with Guy Allott who lived in the back of beyond and he was an enormous help. I once went there in an old Land Rover to see how an engine of mine was coming along. It was the middle of winter and there were snowdrifts everywhere. It was that cold inside that we were lighting newspaper on the floor to keep us warm! Guy was great. I would say: "How does that work, Guy?" and he'd show me and help me understand. I'm not saying I didn't take him an engine and leave it with him to work on but, generally, I'd say: "Guy, can you do this – but can I be there when you build it?"

He was one of the very few people who worked on engines in those days, and all they did was build bog standard engines, but build them properly. Guy used to liken it to buying a car. You could buy a Friday afternoon car or you could buy a Monday morning car – they were both supposed to be the same but one could be fantastic and the other one could be rubbish. It was how I learned the basics of getting things right. It was worth spending a bit more time getting the valve timings right – even if it took five attempts. If it broke, I would want to know why.

I've got some fantastic memories of Middlesbrough and, although it was so long ago, there are things I will never forget. One memory which hasn't faded is of the doctor Reg Fearman used at Cleveland Park on racenights. He always wore green wellies and was always drunk! I was the baby of the team so I was always the butt of everyone else's jokes and they wanted him to give me an enema – but they couldn't catch me! One night Kevin Torpie fell and split his eye open. It was really bad and you could see the bone. They took him off to the changing room, which in those days doubled up as the ambulance room, and I looked at poor Kevin thinking: 'Thank God it's you and not me.'

The doctor stank of whisky, but he sat him down and set about stitching his wound without any anaesthetic. When the meeting was over the rest of us went down to see Kevin and found the doctor had done an absolutely perfect job. When he had the stitches out, you wouldn't have known he'd had any.

"He banged his head. We knew it was serious, but we didn't know it was life-threatening. Helmets were cheap and cheerful in those days"

My last race in Middlesbrough colours at Cleveland Park came in mid-August when we finished our home league programme and after that we were given the chance to go out on loan to other tracks. There were still six weeks of the season to go, so I went to Long Eaton, where Reg Fearman was also in charge. Long Eaton was one of the best-shaped tracks I ever rode on – the corners were the perfect shape and so smooth. Trouble was, the straights were like a motocross track and you had to stand up or the bike would throw you over the top.

So at the end of 1964 it was the end of an era not just for me, but for British speedway as a whole. Reg Fearman closed Cleveland Park because he said he couldn't make it pay – though it's incredible to think that now when you look at some of the photographs and see the crowds on the terraces. He transferred the licence to Halifax and I lined up for the 1965 season, full of trepidation and excitement, as a Dukes rider – in the brand new British League on a purpose-built track 18 miles from home.

③

BETTER THAN WORKING FOR A LIVING

THERE had been rumours a year earlier that Middlesbrough would be closing and that Halifax would be opening, but he played his cards close to his chest did Reg Fearman. He'd never tell you anything if you asked him, but I suppose it's the same today – if you find a new venue, you don't open your mouth about it until you get it signed, sealed and delivered.

But because I was based locally to Halifax, I had heard the whispers and I kept popping across to The Shay find out more, although I thought it best not to tell Reg.

There were certainly signs of activity there and the track was taking shape, but what if Middlesbrough closed down before Halifax opened? That would leave me without a team. My own suspicions, which were confirmed of course, were that the Bears wouldn't be running the following season so, because of all the uncertainty, I handed in a transfer request at the end of 1964 and told Reg that I wanted to join Edinburgh Monarchs.

I always liked riding there. The people were nice and I got very friendly with Doug and Willie Templeton and I used to stay with them. Old Meadowbank was a bit dilapidated but the crowds were at the top end of Provincial League levels and the track was always well prepared. You could always have a go there because the track was consistently good. On top of that, I could call in on my big mate Dave Younghusband on the way up because he lived at Consett, in County Durham.

But, let's face it, who wants to ride in Edinburgh when you live in Wakefield? It's a long way now, and it was an even tougher journey then, so I think that declaring I wanted to join them was a bit tongue in cheek. With the uncertainty over Middlesbrough, I just wanted to get myself fixed up with a job for that season. Who wouldn't? Halifax, of course, is just 25 minutes or so down the road from Wakefield and, although there was no doubt that speedway would be coming to The Shay, nobody knew when the track would be finished.

In the end it was April 17 by the time the first meeting took place there, which isn't actually as late as it sounds now. The season used to start later in those days – people had sense back then! How many meetings were rained off in the first month of the 2006 season? You can see how it made sense to start the season later, although we weren't swamped with FIM international fixtures as we are now.

I spent that winter keeping fit by grass-tracking in a field I carved out with some friends. We rented the field for ten bob a week and used to go over there on a Sunday. It wasn't proper grass-tracking – it was just me, John Dews and about six

other lads having some fun on stripped-down road bikes we had bought for 10 shillings, with speedway tyres on. And we used to ride them until we wrecked 'em!

Always keen to try something new, I bought a Cotton with a Villiers engine and, through Ivan Mauger, got to ride in a scramble down the road in Bentley Springs. This was in the days when scrambling used to be shown on the TV, and the BBC cameras were there. A TV star already! I'd never done scrambling competitively before but, typical me, I wanted to have a go. It was a big meeting too. Joel Roberts, who was world champion, was riding and so were a whole bunch of the sport's top names.

Race day came and it was absolutely freezing – it had been about minus-six and everywhere was white with frost. Practice was scheduled for the morning, but unfortunately my first attempt came to a sudden and painful end. I got to the first corner, but the bike wouldn't stop – and it wouldn't turn either, so I ended up just

A new era dawns with the launch of the amalgamated British League in 1965. Ray Cresp is the Long Eaton No.1 leading his team out alongside myself, Reg Fearman, Dave Younghusband, Clive Hitch and Eric Boothroyd representing newcomers Halifax. Little did I realise then that I'd have so much hassle working at the Station Road track much later in life.

going straight on. One of the ropes used to mark out the track got me round the neck and it felt like I was being hung! I got back on the bike, rode onto the infield and straight into the ambulance tent. My neck was red raw and, in fact, you can still see the mark today if you catch my neck in the light. They dressed it and I carried on, although, it must be said, I didn't do very well. Ivan, his wife Raye, their two kids and his mechanic all came over to my parents' house after the meeting and, after they had gone I decided to have a bath and get the dressing off my neck. I kept having to submerge myself under the water and pull at the corner because they had put two inch Elastoplast tape straight onto my neck! No cotton wool or lint – nothing! I swear it took me all night to get it off because the pain was horrendous. Still, nothing ventured, nothing gained.

By the time my attention switched back to speedway, the new British League had been formed. We were all in one big league with big guns Nigel, Briggo, Ove Fundin, Bjorn Knutsson, Ron How and the like, but I wasn't fazed – I saw it as a chance to improve. Here were 42 riders we had never ridden against and I couldn't wait to test myself against them. It was great for the fans too, as 18 tracks meant much more variety and each one brought with them a top name rider. When Barry Briggs came to Halifax in 1965 he was World Champion – think of the publicity potential that generated.

When I rode for Middlesbrough there were a lot of teams in the Provincial League who were, quite frankly, awful, but I suppose they were the best that could be cobbled together. When we formed one big league it seemed like all the dross had been kicked out and the teams were much better balanced.

I had a bit of a head start when the leagues amalgamated because, for example, I knew how to get to places likes Swindon. I knew where the changing rooms were, where the starting gate was and, although I had never ridden there, I knew the track because I had been there so many times with Nigel. It meant I wasn't apprehensive when I got there – I knew how to find it and knew it was a big track with plenty of room. I knew my way blindfolded to Wimbledon too.

A lot of riders who were visiting Halifax that first year didn't have a clue where the stadium was. Riders today are in the same situation - look at Chris Kerr, for example, the American kid who joined Redcar Bears for the 2006 season. Everywhere he's been this year has been new to him. All he would have known before he set off for a meeting was that there was a track somewhere that he had to ride on. Sometimes you have a mental picture of what it's like because someone has told you but, when you get there, you find it isn't anything like that at all. I also had an advantage when I was preparing my bike for an away match because Nigel would tell me what sprockets I needed. Getting advice from somebody who had been riding – and riding well – at those tracks for a long while was a big plus.

When Halifax opened on Easter Saturday, April 17 against Long Eaton, Maurice Morley – my old boss at Middlesbrough – was team manager and we had the nucleus of the Bears team with Eric Boothroyd appointed captain. It had rained for most of the day but there were 15,000 people at The Shay for the opening night. The only time I've seen a bigger crowd there was for my testimonial. The crowds at Middlesbrough were around 2,000 so, to go from that, was fantastic. We lost 41-36 but it was a great occasion and I won the first race, on my way to a score of 12+2. Pat Phoenix, who played Elsie Tanner in Coronation Street, was the guest of honour because Reg Fearman and Mike Parker used to get celebrities like that to get extra publicity.

> "With its steep banking, The Shay was an awesome sight, one of the best viewing tracks in speedway and there were also plenty of fans there"

They used to have attractions at the interval too. One night he had someone jumping into a pool of water from about 40ft up, and on another occasion he had a bloke who climbed up a flagpole in the middle. He had a bowler hat, suit and dickie bow on and swung around on it, pretending to be drunk. People say we should have more of that sort of thing these days, but it has to be cost effective. If you want to hire someone as an interval attraction, it might cost you £500 – but if you haven't got £500 you can't do it, and, unless you get extra people on the gate to see it, you are losing even more money.

The Shay was a bit of a dump, to be fair. It was a typical speedway stadium – straight from the dark ages. But there were so many people there that nobody noticed it. If you went there on a Sunday morning you would notice it, but on a racenight you wouldn't. In any case, it's no good having an unbelievably modern stadium if nobody goes – White City is a case in point – a brilliant stadium but no atmosphere. People paid their money to watch the racing, not to look at the stadium.

Making a decent start off the inside gate at The Shay, where crowds were fantastic after our 1965 opening.

With its steeped banking at either end, the track at The Shay was an awesome sight. It was one of the best viewing tracks in speedway and there were always plenty of fans there. There was just something about it, down there in that big bowl with the fans right up to the fence. The atmosphere was terrific and, when you had been used to very low crowds everywhere, as we had been in the Provincial League, it was tremendous.

However, had it not been banked, I have to say it would have been a terrible track. It was the banking that got you round the corners, because it was very narrow going into them and narrow coming out due to the football pitch inside. But because you could go up the banking and use the banking to turn, it got you out of the corner quite nicely.

There were a lot of riders who didn't like Halifax. I have no idea why – maybe the banking put them off, and I suppose the steel safety fence didn't help. The fence didn't put me off, though, because you shouldn't get near it, should you? During that first year there, we had an advantage because the other teams had never ridden the place before. They had probably heard the rumours – "that new Halifax track is banked like a cycle-racing track and it's got a steel safety fence." Rumour soon spread, so we had an advantage every week we raced there because as the home meetings went by, we just got better and better on it, while anyone who was riding The Shay for the first time arrived full of trepidation.

Throughout that opening '65 season the fans kept on coming in their thousands and they were treated to some great speedway. Among the early visitors were Coventry and Nigel relieved me of the track record that evening – but he was a world class rider so I expected him to come to Halifax and go quicker than me. I

A social 'do' for Dukes riders Dave Younghusband, Bert Kingston, myself and Dennis Gavros.

had only been riding for three years and he had been riding much longer, but I made a mental note to catch up with the "big fish" – especially Nigel

Clive Hitch was among the former Middlesbrough riders in the Halifax side at the start of the season but he lived in Hertfordshire and didn't stay long before joining Swindon. He was replaced by Tommy Roper who arrived with something of a troublesome reputation because he had a couple of hairdressing shops and Friday night was his busiest of the week – so if we were riding somewhere on a Friday and he didn't want to go, he just didn't turn up. As you can imagine, it was a bit annoying that a member of the team could pick and choose their meetings while the rest of us were there week in, week out. Tommy was a good rider but, unfortunately, he was not a team man. He rode for Tommy Roper, not for the team. These days if you did what he did they would probably fine you £250 and then suspend you if you did it again – but in those days sport was rough and ready and riders could get away with it with a slapped wrist.

Tommy ended up being my partner because he was hard to ride with and no-one else wanted to do it! He knew where he was going to go, but he disregarded where anyone else wanted to be. He used to stuff you into the fence as regular as clockwork, then tell you all innocently: "I didn't know you were there." Then, in the next race, he would do you the same on the other side of the track!

It wasn't long before I'd had enough, so one night I deliberately stuffed him in the fence on the first corner – he was on the outside of me and I didn't turn. Then, just to let him know how it felt, I saw him in the pits and said: "Sorry, Tommy – I didn't see you."

I honestly think I was one of the instigators in getting him moved away from The

Shay. I was always vociferous if I thought something needed to be said. Being a difficult partner was one thing, but failing to turn up for meetings was another, so I told Reg straight: "If he's going to miss meetings, then so am I."

The following season he moved to Belle Vue.

I didn't miss any meetings, of course, and that was something I took great pride in throughout my career. And I carried on scoring well too. My first British maximum came against Exeter at the end of May and my first big individual victory followed in July when I won the Whitaker Brewery Trophy at The Shay. I was pleased with my progress for two reasons – firstly, because my speedway career was most definitely going in the right direction, and secondly because points meant pounds. The more I scored, the more I earned. I started riding speedway primarily because Nigel was doing it so I wanted to have a go, but also because it was better than working for a living.

As Dave Younghusband and I were the top points-scorers at Halifax, we very quickly became local celebrities – me in particular because I lived only 25 minutes away. The football team were rubbish, and so were the rugby team, and all of a sudden they had a new sport in Halifax that was booming. It was great to see so many people getting a buzz out of Saturday nights. Let's put speedway into perspective, it isn't massively popular and it was bigger just after the war than it was in the 1960s. But Halifax is not a big place – it's a little local community, and it's fair to say that, whenever I went into Halifax, people would wave at me. I was, and still am, big mates with a car dealer who lived on the other side of the town and, whenever I drove through the centre someone would always recognise me and sound their horn or give a wave. I would sometimes get asked for my autograph too although, apart from racing, I didn't go into Halifax for anything. Mind you, I could always get a good deal if I went to buy a car or parts for it because of who I was. I was asked to be the special guest at garden parties and church fetes on occasions and, really, it was just part of the job. It was strange because I didn't ever see myself as being a big name, and certainly not a celebrity.

I look back now at the statistical records of my career and I genuinely think "that can't have been me". I still feel like that today. I would come home from meetings and when my wife, Diane, asked how I had got on, I would say: "Crap – I was terrible tonight." I wasn't being big-headed – I never have been like that in my life – although maybe I should have been because, if I had been cocky, I would have gone a lot further. Diane would ask how many points I had scored and I'd say: "12". She couldn't believe it and wondered how on earth I could have been crap if I'd scored a maximum. Other times I would score eight and tell her that I had ridden fantastically well and that I was really on the ball.

Sometimes I'd go unbeaten at Halifax and think that getting money couldn't have been easier if I'd taken it from the collection box at church – it was money for jam! But when things went wrong, it was the hardest sport in the world. The expectations are so high. It's not like you are an athlete competing in one tournament every six weeks – you are expected to come up with the goods every week. The people on the terraces come to see you perform every week – and the first time you have a bad night, it was like an inquisition. Quite simply, you weren't allowed a bad night.

Team-mates at Middlesbrough and then Halifax, Dave Younghusband and me were known as the Terrible Twins.

As I mentioned earlier, Dave Younghusband and I became firm friends at Halifax after getting to know each other at Middlesbrough. He spent more time in the summer at our house than he did at home and we were nicknamed the Terrible Twins – we were always together. I don't think he ever went home after riding at Sheffield – he always came back to our house to stay, then do his bikes ready to ride at Halifax on the Saturday night. He would do the same if he had been riding at Poole on a Wednesday. He was a talented rider too – a good all-rounder.

Dave and I travelled to meetings together too, putting both our bikes on a trailer with us in the one car. It made sense to do that because there were two of us able to do the driving and we shared the expense. We each got paid travel expenses, which helped because the mileage rates weren't that good so we would have otherwise lost a bit of money had we gone independently.

On one Friday evening we were travelling back from Glasgow when we got a puncture on the trailer. Typically it happened miles from anywhere on the A68, so we decided to put both bikes on one side of the trailer to take the weight off the side which had the flat tyre. We didn't have a spare wheel so we stuffed the tyre with an old towel, some cloths and even some socks we had in our bags, then set off again. We must have done all of five miles when the tyre caught fire! There were bits flying everywhere – it was like a giant Catherine wheel! We dragged the thing along for a few miles until we got to a farm. It was late but we knocked on the farmhouse door and explained our problem to the bloke who lived there. I needed to get straight back home so we put my bike in the back of Dave's car and left the trailer and his bike on the farm. We drove back to Dave's where I transferred the bike into

Luxury motorhomes were just a dream when Dave and me hit the road.

my car and drove home, while he returned the next morning with his dad – and a spare wheel – to retrieve the trailer.

Dave and I had some great times together. He was a very funny bloke – and still is. He could take the micky out of somebody and never let his face slip. I would know what he was doing and had to turn away sometimes so that nobody saw me laughing or smiling.

There was a lot of rivalry between us but it was friendly. If he won a race, I wanted to win a race. And if I did win, he had to finish first in his next race, and so it went on. He wanted to be No.1 and I wanted to be No.1, so it kept us on our toes. It's the same when you are playing cricket as a kid – if you are competitive, then you always want to be the best, and that's the way it was between us. But

A proud winner of the Silver Sash.

because we were close friends, Dave and I could swap ideas too and that helped us both.

Anywhere else, I think it's fair to say, Dave would have been a No.1 in his own right. He had a ten-point average nearly every year, but it suited him to ride for Halifax – and he had use of the best bed and breakfast you could find in speedway! Dave kept me on my toes loads and loads of times, and that was fantastic for the club, although he didn't get as much recognition as me because he wasn't local. It is always good having a local rider in your team. It helps you sell it to the local press because they have got another angle.

In the event it was me who ended the year as the Dukes' No 1 rider and one of the honours I achieved in 1965 was becoming the first Halifax rider to win the Silver Sash. I successfully defended it six times and, after one of those victories at The Shay, Dave Younghusband's dad, Joe, was talking to me in the pits. Reg Fearman came over as said: "You won't have that much longer because we're at Poole on Wednesday."

Poole was never one of my favourite tracks, although it never prevented me from giving 100 per cent there. Bill Andrew was the top Poole rider then and he was really flying at the time so, jokingly, Reg told me he was convinced I would lose the Silver Sash to Andrew in my next defence. I was adamant there was no way I was going to lose it, and asked Reg how much he wanted to bet me that I wouldn't win. He suggested £10 but I told him it wasn't even worth trying for a tenner, so we finished up having £100 on it – and that amount of money was a fortune in 1965.

The Poole meeting arrived and I wasn't having a particularly good night. Bill Andrew beat me in heat one by 60 yards at least – I was trying hard but he just disappeared. He won every race by the length of a straight, he was in such good form – but in his last heat his engine blew into a million pieces. I wasn't consciously thinking about the Silver Sash race, but I couldn't help admitting to myself that Bill's engine blow-up certainly boosted my chances of winning £100!

He was Poole's top scorer on the night, which meant he had to come out and ride against me for the Silver Sash. For the match race he borrowed a bike belonging to Geoff Mudge and, knowing that he'd be desperate not to bend it, my plan was to make a good start because he wouldn't want to take any risks trying to pass me on a machine that wasn't his. Sure enough, when the tapes went up, I got a great start and beat him easily. I got back into the pits and there was Reg shaking his head, saying: "You jammy so-and-so", but he paid up at Halifax the following week. He was like that – if he ever said something, he would stick to his word. And if we ever had any arguments, it was history within 24 hours. There were no grudges held by either of us.

I eventually lost the Silver Sash to Jimmy Gooch at Oxford when I blew my engine. In fact it was the biggest engine blow-up I ever had in my career – it even bent the frame and engine plates, and it cost me £130 to put right. There was hardly anything left of it – and I was out in front at the time! I even forgot to take the Sash with me to Cowley that night, although I got it to him a few days later at Wembley, on the night of the World Final.

I'd accepted a guest booking to ride at Edinburgh the evening after my engine blew into pieces, so I came home from Oxford and worked all night in the workshop. borrowed an engine and some engine plates from Charlie Monk and worked round the clock to get the bike ready. I never went to bed, and then drove all the way up to Edinburgh, calling into Dave Younghusband's for some dinner on the way. I finally arrived at the stadium about 20 minutes before the meeting was due to start… and found out it had been called off. It had been pouring with rain for hours and the track was waterlogged, but we didn't have mobile phones in those days, so I didn't know it was off until I got there.

Ian Hoskins was the promoter at Edinburgh and, when he saw me arrive, he called me into the speedway office, which was a little wooden shed next to the pits. I explained how I had blown my engine at Oxford, then worked all night to get the bike ready. Ian told me how much he appreciated me putting in so much effort and gave me £25. "I hope this will make it worth your while," he told me. It was a lovely gesture because 25 quid was a lot of money back then

A fourth place finish in the British League and a final average of just over ten represented a very pleasing year – but 1966 was simply amazing, because that was when we won the British League, the Knockout Cup and Northern Cup in a season which will never be forgotten by Halifax fans of that era.

To me though, it was still just my job. It was a business. I don't ever remember turning a booking down in my life, even if it was a busy week. Some of today's riders won't take an extra ride because they don't want to risk affecting their

The Quiet Lodger, Charlie Monk.

average, but my argument was that it was better to have an improved average in your bank! You ride speedway for one reason, and that is to earn a living. That is why everyone goes to work – to earn a living. If you could earn money for stopping at home, everyone would do that! So although I was happy with the way things had gone, I can't ever remember jumping up and down thinking "this is brilliant" after we did the clean sweep.

What I did find remarkable about our achievement that year, though, was that the bulk of the team had all come up through the Provincial League. They had a very strict rider control policy at that time as well, so any foreign riders who wanted to ride over here were told which team to join. Exeter was a regular port of call for the overseas riders since no Englishman ever wanted the County Ground as their home track. It was rough and scary, although I would have gone there at any time in my career, had it not been 300 miles away. That meant that any foreign rider looking for a British League place would often be allocated to the Falcons or one of the far-flung Scottish tracks and, funnily enough, they soon settled down and plenty of them became big speedway names.

There was no official recognition for our achievements in 1966, but there isn't now so what has changed? Reg Fearman bought us something to commemorate our success, but there was nothing from the BSPA except a round of applause for the winners at the AGM. Even today there is a trophy but that is just for the team – they don't provide mementoes for the riders who made it happen. But, to be honest, I don't think there is anything wrong with that. If you are that desperate to say you won the league, then you should have your own trophy made! In the days when speedway was booming and could afford it, then maybe it should have been different. But today, when the sport is not thriving the way it once was, it makes sense not to spend money you haven't got.

One of the top riders in the mid-60s was Charlie Monk, the Glasgow No.1. I got to know him very well during the 1966 season because he moved in with us. Charlie was an Australian who ended up staying with us for four years while he was plying his trade in the British League and was known as 'The Quiet Man'. He shunned all publicity and when one speedway journalist once tried to take a photograph of him, Charlie threatened to break his camera unless he put it away. "Until I've won something that warrants having a photograph taken, don't ever try to take my picture," he told him. 'Actions speak louder than words,' was his attitude.

Having Charlie around helped me, though, because we shared a workshop for years. I used to call him 'the Mad Professor' because he was very clever and he was always trying things out. He would get a good idea – which he kept to himself, I might add – and get it working very well. But then he would decide to try and make it work that bit better and, by doing that he would mess it up! He would go forward two steps and then end up back at square one. He built a four-valve JAP – it was like a plumber's nightmare! There were wires and pipes everywhere! It worked all right, but why go to all that trouble if it isn't going to be twice as good? He wasn't doing it to save money, he was doing it because he thought it would be a lot better. But he was meticulous in the workshop and that was a very big influence in how I conducted myself throughout my career. He didn't say a lot but, when he said it, he meant it.

Charlie didn't make friends easily and so he didn't have many in speedway. He had his own routine and he didn't want to make friends. One night in an individual meeting at Newcastle he was going into the corner really wide and then turned back inside. I was flying underneath him but he didn't move over an inch. I nearly went into him and, in the pits after the race, I asked him what he thought he was doing. "You didn't even swerve," I shouted at him. But he just said: "If I had, you would have beaten me." And that was it. Full stop. People would say: "Hello Charlie" and all they would get in return was a grunt. That's all they could get out of him. If anyone asked him what gear he had on, they would be told: "The gear that wins races".

But he was fine with the people he did get on with. He had started staying with us because I befriended him in his first year over here – probably because I made the effort. I have always tried to get on well with everyone because I believe that life is for living. I invited him to stay if he was passing on his way down from Glasgow and he took me up on the offer several times. Then one day he phoned my mum and explained he was looking for some digs the following season. He asked if he could stay with us and my mum was happy to oblige. He got on so well with my mum and dad and didn't want any fuss making.

One of the other things I remember about Charlie was that he was so tight! But he had to be because he'd never had that much money and that was the only way he had ever been. He came over from Australia on a five-week passage and in all that time on the boat he spent sixpence on a Coke, which he bought because he couldn't go any longer without a drink. All he had when he arrived at Southampton Docks was enough money to buy a bike. When he bought a car he couldn't afford a blanket so, if it was too far to travel back after a meeting, he used to sleep on the back seat covered in old newspapers. He had nothing and the only way he could make it different was to score points. Points equal pounds!

Ivan Mauger was the same when he first came over. He had an old Morris J2 van with sliding doors and he couldn't afford new tyres, so he used to buy old second-hand ones from a scrapyard under the Tyne Bridge. I went to Ivan's house in Moss Side – a really rough area of Manchester – and his wife, Raye, had an old pram full of bottles. She was taking them back to the shop because you got about threepence back on each bottle and she needed that money to buy some fresh bread and jam. That's what it was like in those days but, looking back, it didn't do Charlie or Ivan any harm and it certainly didn't do me any harm either.

My mum got on with Charlie like a house on fire. They always had some great banter and, if she served up chips with dinner, he would say to her: "Oh no, not chips again," and then he would be told to bugger off if he didn't like it! It was all just a bit of fun, though, and I enjoyed having him stay with us. Even now, every time I go to Australia, I stay with him and his wife.

Charlie married a Sheffield girl – Sandra her name is – and I introduced them. One of her mates had talked her into entering the Miss Sheffield Speedway beauty contest, even though she never usually went to Owlerton. She won the competition and Charlie won the meeting, so she had to present him with his trophy. He asked me in the pits if I knew her and I told him I didn't – but that I would arrange for her to come and talk to him all the same. He was really shy – which a lot of people mistook for being awkward – so I went over to her and explained I had someone I'd like to introduce her to. I took her over to where Charlie was in the pits and left them to it. After that, every Sunday at three o'clock he would be washed and changed and out of the house. He never told us where he was going but we knew he was going to see Sandra.

My dad ended up filling in as timekeeper at The Shay during 1966, although he didn't last very long. I was going best there at the time and kept knocking a fifth of a second or so off the track record – which meant the smart alecs couldn't resist making snide comments to the effect that my dad being timekeeper was no coincidence. They couldn't congratulate me for breaking the track record because I was the best rider at Halifax – oh no, they reckoned it was a fix because my dad had the stopwatch. I didn't care what they said, but I was annoyed for my dad because he was the straightest bloke who ever walked on this planet. He would have rather slowed it down a second than give me a track record unfairly, so I had to ask him to step down. I told him he could come in the pits with me instead if he wanted to, even though I didn't like my father in the pits any more than any other rider did at that time.

> "I'd go unbeaten at Halifax and think that getting money couldn't have been easier if I'd taken it from the collection box at church"

One of the reasons I felt awkward about having him in the pits was that I never swore in the house, and I was prone to the odd expletive or ten on a racenight! Until we were 18 we didn't smoke in the house either – we didn't even tell my mother we smoked, although she must have guessed. My mother was quite strict and even though I thought she was a silly old bat sometimes, there's no doubt that she was right.

My dad, on the other hand, was very soft – he lived for his family and his mill and that was it. And, I have to say, it was good for me to have him in the pits because he never, ever interfered. It was a bit embarrassing early on because I would come back in after a race spitting feathers about something, effing and blinding – and then I'd

Reg is laughing, so it can't be my transfer request that has Dave Younghusband and Eric Boothroyd amused!

notice my dad was stood right there within earshot. I never heard him swear once. When my mother and Charlie Monk were having a go at each other they would use a few choice words and my dad would say: "Mother, if you haven't anything better to say than a swear word, keep your mouth shut." He said it as a joke, but there was an element of truth in his comment.

There was a controversial incident early in that 1966 season when we were riding at home to Newcastle. Going into the final heat Eric Boothroyd and I needed a 4-2 to draw the match, or a 5-1 to win it. Brian Brett touched the tapes and pulled back. I moved forward and, as the tapes went up, they caught my mudguard. Expecting the referee to order a re-run, I pulled onto the centre green while the others shot away – but the race was allowed to continue. Eric road a fantastic race to overhaul Brian Brett and Ivan Mauger but it wasn't enough.

Some fans weren't happy with me – but they expected me to be a robot or some sort of machine who won every race. Then when something went wrong, they weren't happy. They didn't realise that we were just like them. Maybe there were days when they didn't want to go to work because they didn't feel well. But to them, it didn't matter if we felt well or not – Saturday was race day and we were expected to perform. Unless we were really poorly, we turned up to do our job. I can understand people saying "Boocock cost us the match" but it didn't make any difference to me. If I had heard them I would have been disappointed, but they wouldn't say it to my face – and if they had, I would have told them they could ride instead of me.

I know I had some bad nights but a poor night for me was eight points – and that used to hurt me even more than it did our fans.

Our next meeting after the Newcastle defeat was at home to Coventry, who went on to finish second to us in the league that season. The Bees were hard to beat although we did get the better of them that year. They were very fast and had a team of very hard riders – nutcases is perhaps a better description! Ron Mountford, Les Owen, Col Cottrell . . . I could go on. Their side was still made up from the basis of their old National League team and those NL teams were a lot harder. Coventry were the name in British speedway, just like Belle Vue are now and have been for many years. They were the team to beat, and there was the added spice of having two brothers on opposing sides. You could always expect fun and games when Coventry came, and it was always a tough meeting.

Eric Boothroyd was a tough, little rider and had been brought up in the National League era, so he could dish it out. On one occasion there was a bit of aggro between him and Ron Mountford which spilled over into the pits. Eric ended up swinging his crash helmet at him and the pair had to be separated by our friendly policeman who was always in the pits.

The turning point in that title-winning season was after we lost at Poole in May. We then strung together a run of 11 straight victories, which included a win away to West Ham who were the reigning British League champions. The Hammers' Custom House track was big and flat with tons of room on the straights and around the corners – it was a nice stadium. You needed a strong engine to go well there as it was very quick although there wasn't any banking – in fact, on the first and second bends the track sloped the other way a little bit.

We'd been at Exeter the night before our visit to east London and stayed over in a guesthouse. There were four of us to a room and there was such a commotion that night because someone had left a window open and a pigeon had flown in! It frightened the life out of us! But we had won at the County Ground so we were on a roll when we arrived at West Ham and I beat Ken McKinlay from the back in heat one.

He was very good with engines, but he came up to me after the race and said "What engine have you got in that bike? Mine was revving like anything and you came past me". I had the same gear on as he did, but my engine must have had a different valve timing – not that I knew because he was much cleverer than me with engines. We didn't think we would win either of those meetings but we won both and came home feeling chuffed.

Briggo ran the show for ESO.

55

Treble winners! Two different Halifax teams from our great 1966 campaign. Above: Lining up at The Shay – back row, left to right: Greg Kentwell, Bob Jameson, Reg Fearman, Tommy Roper and myself. Front: Eric Boothroyd, Dave Younghusband and Dennis Gavros. Below: After we clinched the KO Cup at Wimbledon. Team manager Maurice Morley (front row, far left) and Maury Robinson (second from left, back row) have joined the Dukes party.

As the British League title came into view, I had a secret weapon to unleash – my new ESO bike. At that time we were all riding JAPs and the first time I had seen an ESO was at the back end of the 1965 season when Halifax were at Swindon and Ray Wilson bought two of them from Barry Briggs, who was the sole importer and had been riding them all year. Wilson took one of his new bikes for a spin after the meeting and he flew round. He looked a completely different rider and I knew then that I had to have one.

At the end of July we beat Exeter at home to maintain contact with pace-setters Coventry Swindon and Wimbledon and I decided it was time to get one. So I placed an order with Briggo and he delivered it on his way up to a meeting at Glasgow. I ran a spanner over it and put a magneto on it on Friday evening and Saturday morning before riding it for the first time at Halifax – where I beat him more than once! He vowed then never to deliver me another bike whenever we were in direct opposition!

It was unreal. The engine revved harder so that made it easier to ride and the handling was so much better too. It was like a toy – a lovely sensation.

My career was going well but once I got my ESO, it gave me an extra 10 percent bonus. ESOs later became known as Jawas, of course, and were more reliable than the JAP because it was a sealed engine – the JAP used to let water and muck in all the time. JAPs were virtually 1930s designs which had never altered, while ESO started from a clean sheet of paper. It cost me £315 and I thought that was the earth, but it turned out to be money very well spent. It was like having a new lease of life – even though things were already going well for me.

> "One of the reasons I felt awkward about having him in the pits was that I never swore in the house...and I was prone to the odd expletive or 10 on race night"

The ESOs were very easy to work on and the spares back-up was great because Briggo ran the show. Very few riders had an account with Barry, but I did so I could ring him up in Southampton and the parts would be with me in two days . . . with a bill inside! His premises were under an old railway arch in Southampton and he worked hard to build the business up. Whatever I wanted, he had it. ESOs soon caught on although there were one or two riders who couldn't get on with them. Colin Pratt was one of them. Because it was a lot busier engine you had to keep the revs on harder. If you knocked the throttle off on a JAP engine, the bike would slow down. An ESO would eventually slow down but nowhere near as quickly. So it didn't suit everyone but, within 12 months, almost everybody was riding one.

The ESO certainly suited me and, soon after taking delivery of my new machine, I went 14 matches without dropping a point to an opposing rider, except for mechanical failure – normally an ignition problem because the magnetos were a weak point. The good riders must have not turned up during that run! Maybe I'm doing myself down by saying that. In fact I think that was my problem – I never believed in myself enough to go up to the next step.

The team were going well too, and we went to the top of the table when we visited

Just look at those shiney knees on the best-kept leathers in speedway!

Newport and recorded our 12th successive league victory. I was unbeaten by an opponent in my previous eight meetings, but in my final race of the night at Somerton Park I had magneto problems and Gote Nordin finished in front of me. I was as sick as a parrot but, driving home, I realised that the pressure was off because I had to lose some time.

I was busy after the racing had finished at The Shay too, because part of my deal with Reg Fearman was that I would stay behind after every home meeting and coach the younger riders. The Shay had a big plunge bath in the changing rooms which would be filled with about 3ft of water. There was also a shower but it never worked, which caused me problems because everyone else had got cleaned and gone by the time I'd finished my training duties. When it was my turn to get cleaned up, the soap would be sitting on top of the water like a scum - 13 other mucky speedway riders had already been in so you can imagine what it was like.

I put up with it for a while but in the end I brought it up with Reg and suggested that one of the directors of Halifax Town FC – who owned the stadium – was a plumber, so he should be able to put it right easily enough. The football club were happy enough to take Reg's rent, so surely this plumber could fix the shower. I told Reg that he certainly wouldn't go in that bath before he jumped in his Rolls Royce to drive home, so why should I?

Nothing was done so, about three weeks later, when Reg asked me if I was taking the training school, I told him: "No, I'm not – and you know why."

The shower never was fixed and I had much earlier baths.

Away from Halifax, I had a good run in the World Championship, although my hopes of getting any further were ended by idiot rules and regulations. I was only reserve for the British-Nordic Final at Sheffield but ended up with six points. Brian Brett of Newcastle finished with the same score, but only one of us could go through to the European Final at Wembley as reserve. Because no run-off was ordered, it was thought that it would be me who progressed as I had the better race results, but in the end it was Brett who went through because he had taken his full quota of races, while I hadn't – although it took the SCB until their meeting the following month to make that decision. Nothing much changes, eh?

Nowadays my recollections of winning the league title are a little vague, but I do know that we wrapped it up with a 52-26 win over Belle Vue. I scored a 12-point maximum while Tommy Roper and Dave Younghusband were both paid for the lot, so we did it in style. Then we followed that up by beating Wimbledon to win the KO Cup. We'd annhialated them 69-27 in the first leg of the final, then only lost by eight points in the return at Plough Lane.

The mayor of Halifax held a civic reception for us to mark our achievements and it was nice to know that the efforts of seven scruffy lads on motorbikes had been appreciated. There was a real buzz for speedway in the town and I'm pleased we were able to reward the supporters with some success. Even now if I am in the town, people will tell me they recognise me because they cheered me on from the terraces at The Shay. It's 40 years ago now, but they remember those days and I still think that if any town could support a speedway team again, it's Halifax. I really believe it could happen.

As much as I liked Halifax, though, it wasn't the best racing track in Britain. For me that honour goes to Sheffield, which was beautifully prepared by Frank Varey. He wasn't just a promoter who took the money on racenights, he lived for speedway and he lived for his track. I've known him to get up at two o'clock in the morning to put some pumps on because it was pouring with rain. In the early days we had probably the best support but, as a race track, Sheffield was the best in Britain and I still think it is today. It was a pleasure to finish last there.

You have got to learn to ride Sheffield, but you can race absolutely anywhere there. People say you need a fast motor to go well there but, I have to say, I'm not convinced when I hear riders talk about needing the right set-up for this track or that track. We had no options in the 60s. Virtually all of us had just one bike – two if I was lucky later on in my career – and we rode that same bike wherever we were. New Cross was tiny – the 'Frying Pan' they called it – but we didn't have a special set-up to go round there. You rode what you had and the rider did the work.

I never had a particular favourite track. Every one I had to go to was somewhere I had to earn my living. It's like being a scaffolder – you might go to work today and be climbing up a bungalow to get to the roof. Tomorrow you might be working on an eight-storey block of flats – but it's all work. I used to say "what's the point in going there if you've got a hang-up about the place? You might as well stay at home and chop firewood." That used to be my favourite saying.

The equivalent of that eight-storey block of flats to me was Glasgow White City. It was a great big circuit with unbelievably long straights. You needed another gear to go down them – you wanted to change up into second! But if you put a higher gear on, you wouldn't have got round the corners because they were so tight and the straights were so wavy that the wheels came off the ground.

You had to drive through the Gorbals to get there too and, if you haven't ever sampled the delights of that area of Glasgow, let me assure you it was not somewhere you wanted to spend much time in! On one occasion after Halifax had raced at White City Dave Younghusband and I found a Chinese restaurant in the Gorbals and decided to stop there for something to eat. There was a big football match coming up and the locals were demanding to know who we supported – we played safe and told them that motorbikes were our passion and we didn't care who won. When we'd finished our meal we got back to the car and some idiot was sat astride the bike on my bike rack and he wouldn't get off. The only option was to drive away with him still sitting on the bike and when we eventually stopped, at some traffic light, he wanted a fight so we just roared away before the lights had changed to green. We didn't stop again on that journey home and, needless to say, next time we were in Glasgow we found somewhere else to eat a post-match meal.

Wherever I rode, though, I seemed to score well, and 1967 was another terrific season. We didn't retain our league or KO Cup trophies but, on a personal level, I improved my average again and reached my first World Final. There was plenty to celebrate off the track too, because on April 3 I married my finacee, Diane Miller, at St Luke's Church in Middlestown.

❹
FOR BETTER OR FOR WORSE

THE first time I ever saw my future wife, she was standing in a pile of horse manure! She lived very close to the house where I grew up and her parents had a pony. The stables were next to a pig farm and, when I went past there with a friend one Sunday morning, we found two girls stood in a muck heap in their Wellington boots. We asked them what they were doing and they told us they were warming their feet. That was in 1964 and I saw her quite a lot after that. We started going to the Mecca ballroom on a Sunday evening, which was very big in our day. All the kids went – it was our big night out.

When I first met Diane she didn't know what I did for a living. In fact when I told her, she didn't know what speedway was. However, her father was a proper Cockney and had been a very big speedway supporter when he lived in London – New Cross, White City, West Ham, Wembley, Harringay, he used to go to them all. His name was Dusty and he was a lovely fella. If I was really busy I used to dump my leathers off at their house and he used to get up and clean them for me. I never, ever rode in dirty leathers so it was important to me for them to be cleaned.

He used to work for Slazenger just down the road which, in its heyday, had 2,200 employees. They used to make the old leather footballs there and that proved very handy because, if I ever crashed and needed my leathers or boots repairing, he used to take them in and get then stitched up. The same went for Charlie Monk or any of the other riders we had staying with us. I had a bad back one season and they made me a really good body support belt.

Diane was my first long-term, serious girlfriend – and I don't know why she's still with me! She needs more than a medal because she has put up with a lot over the years. She took her marriage vows like they should be – for better or for worse, for richer or for poorer. My mother liked her a lot and was very keen for us to tie the knot. I came home one day and she said she had seen a lovely engagement ring in a shop in Wakefield. I jokingly told her that she should buy it because her own was looking a bit tatty! I tried to explain that I wasn't ready to buy an engagement ring, but I took the hint and went to have a look at it anyway. She was right, it was a nice ring, so I said to Diane: "I've seen a nice ring. Do you think we ought to become engaged?" She said "yes" and I bought it. I knew I didn't need to but I had already asked her dad. They were a lovely family – very polite – so I thought it best.

Eventually we went to see the vicar about getting married. He asked us when we

I don't know how Diane has put up with me for so long, but thank God she has! Our wedding day was a great occasion and (right) we're joined by Best Man Dave Younghusband.

were thinking of having the ceremony and, acting like we were millionaire big-hitters, we told him just before the end of the tax year. "That's good," he said, "because after April the church is being pulled down."

> "Diane rarely came to watch me race. I used to ask her if she would want to come and hold my ladders if I were a painter and decorator"

As it turned out, ours was the last ever wedding at St Luke's and, because it was being demolished shortly afterwards, it was covered in scaffolding when the service took place. So my mother took some chicken netting along to cover the poles, then decorated the scaffolding with greenery and flowers. She made a really good job of it.

Dave Younghusband was my best man. Frank Varey was there too, along with Charlie Monk and Alan Smith, who was right-winger for the Leeds rugby league club. Alan was a good friend of mine. We went to school together and we still see each other to this day. His ambition was to play at Wembley in a rugby league cup final, and mine was to be good enough to ride in a speedway World Final at Wembley – and we both realised our ambitions. He played for Leeds all through his career – 20-odd years – and they only got paid if they won. If they lost, they didn't get a penny. Leeds were, and still are, one of the top rugby league clubs and on a Saturday I often used to get my bike done, load up the car, then go to watch Alan play at Headingley as his guest. Then I'd pop home before heading off to ride at Halifax, where quite a lot of rugby players would go to watch me race.

Throughout my career I had a few crashes – some of them real beauties, in fact - but I never broke anything until that night at Newport in 1973. But I did get knocked about a bit, just like the rugby league players I used to watch because it's a rough old sport they play. And the technology they had to help players get over their injuries, even back then, was incredible. I never missed meetings – my view was that if it hurt, I should just get on with it because races only last a minute. When I crashed, I was more worried about my bike. I can't understand riders who pull out of a meeting because they have got a cold. What's wrong with them? And, much later on, it wasn't unknown for me to go over to a rider who had fallen during a race and start shouting at them to get up and get on with it because we had a 10pm curfew to stick to!

I always said that, if I ever broke my leg, I would crawl onto the centre green. So keen was I to avoid missing a meeting that Alan used to arrange for me to go to Headingley for treatment if I needed it. One occasion when the rugby club came to my aid was after a crash which left me with a big lump on my groin. I'd gone to the doctor and he sent me to hospital – where they told me I had to stay in for 24 hours under observation. A day in hospital? No way – I told them I couldn't possibly do that because I had to ride, so that's when I went home to phone Alan, and he arranged for me to go to see his club doctor that night. When I got there the doctor put this big black cable around my groin area, switched his machine on, and an hour later the lump had gone. It was better than spending a day on a hospital ward!

It's a shame more riders can't benefit from a bit of co-operation like that, and I still feel that speedway should have a lot more affinity with other sports. When I was at

Hull we had two rugby league teams in the town – we shared the stadium with one of them – but we never had so much as a social get-together with them. We should share our facilities more. Mind you, I'm not certain the Leeds RLFC directors knew what was going on! When I was in the VIP lounge with Alan after the match, I'm sure they knew that I raced speedway because speedway was big in those days. But I'm not sure they were aware I was getting intensive treatment from their club! I don't think they would have minded, though.

Diane and I bought a little semi-detached bungalow for £2,650 to move into when we were married and, funnily enough, John Dews bought a place about 100 yards up the road so we were neighbours for a long time. When we applied for a mortgage we put about £400 down but, being a speedway rider was considered a very dodgy job – unlike a coalminer which, apparently, wasn't dangerous – so my parents had to sign as guarantors in case anything bad should happen to me. They signed quite glibly because there was no way they could have afforded to make the payments if anything did happen.

Diane rarely came to watch me race and I don't think she was particularly happy about that, but I used to ask her if she would want to come and hold my ladders if I were a painter and decorator. Or if I were a milkman, would she want to come along just to walk around carrying bottles? "What's the difference?" I used to ask her. I was paid as a speedway rider – that was my job and I went to meetings to earn a crust for us both. How bigoted does that sound today?

Throughout my career I never phoned home after a meeting either – but before you start to think that I'm cruel and heartless, let me explain. I told Diane that if anything ever happened to me during a meeting, the promoter would be sure to let her know. So if the phone didn't ring, she would know I was OK. Imagine if we had an arrangement that I would phone home every meeting and, for some reason or the other, I wasn't able to – she would be up all night worried sick. Remember, we didn't have mobile phones in those days and it wasn't unusual to stop at a phonebox, only to find the phone out of order.

I remember one night I was coming home from Newport with my mechanic, Bernard Harrison, and he had arranged to ring his wife when we set off home. We went all round Newport and found three phone boxes… but not one of them worked. That's the sort of situation I wanted to avoid.

But I appreciated all the support Diane gave me – as I still do – and with the wedding bells still ringing in my ears, I was ready to start my first season as a married man.

5
'I KILL YOU'

I MADE a quiet start to the 1967 season and it took me a month to score my first maximum. By the time mid-May came around I was in the unfamiliar position of being third in the Halifax averages – but, a month after the wedding, I think the penny suddenly dropped that I was feeding two people now and that I had a mortgage to pay.

Once I got going, I really started flying and I rode myself into the history books after taking a guest booking for King's Lynn at Glasgow White City and scored an 18-point maximum. Only one other visiting rider had previously scored a six-ride full house in the British League at that stage, and the next time I was at Saddlebow Road, Stars promoter Maury Littlechild gave me a £20 bonus as a 'thank you'. We were on £4 a point then, so that was the equivalent of scoring another five points without doing anything except for turning up to do my job.

I had a lot of time for Maury. He opened a track in a field, just like Scunthorpe and Redcar have in the past couple of years, and look at King's Lynn Speedway now. He knew he could rely on me too, because I must have been a promoters' dream as a guest throughout my career – I never turned a booking down and always gave 100 percent.

BSPA regulations meant that our title-winning team had to be broken up ahead of the 1967 season and Dennis Gavros became my new riding partner after Tommy Roper went to Belle Vue. He was a mechanic by trade so he had some good equipment and we had a very good partnership that year. He won loads of bonus points – if I was winning and he was second, I made sure I was just in front so that nobody could get past either of us. They called it team riding – you don't see much of that these days.

One of the big individual meetings at this time was the Internationale at Wimbledon. It was by invitation only and used to attract the best riders in the world. My first invitation to take part in that prestigious spring Bank Holiday Monday event came in 1967 when I went on to finish third. I actually led Gote Nordin, who won the meeting with a 15-point maximum, for two laps but at least I had the satisfaction of being the top British rider on the night.

Nordin was always immaculately dressed and was known as 'Gentleman Gote' but on the track he was no gentleman. He was a typically hard Swedish rider – a crafty old fox. They ran stock cars at Wimbledon as well as speedway and, if you raced there on the Thursday after a Monday night stock car meeting, the track was always terrible. They ran stock cars once a month and, if you were there three weeks after the last meting, the track was very good. But, for the Internationale that night the track was awful. It was deep and patchy, and it reminded me of the field we rode in near home when we were kids. I thought to myself: 'This is just like riding in Coxley Woods.' You couldn't slide your bike into one of the corners on that track we made, and the pit bend was just like that at Plough Lane. Riders were missing the corner because they couldn't turn – but it suited me!

Another occasion when conditions were bad that season was at Poole where we were knocked out of the KO Cup. In fact they were so bad that Eric Boothroyd fell off on the parade lap, and it was unheard of for him to fall off anywhere. I'll openly admit that I was vociferous about bad tracks. If they were terrible, I would say so! I didn't care what the promoters thought.

My argument was that I had a lot of time, money and effort invested in being a speedway rider. I always made the effort to turn up looking immaculate every meeting and with immaculate machinery – in fact Ivan Mauger and I used to have a competition to see who could keep the cleanest bike and, when we were riding in the same meeting, we used to tip our machines on their side to inspect every nook and cranny. He said to me at Halifax one night: "I've got a lad employed full-time to clean my bikes and yours is still cleaner than mine'.

So if I thought a track was a disgrace and not fit to ride on, I would say so. But if the meeting still went ahead, I would ride – albeit after I had made my opinions known. Looking back, maybe it didn't do me any good at all. Perhaps I should have just kow-towed along and done what I was told without saying a word, but that has never been me. I was risking my neck to take part – the only risk the promoters took was that they might lose a few quid.

Poole wasn't an easy track to adapt to from Halifax in any case and only an appeal from Reg Fearman stopped the whole Halifax team from walking out. We ended up on the wrong end of a 60-36 scoreline and that was the first of our trophies from 1966 gone.

It must have been a very wet summer, because in August of that year Dennis Gavros, Dave Younghusband and I withdrew from our home match against Cradley

An individual meeting at The Shay and we were wary of the new tape exclusion rules.

after just one race due to bad track conditions. The track was atrocious and we wanted the meeting called off, but Reg Fearman suggested we all took one ride each to see what it was like. That's what all the promoters used to do – send you out for one race and then say: "You're all dirty now and so is your bike, why don't you finish the meeting?" All the promoters were like that – they wanted you to turn up and race in conditions that today's riders certainly wouldn't tolerate.

Bob Jameson's extra rides at reserve came at a hefty price.

One night at Halifax I got so filled-in that I took my goggles off. I couldn't see a thing, so I pulled up. Where do you get a spare pair of eyes from? You can't go to the supermarket and buy some! Drive down the motorway at 60mph in heavy rain and turn the wipers off, then imagine someone in front of you throwing a bucket of wet shale onto your windscreen, and you'll get the picture.

To appease Reg, we agreed to take one ride apiece, but we still felt the track was dangerous so, after that one ride, we went and sat in the grandstand. Bob Jameson was one of the reserves and he had plenty of extra rides that night. He was so excited about all the extra points money he was getting – but in the last race he came a real cropper and totally wrecked his bike. When we went into the changing rooms after the meeting we all said: "Well done, Bob, you had a great night. You rode really well – but it's going to cost you twice as much as you earned to put your bike right and all week to get over your almost broken ankle."

"If I thought a track was a disgrace, I would say so. But if the meeting still went ahead I'd ride. Maybe it didn't do me any good at all"

I might have pulled out on that occasion but, if you look at the averages I recorded over 10 years at Halifax, it's obvious that I rode in a lot meetings where the conditions were pretty awful, yet I scored the points just the same. Another meeting that springs to mind is my World Championship qualifying round at Newport.

Somerton Park was a track I hated. It was awful. It was square! There was one line around it, unless you wanted to put your neck right on the line and ride like a lunatic. I didn't like it at all, but I won my World Championship round there in 1967 with a 15-point maximum. The meeting had been rained off two weeks running and on the third occasion it was chucking it down again. I stood there in the changing rooms and, because I had a reputation for speaking my mind, everyone was waiting to hear what I had to say. So I told them: "I don't care what the weather is like, I'm not coming all this way again."

When you walked on the track it was like a giant sponge. There was sawdust on the track and I couldn't slide the bike at all – but I still knocked two seconds off the track record. It was so deep that I just road-raced it round. I made a terrific start and stayed in the same tyremarks for all four laps but nobody could get past because there wasn't anywhere to overtake.

Maurice Morley was track manager there at the time and, after I'd won that race, he tried to tell me he was right and that there was nothing wrong with the track. I was having none of it and told him he didn't know what he was talking about! He was happy to point out that I had knocked two seconds off the track record, but he didn't say anything about the bloke behind me being about 10 seconds outside the track record! Chris Pusey and I were unbeaten going into the last race and, before we made our way out onto the track, I told him not to worry about me if he got out of the start ahead of me because I wasn't going to chase him. He just looked at me and said: "I was just about to say exactly the same to you!"

Some people thought I was a trouble-causer but I wasn't. I had a voice and I used it. Eric Boothroyd went to Newport for a World Championship qualifier one year. He walked round the track once and headed straight to his car where he picked up a polythene bag. Then he went back out onto the track and filled his bag with stones he'd found there. He took them back to his car and drove straight home without racing.

That's the sort of thing I wanted to bring to the attention of the promoters. It still bugs me today that you put so much effort into turning up with fantastic equipment to put on a show, and some of the tracks weren't even touched until lunchtime on race-day.

It could be very hard to make yourself heard in those days too. The promoters and riders weren't close friends like they are today – it was very much a worker and boss situation. It was Mr Ochiltree at Coventry, Mr Greene at Wimbledon, Mr Foot at Poole, Mr Fearman at Halifax – no first name like today. The first time I met Ronnie Greene, Our Nigel was mortified that I'd called him Ronnie and not Mr Greene, because you simply didn't do that. You were told what to do and the riders didn't have a say in it – only I was Boocock and I was a Yorkshireman so I was definitely going to have a say in it! I'm the same today. If someone asks me my opinion on something, I'll give a truthful answer and I can't help if they don't like what I say! Sometimes I go over the top – I know that – but speedway has been my life for as long as I can remember so, of course, I'm passionate about it.

Some tracks were disgraceful whatever the weather and Newport was one of them. You rode it like a diamond – you would go tight into the corner and head towards the fence, then come straight back again and lift your foot up as you went into the straight. It was impossible to pass someone round the corners because you couldn't go underneath them and you couldn't go round them because once you got to the middle of the turn you were in the fence because that is where the bloke in front was going. It was a wire safety fence but, on the other side of the dog track, was a bright green hooped fence. So when you were coming down the straight you couldn't see the wire mesh fence, only the green thing behind it. It was very deceptive to ride – it appeared as though the fence was further back than it actually was.

Happily, though, the conditions were better in September when I made my World Final debut at Wembley. And, just as I had done at the Internationale, I finished the night as the top British rider after scoring nine points. I had to buy a new motor for the big night because, during practice on the Thursday, the one I had blew sky high. Wayne Briggs was going up to ride at Edinburgh on the Friday night so his dad,

Barry, the Jawa main dealer, arranged for him to drop an engine of at my house on the way. I stripped it down, checked it over, put a magneto on it, fitted it and went back to Wembley on the Saturday. I had explained to Reg Fearman that I'd blown my only engine so I didn't have one to use in the World Final, and asked if he would buy me one.

Typically for a promoter, he said "Where am I going to get the money from?" and I suggested he might well have a bit more than I did! But he wouldn't budge and I paid for the engine from Briggo myself. Reg rang me again on Saturday and eventually said he'd chip in £50 towards the £125 it cost me for a new motor. But I still wasn't happy and told him to stick his £50 where the sun didn't shine!

What I discovered many years later, though, was that every track that sold World Final tickets kept ten per cent of the value – and there were thousands sold at The Shay because I was the first Halifax rider ever to qualify for a World Final. Reg would therefore have earned far more than £125 in ticket sales and, of course, he paid nowt!

Despite a decent score on my World Final debut, I told the speedway press I felt I'd performed terribly and wished I could ride the meeting again. I'd complained that the JAPs were faster than the ESOs, but I think that was just an excuse because I hadn't done as well as I'd hoped. The big let-down in my career was that every meeting was just another meeting to me, whether it was an open meeting, league or KO Cup. Or even a World Final. It was a job – I went there, did my best, then went home.

If you want to get to the top, you have got to raise your game. My record shows that I was good, but to be the best you have to be mentally prepared and I wasn't. It was my own fault. The atmosphere at Wembley was amazing, but I should have been mentally smart enough to know it wasn't just another meeting – it was the main speedway meeting of the year anywhere in the world. I should have been more switched on to know what that meeting meant.

I'm not big-headed enough to say that I could have been world champion but I had 99 percent of the equation right and maybe, if I had got the mental preparation right, I could have done a lot better than finish sixth. I had great equipment, a nice style, a good speedway brain – all the attributes that make up a World Champion – but whether I could have ever done it, I don't know.

I was certainly relaxed before the meeting – so much so than when I arrived at Wembley I had a sleep in the back of my car. And, when the racing began, I savoured the moment. I stopped Igor Plechanov getting on the rostrum and I passed Colin Pratt from the back in the first race, even though there weren't too many passing lines at Wembley, certainly favouring the good gaters.

At the end of that season Halifax were seventh in the British League table. I had only been unplaced six times throughout the British League season and I finished with an average of 10.38, just behind Nigel (10.46), so I was closing the gap. I also managed to claim the scalp of Ove Fundin, the newly-crowned World Champion, in the British League Riders' Championship at Belle Vue where I finished fourth.

One of my duties at Halifax – which earned me an extra £5 a week – was to maintain the track spare and take it with me to all the meetings. That's the bike I rode in the BLRC while my own was on its way to Australia, where I was riding that winter.

For the start of the 1968 season I invested in a new Ford Cortina 100E. In fact, it wasn't unusual for me to start the new year with a new car because I saw it as being an extension of the job. I was fortunate that The Shay was very close to my home, but I covered a lot of miles travelling to away matches and World Championship rounds. Nigel thought I was being extravagant but I wasn't. The motorway network was only just getting underway, so we spent a lot of time in our cars. What was the point it driving all that way and then getting out of your car with a terrible back-ache or if the backs of your legs were hurting? I used to get a good deal because I was a local celebrity so, by the time I came to sell it, I hadn't lost too much in depreciation.

Unfortunately the Cortina wasn't one of my best buys. It was always in the garage and we used to call it the Friday Afternoon Car – it seemed to have been put together without too much thought and whoever built it was too busy thinking about the weekend. It had the wrong speedo drive on the diff so, when you were doing 70mph, it reckoned you were doing about 95mph!

That wasn't the only transport trouble I had that year. Eric Boothroyd was in a consortium which owned a little Cessna light aircraft and he offered to fly me and Dennis Gavros from Leeds-Bradford Airport down to High Beech for the 40th anniversary of speedway celebrations. We took off and the next thing we knew there was a noise like we were being machine-gunned. I was looking round for the Red Baron! It was scary because, once you're up there, there's only one way to go and that's down. Eric radioed back and told the airport we were coming back. As we approached the runway we saw a fire engine racing along the runway to where we

I was quite content to be third behind Barry Briggs and Ivan Mauger at the 1968 British Final.

were going to land. It turned out that the fuel tank filler cap on the wing was on a chain and it had come undone. So we tightened it up and went on our way again, following the M1 motorway most of the way.

Speedway was booming at that time. Tracks were springing up all over the place and 1968 saw the launch of the British League Second Division. There were the usual changes to the team for the start of the season, one of which saw Les Sharpe arrive from Australia on the recommendation of Aub Lawson. Les was an enigma. He could ride a speedway bike but he couldn't ever find any form of consistency. I don't think he ever developed to his full potential, although he made me ride hard and kept me on my toes for quite a long while. Eventually, though,

Eric Boothroyd flew us to High Beech.

he went back to Australia – I don't think he could hack it. I think the pressure got to him.

There was a story that he drove all the way down to London for a match at Wimbledon. He was almost there because he'd driven over Kew Bridge, but he couldn't find a toilet so he drove home.

Reg Fearman was fond of bringing Australian riders over - perhaps because they liked the big tracks and could adapt to Halifax quicker than some of the others in this country. Before the first race he would often stage a race between four Aussies and whoever won would take one of the reserve berths for the meeting – vultures races we used to call them. It was often one of the best races of the night until the Speedway Control Board stopped the practice. Competition is what speedway is all about but trust the SCB to come up with another nonsensical rule.

Having got to the World Final in 1967, I was naturally only too keen to book my place for the big night again in '68. By finishing behind Briggo and Ivan Mauger in the British Final at Wimbledon, I qualified for the British-Nordic Final at West Ham. Dave Younghusband, who was still a team-mate after withdrawing a transfer request in the close season, qualified too and we went down to London in style… in a Rolls Royce. It belonged to Henry Nelson, who was Greg Kentwell's sponsor, and he offered to drive the three of us down to Custom House in it. We put a trailer on the back with my bike, plus Dave's machine and Greg's as a spare, and off we set for West Ham. About a mile from the stadium we stopped. Greg, Dave and I all got in the back and Henry put a chauffeur's cap on – you should have seen the looks we got when we pulled into the stadium.

It rained on and off throughout the meting at Custom House and Dave only scored one point. I failed to win a race all meeting too, but my eight-point total was enough to put me through to the European Final at Wroclaw in Poland.

Unfortunately, though, I never got to ride in that meeting because, despite going all the way to Poland, I was ill and had to pull out. Barry Briggs had only qualified as reserve and he took my place. There were insinuations that Briggo had paid me not to ride, but that was most certainly NOT the case. Unfortunately, you are never going to stop that sort of talk, but I was genuinely ill and I withdrew from the meeting on the orders of the track doctor.

The problems began when we had to swap planes for our flight out to Poland and we ended up in a little 14-seater with leather seatbelts with a little peg attached to it. Talk about looking ominous. I wasn't a good traveller anyway, and it was a bad flight. When we landed it was as though the pilot hadn't decided to head for the runway until he'd seen it. As we made this sudden descent, the snot came gushing out of my nose, my ears were bursting and my eyes were pouring. My head felt like it was exploding so, when we arrived at our hotel, I took the opportunity to get some rest. The track doctor came to see me and, even though I felt terrible, I told him I was going to practice the following day along with everybody else. So practise I did, and I went very well.

However when I got back into the changing rooms afterwards, I bent down to take my steel shoe off and – bang! I collapsed. The track doctor came to see me and visited me again at the hotel the next morning. He gave me an injection and stuffed cotton wool so far up my nose I thought it was going to end up in my brain – he then told me I wouldn't be riding. Polish hospitals had a very bad reputation – I remember Sverre Harrfeldt being taken to one after a crash one year. About four hours later, after the meeting had finished, Briggo went to see him… and he was still on a trolley, in his leathers, in a dingy waiting room that looked like a dungeon – so I certainly didn't want to end up in that sort of situation.

In hindsight, maybe I should have ridden, but I wasn't well and my loss was Briggo's gain. In fact he seized the opportunity with both hands and went on to qualify for the World Final at Gothenburg, where he finished second as Ivan Mauger won the first of his six titles.

I was never a good air traveller and, after any length of time in a plane, I would get dizzy. After I got home from a trip to Australia it used to take me two weeks to get my sense of balance back. The first time I got back from Australia I had to spend two days in bed because I couldn't stand up. I'm not sure of the exact medical description but it's something to do with pressure being put on the inner ear – and there was some pressure that day we landed in Poland, I can tell you! Even today I have to get tablets from the doctor to get my balance back although, as the pressurisation has improved in aircraft, I have become a better traveller.

Another thing I won't ever forget from that trip to Poland is that Nigel sold my jacket! It was a leather one I had bought in Sweden and, after I had been resting following one of my visits from the doctor, Nigel came up to me and said: "The good news is that while you have been in bed all day, I've sold your jacket." He'd got a good deal for it apparently, but I wasn't too happy and asked him: "Why didn't you sell your own then – or, better still, why don't you sell the bed I'm in?"

Another overseas trip I made that year was when I broke new ground by competing in the Dutch Golden Helmet in Amsterdam. Geoff Mudge, me, Colin Pratt, Charlie Monk, Terry Betts, Roy Trigg, Norman Hunter and Bruce Cribb all stayed in one hotel room – it was like a school dormitory. Geoff Mudge had a book with him and, as we walked back to the hotel at about midnight after having something to eat, he was reading us extracts from it. He was so engrossed in it that he walked into a lamp post! It was so funny – just like something you see in a film. The book was about slavery and he read out a chapter in which somebody was getting whipped. We all wanted to hear more and, for about half an hour after we had got back to our room, we insisted he carried on reading to us. Eventually we turned our lights out and went to sleep, but we hadn't been settled down long when suddenly we heard a loud scream. Charlie sat bolt upright and sent his blankets flying everywhere. He was having a nightmare that somebody was whipping him! Charlie wasn't amused but the rest of us had a good laugh about it.

The day of the meeting wasn't without its laughs at someone's expense either. It was a lovely hot day and we arrived at the stadium early, so we all laid down on some grass banking, drinking pop and chatting. When Bruce Cribb stood up we realised he had been lying in the biggest pile of dog poo imaginable! He had been

"Sometimes I go over the top – I know that – but speedway has been my life for as long as I can remember so, of course, I'm passionate about it"

convinced he could smell something all the time we'd been there, and he was right. We had to get a bucket full of cold water to wash it because, boy, did it smell!

On the domestic front, 1968 was the year when compulsory exclusions were introduced for breaking the tapes. I became a victim of the rule during Halifax's home meeting against West Ham. There had already been two false starts and, at the third attempt the referee saw fit to exclude me for breaking the tapes. I was absolutely livid because I was convinced I shouldn't have been thrown out of the race, but there wasn't much I could do. I went back to the pits while Reg Fearman got onto the phone to the referee and, while I was in there, a big cheer went up around the stadium. I turned to Bernard Harrison, my mechanic, and asked if the ref and changed his mind and put me backing the race.

Bernard told me not to get too excited because the cheer was for a woman who had climbed up to the referee's box. The referee's box at Halifax was right up in the gods – in a vertical line upwards it must have been 40ft. There was an old steel ladder which was bolted at the top and bottom, and this woman had apparently tottered up there in her pleated skirt and high-heel shoes to confront the referee. I didn't want to know about that, though because I was still feeling aggrieved at being excluded.

I just sat on my toolbox and sulked but, during the interval when things were a little quieter, I decided to ring the referee and ask him why he excluded me. So I picked up the phone in the pits and rang the box. When the referee picked up the phone I told him who I was and said: "It's a bit quieter now, so could you please tell me why you excluded me from that race?" He just gave a sigh and said: "Eric, I'm not going through it all again – I've just explained it to your mother!"

It was my own mum who had climbed up to the referee's box! I couldn't believe it

– I was twice as mad then. I didn't laugh about it then, but I can see the funny side now. Dougie Adams was the timekeeper and he told me the full story – apparently my mother really had the referee worried. She said afterwards that she was all right until she went to climb back down the ladder. She looked down and there were 3,000 pairs of eyes gazing up, cheering and shouting.

Once again at the end of the season I headed off to Belle Vue for the British League Riders' Championship – and got as close as I ever managed to winning it. Right up until the last race things were going my way. I had never won a major title but I won my first four races, beat World Champion Ivan Mauger and pre-meeting favourite Barry Briggs and set the fastest time at Hyde Road for two years. But in my last heat of the night Soren Sjosten, who was well out of the running, got out of the start in front of me and I just couldn't get past. I'd even lent him a spark plug because he couldn't get his bike going! I tried everything in the book to get past him but he was a wily old bugger and I just couldn't do it, even though I'd already beaten Briggo and Ivan from the back earlier in the meeting.

Charlie Monk was in that race too and, before we went out, he came over and said: "Don't worry about me – I'll keep out of your way." And, I can't lie, I did think about going over to Sjosten and asking him to keep out of my way too, because I stood to win the meeting if I finished first. But if I couldn't win it fair and square, it would be a false victory. I could have gone to Sjosten no bother and said: "Soren, here's £20 – stay out of my way."

That sort of thing certainly went on, and I know that Malcolm Simmons has made reference to it in his new book, Simmo: The Whole Truth. The biggest culprit I knew was an England international – I don't want to name him – who used to buy points in World Championship rounds right from the first qualifying meeting if he was struggling. He never tried to buy points from me and I never, ever attempted to buy

Racing with Briggo at Swindon. He was like a mentor and, for me, the best rider around in my day.

points from anyone, but I was aware that this sort of thing went on, albeit on a small scale.

So after finishing second in my last heat at the BLRC, I ended up in a run-off for the title with Briggo. It was my last race in England that year and I had a brand new tyre, cut on one side, and I thought that would just do me for five rides at Belle Vue. It did, but the trouble was, I had six because of the run-off. Briggo, on the other hand, put a brand new tyre on for the run-off.

But, I have to say, even if I'd had a new back tyre and a new front tyre on, Briggo would still have beaten me. After the race we went out to the starting gate for the presentations and he had his arm around me all the way. Then, when he was given the winner's laurel wreath, he put it round my neck and said: "You deserve this". It was a lovely gesture from a lovely man.

I had a lot of time for Briggo and, I think, he had a lot of time for me. He was like my mentor. He was a rival and he was twice as good as I was, but I admired the way he raced. I admired Ivan Mauger for being the total professional he was and for being way ahead of everyone else. But I liked the way Briggo raced and, for me, he was the best rider in my day.

If he came out of the start last, he would fight for everything and win races. He told me that he thrived on panic and that he lived on that supercharged atmosphere of things going wrong.

I rode in a Test match against Sweden at Glasgow White City one year early in my international career and my partner was Briggo. In one race Olle Nygren stuffed me right into the fence. Briggo looked behind to see where I was so, on the last corner of the last lap, he ran Nygren so wide he nearly put him into the fence, which allowed me to nip inside. I could have won easily but I just knocked the throttle off so that Barry got the win. When Briggo got off his bike he never said a word to me – he went straight over to Nygren. He said to him: "If you want to pick on someone, pick on me or one of the old hands. This kid has just started in speedway." I told him how much I appreciated that and he said: "Don't worry, he won't do that again."

Briggo often used to stay at my parents' house if he was passing, as a lot of the riders did. They all knew where to find the keys and they used to let themselves in. One night he had quite a surprise when he got into the spare bedroom where all the riders used to stay. My mum had been doing some work for the Co-op which was closing down and she got hold of a mannequin which had been used as a window display. My sister put a wig on it and we put it in Briggo's bed before he arrived. When we got up the next morning we found Briggo fast asleep on the settee! My dad asked him what he was doing there and he said: "There's a woman in my bed". The joke backfired on us really, because we all felt really guilty for making poor old Barry sleep on the settee.

At the end of 1968 Halifax were seventh in the First Division table, so we began 1969 with the aim of improving upon that. We did so with a new team captain – me. Eric Boothroyd had finally retired and joined Northern Speedways Ltd as co-promoter and team manager at Halifax. That meant I replaced him as the skipper although, to be honest, I can't say it was much of a big deal to me. Someone had to do the job and, because I'd been the top points-scorer for several years, I was the obvious choice.

We all make a meal of being appointed captain in the press, but it's not that important really. Apart from tossing a coin and choosing a gate position, you don't have a lot to say. There was more camaraderie than there seems to be now. These days you see a rider with mechanical problems on the two-minute time allowance and everyone else is looking in their

Chasing after Norwegian No.1 Reidar Eide in the British-Nordic Final at Hampden Park. He threatened to kill me.

toolbox or heading off to the loo. In my day there would be three riders offering their bike for you to use – and you would fall out with two of them because you didn't choose theirs!

So there wasn't as much need for a team leader then. And, to be fair, I always made my feelings known before that, so I might as well have been captain anyway. Even when Eric was captain it was me who said it all and I'd always tried to help everyone in the team – I didn't just turn up, do my own thing and go home. If anyone got into any trouble, I was always there first.

Fortunately by the time the season started I had recovered from having my tonsils out. Now that's something I wouldn't recommend to anybody! The pain was terrible. It feels like your throat has been cut – because, inside, it has. You can't swallow at all to start with and it takes about 14 days to get right afterwards. You lose a lot of blood too and all they give you are ice cubes or lollipops for three days afterwards because your throat is red raw inside. The pain for the first three days was worse than when I broke my arm at Newport. But I needed to have it done because I was so sick of getting tonsillitis and I've never had it since!

> "She said afterwards that she was all right until she went to climb back down the ladder and there were 3,000 pairs of eyes gazing up at her"

The season started well for me and by May I had an average of 11.45. Some people would kill for that – and in fact Reidar Eide did threaten to kill me - and I am absolutely certain he meant it! Eide was, as we say in Yorkshire, a bit puddled! I genuinely thought that, the first chance he had, he would kill himself to kill me!

The situation developed during the Dairy Festival Trophy at The Shay in June – a meeting I won, incidentally. I can remember it as though it was yesterday. When someone tells you they are going to kill you, you don't forget it in a hurry! Eide was on gate three, I was on gate two and Ronnie Moore was on gate one. Eide made the best start and was mid-track on the banking as we went into the first corner. I was underneath him and Ronnie Moore came right round the grass on the inside. Coming out of the corner, where it went square, we all collided. The track at Halifax narrowed coming out of the corners and it wasn't as if Ronnie was trying to run us wide – he simply had to move out. There was lots of room but Eide wasn't moving

Looking out over the steeply banked Shay track – it was home to me for 10 years.

out, he was chopping back. What a crash! My bike was wrecked and I had to borrow one from Pete Smith of Poole for the rerun. I, along with my bike, ended up by the changing room gates halfway down the back straight . . . and Eide ENDED UP IN THE CROWD!

He climbed back over the fence and came marching towards me. He was so angry his eyes were bulging out of his head. It looked like his eyes were on stalks, like a snail's! As we walked back to the pits he pointed straight at me and, in his heavy Norwegian accent, said: "I kill you." Sometimes riders would say things they didn't mean in the heat of the moment, but I've no doubt he meant what he said. It was just a racing incident and there was no reason for him to get so worked up. We were all going for it and, even if I had knocked the throttle off,

Wimbledon legend Ronnie Moore became the target of Reidar Eide after he realised that I wasn't to blame for him crashing.

Ronnie would still have come through and collided with him instead of me.

Eide was the No.1 at Coatbridge and, after that incident, I really didn't want to go up there and race with Halifax later in the season. I'd thought a lot about what he had said to me but, needless to say, I had to go. And that was the only time I ever thought about my average. I had an 11.02 average at the time – it had been as high as 11.53 at one point - and I was determined not to let it dip below 11 by the end of the season. We won the toss and I chose gates one and three which meant, for the first race, I was on gate one and he was next to me on gate two.

When the tapes went up I must have made the best start I ever made in my life! I went so fast out of that start and into the first bend I could believe it. I left him miles behind me – it was either that or finish miles behind him! I went through the meeting without dropping a point and I wouldn't take an extra ride because I didn't want it to affect my average.

It was the first time I ever said 'no' to an extra ride

Eventually Eide realised I wasn't to blame for his crash. He came up to me at Halifax one day and told me he wanted a word with me. "Eric, I speak to many people after this crash," he said in his stunted English, "and I not kill you now. I now kill Ronnie Moore!"

I told him to be careful, because Ronnie was a much better rider than me and had a lot of influential friends. Sure enough, later that season he stuck Ronnie Moore right on the centre green at Coventry. But, as Ronnie came back onto the track, he revved his bike up flat out, dropped the clutch and went flying into Eide. As Eide went all ends up onto the track, Ronnie dived on him so he had the last laugh.

There were some nasty vendettas in those days. People genuinely had little black

Halifax v Belle Vue in 1969 with Ivan Mauger and myself leading out the teams.

books to mark down the names of riders they wanted to settle a score with.

Exeter was always a favourite track of mine, even though it was very rough. I won the Westernapolis there in 1967 and 1968 – and I would have won it again in 1969 if it hadn't been for my brother! I'd gone down to his house in Rugby on the Monday morning and we travelled down to the County Ground together. We met in the last race and he beat me. If I had finished in front of him I would have won the trophy for the third time on the trot, so I might well have been able to keep it. I pointed that out to Nigel as we walked out to the presentations, but he acted all innocent and claimed he had no idea I'd won the event for the last two years. "Oh, you should have told me," he said – like he didn't know!

Nigel liked Exeter as much as I did. The first time I went there I was talking to Howdy Byford in the pits. He rode there at the time and was a mate of Nigel's, so he was giving me some advice. In my first race I ended up riding against him and I remember saying to him: "Don't run over me." After the race Nigel said to me: "Young Un, you're just not going hard enough. If you hit the first bump, you will clear the next six!"

The harder you rode it, the better you went there. It was just a case of having the confidence because it was always bumpy. It was so rough that your foot used to come out of the foot rest – your privates would slam onto the seat and you would be out of control! So I used to cut a rubber band off an inner tube about an inch wide, pull it round the foot rest and over my foot. It was so much safer because at least when your foot came out of the foot rest, it went back in.

On the team front, I accomplished my aim of finishing with an average of over 11 and, for the first time since I joined the Dukes, I didn't miss a match all season. My final average that year was 11.02 and, statistically, I had enjoyed the best ever season by a Halifax rider. Out of 18 home meetings I scored 16 maximums, and I rattled off four more full houses away from home – so it must have been a shock for the manager and fans to pick up the local paper the following February and read the headline "Eric Boocock to quit British speedway".

⑥
WHAT ABOUT THE TRACK RECORD?

T HE 1970s were barely two months old when the Halifax Evening Courier ran the story than I was considering an offer to ride full-time in America. I had been to Australia again that winter and I came home via the States where I stayed in Los Angeles with DeWayne Keeter, who was one of the top American riders of the time.

I met a few of the other riders over there and also some of the promoters, and they offered me a contract to go and ride there. It was nothing in writing, just a verbal offer and something to think about when I got back home.

At the time I was having another difference of opinion with Reg Fearman over money for the following season. I was no different to any other rider – we all used to try our hardest to get the best possible deal, while the promoters would dig their heels in to pay us what they wanted to which was normally no increase on standard pay. Dave Younghusband was in dispute with the club over money as well that winter, but this sort of situation was no different to what happens today.

Promoters have always tried to pay their riders as little as they can get away with. Reg always used to say that if I didn't agree the deal I had been offered I would have to go back to working with my dad in the mill – but on this occasion I told him I wasn't worried about that because I'd had an offer to go and ride in the States. Then it got picked up by the press and the story was out. But I don't think it was ever a serious proposition, it was something to think about and I've no doubt it would have been a nice life for seven months, but it was just another string to my bow when it came to negotiating a contract really.

I missed the first two matches of that season because I hadn't agreed a deal with Reg. It's fair to say there were a few heated arguments that winter – but once you struck a deal with him, that was it. He was a man of his word and, if he said he was going to do something, he would do it. You didn't need it in writing. My feeling at the time was that I had carried the team year after

Leicester's DeWayne Keeter – the first American to race in the British League.

year and it seemed like I was being taken for granted – particularly when I saw all the Aussies coming over. There was no way they could have afforded their own air fare over – which must have been around £900 at the time – so it was reasonable to assume the promoters were paying it. Meanwhile here was I, a lad from 20 minutes down the road who had come good, and I couldn't get the deal I thought I was worth.

The issue was finally resolved when Reg phoned me from the Grand Hotel in Huddersfield one Sunday morning. Halifax had ridden their first challenge match of the season the previous evening and I was nowhere to be seen. "Where were you last night?" he asked me. I told him I was at a 21st birthday party, which was absolutely true, and pointed out that I had warned him I wouldn't be riding. What is more, I told him, I wasn't planning on being at the next meeting either.

But Reg was keen to talk and suggested I jumped into my car and meet him in Huddersfield. I was still playing it cool and told him a better idea would be if he drove over to me, but in the end I did go to his hotel. We had breakfast together and agreed a deal without falling out. In his defence, Reg was very good at making a penny stretch to tuppence and, years later when I was involved in promoting, my dealings with him stood me in good stead for when I became a promoter.

Reports of my offer to ride in America made it onto the Yorkshire TV news, but that wasn't the only time I was on the small screen early that year. Nigel and I were the mystery celebrities on BBC's A Question of Sport. Ivan Mauger, who was reigning world champion at the time, was one of the panellists – but he couldn't identify the two Boococks! The BBC had me and Nigel typing – well, pretending to – in promoter Charles Ochiltree's office at Coventry Stadium and I enjoyed doing

Northern Riders' Champion at Sheffield.

it. Speedway was high profile then, and it was a good plug for the sport.

On the track it was another decent season, although my World Championship hopes were ended when I failed to make it past the British semi-final at Sheffield. I did, however, enjoy a happy return to Owlerton when I won the Northern Riders' Championship there in September. I had already won the Dews Trophy at Halifax that season so it was good to earn another individual honour, especially as the Northern Riders' Championship was a prestigious title, with qualifying rounds to get into the final. Mind you, it was very wet and I was the first one to tell the referee the track was too slippery and that he should postpone it. I had some good fortune in the first race when Oyvind Berg fell and forced a rerun – I was second to Jim Airey at the time, but I won at the second attempt. But

So close again in the BLRC, but this time Briggo and Anders Michanek beat me in the run-off.

that's the way it goes, isn't it? The tide goes in and the tide goes out. When you're on the crest of a wave you have to make the most of it because when you're in the trough you have to climb back out of it.

Once again I almost won the British League Riders' Championship that year, but in the event I was third behind Barry Briggs and Anders Michanek in a three-man run-off. They were two of the best riders in the world while I considered myself a minnow and I still found it difficult to believe it was me who was rattling up such big scores. I used to go home and think: "That can't have been me on that bike – I'm not good enough".

I should, however, have come home from Wembley with a very nice prize – but I still have no idea where it disappeared to! Trevor Redmond had relaunched Wembley Lions and I was there with Halifax for a British League match. As the meeting went on, I got better and better. By the time the second half came, I was flying. Redmond had set out a table with some very nice trophies to be presented after the scratch race final, which I won. But, when the end of the meeting came, there were no prizes to be seen! He had been expecting one of his own riders to win it but, unfortunately, I did so I got nothing. Redmond's nickname was Billy Liar – and I think that's a good example of how he earned it!

Another time I got short-changed was at Leicester. I broke the

"I broke a few track records in my time and, apart from that occasion at Leicester, I always got the extra fiver. But wasn't that just so childish?"

track record there when Ron Wilson was the promoter and it was the accepted practice throughout speedway that, if you had done that, you were given a fiver extra. When my pay sheet arrived in the post, there was no mention of the track record. So I wrote on the pay sheet: "Dear Ron, I think you may have made a mistake – what about the track record?" and sent it back to him. He sent it straight back to me and wrote underneath: "What about the track record?"

I then returned to him a second time. This time I wrote on it: "Normally, good promoters pay £5." He returned it again and had written on it: "Not at Leicester."

When you were riding for £1 a point, an extra fiver was worth having. But wasn't that just so childish? They were making money and it's not as if I was asking for £100 or £200. I broke a few track records in my time and, apart from that occasion at Leicester, I always got the extra fiver.

Compare that to the time I was in a scratch race final at Poole. The rider in front of me stopped so, going into the very last corner of the very last lap, I was third. But suddenly, I went from third to first! I dived into the white line and hit a great big rut. The bike took off and landed sideways. The next thing I knew, I was coming out of the corner and passed both the riders in front of me, one of whom was Gote Nordin. Poole promoter Charlie Foot had a gold watch he had planned to present to the top scorer in the Pirates team that evening – but he gave it to me because I had brought the house down with that move. He said: "Don't worry, I'll get another one. What you did was tremendous". That was proper speedway.

By the end of 1970 my career was in full flight and, although I decided to work at the mill instead of going to race in Australia that winter, I was still eager for some competitive action. So I bought a Bultaco and did some trials riding as a bit of fun. I hadn't had a winter at home for years and I wanted to keep my hand in. Then the ACU asked for some nominations to ride in an ice speedway meeting in Grenoble and, always keen to try something different, I put my name down.

There wasn't much interest from the other riders so Andy Ross and I were the only two Brits to make the trip. I had only ever seen a photograph of an ice bike before and I'd certainly never ridden one. But we travelled out in an Austin A55 pick-up and I was well up for it. The journey took us up into the mountains through Switzerland and, while we were on our way we noticed a ski resort. It was closed, so we pulled into this huge empty car park which was all frozen over. We unloaded the bikes and had a blast round the car park – what a place for my first ride on an ice bike!

Before the meeting we were allowed to practice on the track – and I couldn't believe what I had let myself in for. I walked into the stadium and stood at the end of one of the straights to watch one of the better riders who was out on the track at the time. I was convinced he was never going to get round the corner! I was weighing up which way to run! I couldn't believe it, but after I had been out for a practice, I thought: 'It's not so bad.'

I finished 12th overall and came home with the best newcomer trophy – although neither Andy nor I returned with any money. It was a 2,400-mile round trip, we were away for a week and we didn't earn a penny. The promoter arranged to give us what he had agreed to pay us when we got back at the hotel after the meeting. We caught

up with him the following morning and he told Andy he would sort us out as soon as he had been up to his room after breakfast. We never saw him again! He did a runner. The meeting hadn't attracted a particularly big crowd and we weren't the only riders he hadn't paid, but it was another valuable lesson I had learned – don't trust anybody, at least not with money!

To make it worse, on our way back home we ran out of petrol. It was pitch dark and we were in the middle of nowhere in Europe. So we drained the methanol out of both bikes and mixed it with a bottle of Scotch which we had bought and poured it into the tank. The car, on full choke, coughed and spluttered a bit but we got it to the next filling station where we could fill it up with petrol.

The next time I was back on shale, the Halifax track had a different look to it. The Football League had ruled that all four corners of the football pitch had to be laid down permanently from the start of the 1971 season. Prior to that they used to be lifted up for each speedway meeting. The track was never wide at The Shay but when they altered it, it was narrower still going into the corners and, if they hadn't been banked up, you wouldn't have got round them. It made it more difficult to get round the white line and Colin Pratt, who was known as an inside line rider, used to be able to get round it really well by hugging the white line. But when they changed the track, it made it twice as hard for riders like Pratty. You had to go past the corner before you could turn in because it was square.

The newly-reshaped track didn't cause me too many problems – but my machinery did. I had invested in two brand new ESOs and the trouble I was having affected me so badly that I lost weight with worry. Even though I had two bikes, I had my favourite – I think that most speedway riders are the same. It happens so many times – the main bike has a problem so you take bits off the spare to repair it.

I was happy enough with the way I was riding, but the bike would run perfectly for a race and then it would suddenly cut out. Then it would start going again. This was happening on a regular basis – one minute I would be flying and the next I'd be slowing down. I was meticulous with my equipment and I couldn't believe it. I tried absolutely everything and got so worked up about it that I used to come home from meetings, put my overalls on and start stripping the engine down trying to find the problem. It would be one or two o'clock in the morning sometimes and I would be there in the workshop trying to get to the bottom of it.

One of the occasions when the problem surfaced was when Halifax were riding against Coventry. I was beating Nigel and, as we went down the back straight, the engine died. Then, just as it always did, it started going again. I still beat Nigel but he almost ran into me and, when he rode back into the pits he was furious. He accused me of showing off in front of my home supporters and trying to make him look stupid because he thought I was slowing down deliberately. We had a huge row about it and I told him, just as I had been doing for weeks, that it was my bike which was causing me problems.

At the end of the meeting I told Reg Fearman I was going to take a month off to sort it out. It annoyed me that I was falling out with my own brother over it and my parents were worried because they had seen how much money I was spending trying to put it right. Bernard, my mechanic, used to come over every Sunday morning to help me wash the bikes, but I told him not to come the following day because I was going to leave the bikes on the trailer and have a lie-in, which was unheard of for me. The following day Bernard came round anyway and, sure enough, both bikes were still on the trailer where I'd left them. I had no intention at all of doing anything with them, but Bernard convinced me that the bikes needed to be cleaned whether I needed to get them ready for the next meeting or not.

He took the main bike to clean because I refused to touch it after all the grief it had caused me. On the crankshaft there was between 25/35 thou end-float. Out of habit we used to make the flywheel clonk. When Bernard set to work he noticed there was no end-float, so we washed it quickly and stripped the engine down. The pins from the crankshaft were pressed in and the main shaft which drove the chain had moved. When the engine got red hot it would take all the end-float out, which made the engine die, and then go back in, which allowed it to go again.

That was why we could never find the problem, but luckily on this occasion it had stopped out. It was simple enough to put right and went like a rocket after that. Eight weeks it took us to find that and I was like a new bloke after that. That was probably the worst period in my career.

After the previous year's disappointment, I had a far better run in the World Championship in 1971. Mind you, I left it late to qualify from the British-Nordic Final at Hampden Park. I needed a win from my final race, and I beat Ivan Mauger from the back to get it and I'm certain that was on Ivan's No 2 bike!

Now Hampden Park was a track I didn't like. The dressing rooms were amazing –

Leading Ivan and Briggo in the 1970 Internationale at Wimbledon.

they even had under-floor heating – but the track was rubbish. It was square, like Newport, and on the back straight into turn three you actually rode under the overhang of the stand, so you would come out of sunshine behind you into a big, dark shadow, round the next corner and back into brilliant sunshine on the home straight. The stadium was first class but it was purpose-built for football and you can't expect people to watch speedway unless the product is right. You can't go round corners at 90 degrees and call it speedway. At places like Scunthorpe and Somerset today there aren't many facilities but the racing is first class. I admire any promoter for having a go and I take my hat off to anyone who does that, but the racing has to be good for it to work.

But whether you like a track or not, you have to go there and that do or die effort in my last race was good enough to earn me a place in the European Final. I was beginning to get a little worried earlier, however, because the countershaft on my bike broke – but fortunately Ivan leant me his spare machine. It reminded me of the time I let Soren Sjosten have a spark plug before the final race of the BLRC and he beat me.

At the time, I guess Ivan was using nitro in his fuel because it hadn't yet been banned in the British League. A lot of riders were experimenting with it at the time and its biggest advantage was that it was definitely better out of the start. But the biggest disadvantage was that it was volatile. It was unbelievable stuff and you had to get the mix dead right. I played around with it for a while but, for me, the advantage it gave you wasn't worth the risk of blowing your engine all over the grandstand every time you came out for a race. We were all on two-valve Jawas at the time, which were so reliable, and there seemed no point in risking that. When I tried it I didn't put as much in as some of the other riders because I wanted some reliability. I could have put more in but I didn't want my engine blowing sky high.

The way I looked at it was that if someone had an advantage, I wanted to find out what it was. It didn't mean I necessarily thought it was a good idea, I just wanted it

> "Charlie Foot had a gold watch he had planned to present to the top scorer in the Poole team – but he gave it to me because I'd brought the house down"

to be a level playing field. You got sucked into it in a sense whether you liked it or not, because if someone is gaining an advantage, you can either get left behind or catch up. And it wasn't as if everyone was using it – it was only a few of the top lads and once they had tried it, a few of the other top lads wanted to give it a go.

I remember the time Greg Kentwell experimented with it at Halifax. He was quick, there are no two ways about that, but then the engine blew so dramatically that I'm sure the pieces landed in Bradford! The whole lot disintegrated. They use it in drag racing and sprints now, but it's technical stuff. We were just a bunch of rough and ready lads – nobody really knew what they were doing. Somebody had an idea and everyone else jumped on it.

It was eventually banned before the start of the 1973 season because it was highly explosive and therefore more than a little bit dangerous to have in the pits. But I think the biggest problem was that nobody knew enough about it. The powers that be were trying to keep the costs down so it didn't make any sense to let riders use something that was going to blow their engine into a million pieces.

The funny thing is that Ivan was getting so good that he didn't need to use nitro, but he was a trend-setter and was always being copied. Who put the first spoilers on his bikes? Ivan did. The joke was that it was better when you rode near the fence because it acted as a cushion – rubbish! It was just somewhere to put his sponsors' names. If Ivan had come out with two pairs of handlebars, there would have been at least 10 kids out on the track with the same. They wouldn't have a clue why they were doing it, but they would have seen Ivan do it and copied him.

Ivan was certainly a good role model and he was on top form in the next round of the World Championship – the European Final at Wembley. One notable absentee, though, was Barry Briggs. He failed to get further than the British Nordic Final after qualifying for 17 consecutive World Finals. I was there, though, and I even beat Nigel in heat 15 to qualify for my second World Final.

I was delighted with my 10-point return at Wembley but, unfortunately, the big night in Gothenburg was one to forget. The track looked as though it had been tarmaced! There was more dust on my living room carpet – it was as slick as a board. I was trying my guts out but I was getting nowhere. You couldn't leave the inside. If you moved out to try and challenge for second place, you would end up last. There were people cheating on the start-line like you wouldn't believe and I wasn't happy. So before I went out for my final race I said to Bernard Harrison: "As soon as that green light comes on, I'm going!" I knew I would either get a flier or be excluded so, as soon as the green light came on, I dropped the clutch – and at that exact moment the tapes went up. I won it by a mile.

Ole Olsen won that final and he was a good champion. We came across each other quite a lot and he was a superb rider – a lovely stylist and a great racer.

I was, however, less than impressed by having to ride at West Ham the night before the meeting. Can you imagine that? I was riding in the World Final, the showpiece event of the year, in Sweden on the Saturday night and the BSPA wouldn't give me permission to miss a British League match in London 24 hours earlier because they reckoned it wouldn't affect my performance! So much for the powers that be. It's certainly a lot different now, where the top riders take nearly a week off from the

Greg Kentwell, who had an expensive experiment with Nitro, with me and Sheffield's Jim Airey.

Elite League before a GP.

In between the European Final and World Final I rode in a grass-track meeting at Cranwell in Lincolnshire one Sunday – and rode over my own foot in the first race! I had borrowed a JAP for the meeting and, when I changed gear, I was a little too heavy-handed and my foot went under the foot rest. I honestly thought it had smashed and I rode onto the centre green, where I parked up and fell onto a straw bale. I went straight to hospital back home in Wakefield and, although they confirmed nothing was broken, I couldn't stand on it.

That meant I had to ring Reg and tell him I wouldn't be able to ride for Halifax at Cradley the following night. It's fair to say he wasn't pleased – but I told him I could do exactly what I wanted to on a Sunday. I said to him that if I wanted to go mountain climbing on a Sunday I was perfectly entitled to do so because he didn't pay me to stay at home on a Sunday. In any case, I wasn't best pleased at being injured myself because I'd be losing points money if I wasn't riding. One again the rugby league club came to my rescue and I was soon back on the track.

By the end of that year I was no longer classified as the British No 1. Ray Wilson of Leicester was emerging then and becoming a very good rider. He finished ahead of me in the World Final and ended the year with a higher average than me – mine was 10.56 and his was 10.90. Not that it bothered me – in fact quite the opposite. It was a case of the more the merrier as far as I was concerned. We need to give every encouragement to the English kids, even today.

On the team front, Halifax finished 14th out of 19 in the British League, which was the lowest since we had joined the league. What is more, we failed to win a single away match all season, which wasn't very impressive, but the finger couldn't be pointed at me! It's funny because speedway is a team sport but you don't think about it too much. If the team is going well, it's fantastic. But as long as you have

Getting down to business in the workshop, where the two-valve ESO/Jawa was easy to maintain. I prided myself on good mechanical preparation, which made it so hard to bear when things occasionally went wrong.

done all right and you're earning a living, it's not the end of the world. It's disappointing but you don't go home with your head in your hands thinking: "Oh no, we've lost again". It sounds a bit arrogant but I was always happy if I'd had a good night, whether the side I was riding for had won or lost.

I finished the year on a high note, winning the Autumn Classic open meeting at The Shay. There was a £100 top prize on offer, which made it the richest meeting held at Halifax to date and I even had the satisfaction of beating Ray Wilson, the new England No.1. But it didn't stop me asking for a transfer in December.

ALL IN ROUBLES

I TOLD the Speedway Star I had no axe to grind with the Halifax management, but that I felt my career could benefit from a move after seven years as the No 1 rider at The Shay. I'd had disagreements with Reg Fearman over money in the past, but I don't think this had anything to do with pay, even though I knew I could probably get a better deal if I went somewhere else.

I had been thinking about it for a while and my opinion was that I got taken for granted. The fans were superb – lovely people – but some of them would start pointing the finger at me if I had lost to someone they felt I should have beaten. They couldn't understand that, like everyone else, I could have a good day at work and a bad day at work.

I felt I was getting stale and that a change would be as good as a rest, so I asked for a transfer. But then, when I analysed it in the cold light of say, I began to realise that going to another track probably wouldn't be such a good idea. I'm sure I could have got a transfer, but what if it was to Wimbledon? There I was, 20 minutes away from my home track, so why on earth would I want to make a 400-mile round trip on a Thursday when I could do a 32-mile trip on a Saturday to do the same job and earn the same money? I could be at home by 11.30 – even after picking up fish and chips on the way in.

I don't think I ever put the request in writing, though, and I eventually agreed a deal with Reg at Leicester Forest services on the M1. We talked all day about everything but speedway and then, in the final half-an-hour, we finally got round to discussing my contract. I got it all off my chest, Reg gave me some of his points of view and the deal was done.

With my immediate future sorted out, I decided to have another crack at ice racing. Once again the ACU had sent some nominations out and the only two idiots they thought might be up for it were me and Dougie Wyer. Having only ever ridden an ice bike on a frozen car park prior to my last experience of ice racing, I thought it would be a good idea to get some serious practice in – so me, Dougie, Dave Younghusband and Richard Greer headed off to a frozen lake at Whittsey Wash, near Peterborough. Unfortunately when Dougie wheeled his bike onto the ice, a huge crack appeared and the back wheel disappeared into the water. Great start!

Fortunately, it wasn't too deep because we were near the edge, but we struggled like anything to get it out. The exhaust was under the water and it sounded like a barge! We eventually managed to drag it to the edge and get it out before getting a few laps in on thicker ice.

There were a group of ice-skaters on the lake but none of them offered to help, even though it was obvious we were having a bit of trouble. In fact they thought it was hilarious and couldn't stop laughing. But the boot was soon on the other foot because one of these ice-skaters, who obviously fancied himself as an Olympic champion, came running along the grass bank in his skates and leapt onto the ice. He thought he looked so cool but, when he landed on the ice, it gave way and he was stood there with water up to his chest! Now it was our turn to laugh and he certainly was cool then - literally.

Our ice-racing call-up was for the world semi-finals at Ufa in the Soviet Union, but we were actually part of a travelling troupe. We competed in nine meetings all over Russia and we were away for seven weeks in total. When we arrived in Russia there were two brand new bikes waiting for us – all we had to do was take them out of their packing cases and assemble them. Andy Ross was not riding at the time because he had a broken leg, so he was our manager. It was an amazing adventure and I wish now that I had taken a map and taken more notice of where we had been.

We started off in Moscow and we rode in the Olympic Stadium. I have ridden virtually everything that has got wheels on it and the most exhilarating feeling I have ever had is riding an ice bike. It is amazing. When you go out for a practice early on and the ice is brand new, it's just like being on an ice rink. You go belting down the straight flat out and just lean the bike into the corner. The handlebars are literally just a couple of inches off the ice. But what people don't ever realise is that the ice really chops up badly after a while and it gets unbelievably rough. As you go down the straight there will be chunks of ice as big as a cigarette packet coming off your front wheel.

At the end of the first meeting we were black and blue from where these chunks of ice had hit us, but we quickly twigged on and put pieces of cardboard inside our leathers to protect ourselves. It used to take us an hour to get ready, but it was time well spent.

Ice racing is perfectly safe though – unless you crash and then you haven't got a chance. The guards over the wheels go right down to the ice, but the spikes have still got to be touching something to get the grip, so if you get run over you don't half know about it. When we went in the showers after meetings we looked at the lads who had been riding for a while and they all had tramlines down their backs and across their thighs where they had been spiked after falling off and then been stitched up. They looked like they had been run over by a sewing machine!

Because we were heading behind the Iron Curtain, we took all our own food. We took so much of it that we were way over our weight limit when we went to check in at the airport, but we got away with it because we were British sportsmen representing our country. Ryvitas, tins of beans, Mars bars, dried soups, it was all in our suitcases – but it was a good job too because, if we hadn't taken it, we would have starved! The food out there was terrible.

When we left Moscow we caught a train up into Siberia, and we were on it for about three days. I don't think it went any faster than 30mph the whole time. The carriages were the like the ones we used to have over here in the 1950s with a corridor down one side. Off the corridors were your rooms where four of us ate and slept as well. At the end of every carriage was an old Russian lady, dressed all in black with an apron on, and she had a coal-fired pot-bellied stove. When she used to shovel more coal on, the smoke would drift down the corridor so we would have to slam the door shut so we could breathe. Every time we wanted hot water to make some soup, we would go to see her and she would give us some from her pot-bellied stove.

Being stuck in a railway carriage was incredibly boring and the journey seemed to last forever. We had an interpreter with us and we tried to beat him at chess but couldn't. Dougie and I tried cheating but we still lost. All you could see out of the window for the whole three days was snow, snow and more snow, although at one point we looked out and we could see row after row of combine harvesters in the grounds of a collective farm - 186 of them we counted.

All the time we were out there we kept going from one extreme to the other. One night we would be in the best hotel you could imagine, probably western-owned, and the next we would be staying somewhere straight out of the dark ages. Sometimes they provided a brand, spanking new coach to take us from one place to another, while on other occasions we would be put on a right old banger that was 25-years-old.

One hotel we stayed in was particularly basic. All the room had in it was two beds, each with a duvet, and a sink in the corner with one brass tap. If you wanted a shower you had to go three floors down into the hotel basement. The trouble with that was that there was so much steam and condensation that you couldn't see anything! The duvet was warm though, and the windows were triple-glazed, with the panes two feet apart.

"He pointed all around the room and then went over to the TV and turned the volume up before talking in a hushed voice"

The temperature was minus-42 degrees when we raced in one meeting – you could have a pee and watch it freeze! It was so cold that we had to warm up the cylinder head, the cylinder and the crankcase with a blowtorch before starting our bikes up, while the oil was so thick and heavy that we couldn't turn the engines over. Both Dougie and I had sideburns at the time and, when we came back to the pits, they were all frozen up.

The pits were heated and the first thing we did after every race was go and sit on the radiator. The track was in a dip and there must have been about 8,000 people there to watch. Just above their heads was what looked like a giant halo because it was so cold that their breath had only risen that far.

Our interpreter explained to us that, during the interval, the organisers would make a new track. 'That's interesting,' we thought – and it was. A huge tractor towing a 4,000-gallon tank full of boiling water from the local power station appeared. The driver turned the sprinkler on at the back, did one complete lap of the circuit, and five minutes later we had a new track. Easy as that – hot water freezes quicker than cold water, or so I'm told!

For the duration of our trip we had an interpreter who had been found for us by the Russian federation. He was a great kid – about 23-years-old and not long out of university. At the time, one of the catchphrases we had was "Oh bollocks." Our interpreter hadn't heard of this phrase before and was keen to know what it meant - he was very amused when we told him. When we had finished the parade before our next meeting, he seemed particularly keen to make sure Dougie and I didn't forget where our area of the pits was. There were riders from all over Europe there and we all had big signs in the pits, so we thought it was a bit strange that he should be so concerned. But then we got to our pit area and saw that, on the wall he had sprayed in big letters BOLLOX. "Now you cannot miss your pit," he said.

All our expenses were paid and, when we got out there, we were given a daily allowance – all in roubles. Then, when we got paid our start money and points money, that was all in roubles too. We'd never had so much money but it was no good to us because it was all in Soviet currency and there was nothing to spend it on. But we realised that the clutch, countershaft, engines, carburettors, and even the wheels on an ice bike were exactly the same as on a conventional speedway bike, so when we got back to Moscow for our final meeting, we told the interpreter that we wanted to use our roubles to buy some spare parts to take home.

The Russians were so keen to buy our equipment that I sold my leathers, goggles, helmet, the lot – although that, of course, meant I had even more roubles to get rid of. Our interpreter told us that he wanted a short-wave radio so he could listen to the BBC and learn more English, but the only shops where you could buy such a thing were out-of-bounds to the Russians. Only westerners could go in there and you had to show your passport to be allowed in, so we agreed that if he helped us buy some spare parts, we would get him a radio.

He told us he would need to go home and see his wife because he had only recently been married but, because Russia was still in the grip of Communism then, he made us promise we wouldn't leave the hotel until he had returned the following day. "People are watching everything," he warned us.

When he arrived back at the hotel, which was a big modern place in the middle of Moscow, we asked him if he'd had any success with our request. He just glared at us and went: "Ssssshhhhh." He pointed all around the room then went over to the TV and turned the volume up before talking to us in a hushed voice. It was like something out of a James Bond film! There were funny things that looked like microphones in the wall – they may have been sensors for the radiators, but on the other hand, maybe we were being bugged.

Before we came home, where we knew we would be able to eat some decent food at last, we binned or gave away all the left over food we had taken – but we still went home with as much excess baggage as when we had left because of all the spare parts we had bought from the Russian lads. We took back so much that I had enough to run my bike for the whole season without having to buy any more. In return we bought our translator a short-wave radio – it cost £15 so Dougie and I went half each.

The riders we bought the gear from got a good deal too. They were quids in – or

With The Shay re-shaped and the corners taken in, I manage to squeeze up the inside of King's Lynn's Malcolm Simmons during the 1972 season. Below: With Diane and young Ritchie, who had some new toys to play with on my return from Russia.

rather roubles in – because they were all sponsored by the state, so it had all been bought for them in the first place. They sold so much that by the end of the tour one bike had gone missing completely. Everyone was wheeling and dealing, different people wanted different parts, and eventually the whole lot had gone.

I also brought home some toys for my son, Ritchie, who wasn't very old at the time. I went into the main department store in Moscow and they were still adding up using an abacus, quick as lightning. There wasn't a till in sight! And the only toys I could find were model Army vehicles like tanks and jet launchers. I think we've still got them at home – they certainly wouldn't wear out because they were made out of 2mm thick cast metal!

Neither Dougie nor I qualified for the World Ice Final and, in fact, I only scored two at Ufa. Looking back, I think I must have been mad to put my name down to do it, but I am very glad that I did. The Russians were absolutely wonderful and they looked after us from the moment we arrived to the moment we left. They say that sport has no boundaries and I think that trip was proof because it was a wonderful experience.

When the conventional season got underway, Britain was coming to terms with a world energy crisis. Workers were reduced to a three-day week, lighting and fuel were in short supply. There was a power shortage in the Halifax team too. Along with John Titman, we had signed Mike Hiftle and young Dane Preben Rosenkilde who were both nice enough people but not particularly good. Rosenkilde didn't last long before joining Oxford and Tommy Roper came back for a short spell. Gote Nordin was signed in July when Dave Younghusband broke his leg at Poole but we still lacked a quality third heat leader all season.

On a personal level, though, things were going well for me. I scored 10 points in the British Final at Coventry, which put me into a run-off with Jimmy McMillan. I won that, which put me straight through to the World Final which was at Wembley that season. The story at the time was that I had given up beer for two months and smoking for a month to get fully fit for the meeting, but in truth that was just something concocted by the press. I've never been a big drinker and, if I'd had two pints in a week, that would have been a lot for me. I've never been drunk since George Hunter's wedding!

As for smoking, well I smoked from before I left school but not heavily. I don't even smoke 20 a day now, and I smoked much less when I was riding. I wasn't a fitness fanatic, but I did like to think I was reasonably fit and in my early days with the Dukes I used to train with Halifax Town.

No, cutting down on booze and fags had nothing to do with me qualifying – but what did help me was the bike I borrowed from Ole Olsen. I'd been unhappy with the performances I had been getting out of my own machines before the meeting so I was very grateful to Ole.

Having lost our fight for more appearance money, I look nervous as we're about to go on parade before the 1972 World Final at Wembley. While I have a quiet word with Reg Fearman, Russian Gregori Chlinovsky and Poland's Pawel Waloszek seem amazed by the 80,000 crowd. The thrills – and spills! – were about to begin . . .

Once again, however, the World Final was a frustrating one for me. Myself and the four other British licence holders – my brother Nigel, John Louis, Barry Briggs and Ivan Mauger – who had qualified for Wembley were in dispute with the SCB over the pay rates for the big night – a paltry £3 per start and £6 a point. And that was to race in front of 72,000 fans plus millions more tuning into ITV that night. We demanded £1,000 a man appearance money and threatened to go on strike if we didn't get it. The World Final, especially when it was at Wembley, was making a lot of money for somebody and, so it wouldn't have hurt them to give us a bonus – even if it was, say, £2,500 between the five of us, and in future years British World Finalists would also have benefited.

We eventually dropped our threat to go on strike when the SCB promised that the issue of World Final prize money would be brought up at the next FIM meeting, which in truth was just another way of them getting away without doing anything about it.

The World Final was on a three-year roster, with Wembley, Poland and Sweden taking the event in order and, when it was over here, the SCB were the promoting partners which meant they took the bulk of the profits. What we were asking was that the SCB rewarded us when it was staged in England because, if you had five good British or English riders there, they would attract a huge crowd – and a reported 80,000 turned out to see this final. When someone goes to watch a World Final, they're not going there to see a promoter, are they? They're going to watch the riders.

In the end, the SCB papered over our protest by saying they would bring it up with the FIM – an organisation that wasn't in a position to address the issue in Britain! Once again, how typical of the SCB.

> "If you believe in something very strongly, you have to say your piece – and I don't just mean about track conditions either"

I was chairman of the Speedway Riders' Association – the riders' union – at the time, which wouldn't have done me any favours. The assumption would be that I was only speaking up because it affected me, although that clearly wasn't the case. The reason I ended up as SRA chairman was down to the fact that I would always speak my mind – that and the fact I was mug enough to take it on.

To be fair, though, the SRA had a lot of respect in those days. We didn't do a great deal but I enjoyed working with the BSPA and we tried to bridge the gap between them and us. We needed them so we could ride on their tracks and they needed us to earn them some money. It's the same today, and there's no doubt that a good SRA will benefit the sport. What won't do it any good is a bolshy SRA – there's no point in going about the job like a bull in a china shop.

I think that if half the promoters, back then and today, had been half as passionate as I was about speedway, the sport would have moved with the times. If somebody asked my opinion, I told them. I've never, ever gone out to deliberately upset anybody. If ever I told someone that their track was crap, it was because it was. I think the BSPA understood that I wasn't a trouble-causer and that I was simply being honest and saying it for the right reasons. Not that I really cared what they

The start of a bad night for me at the 1972 World Final. On a diabolical Wembley track, I slid off in heat one and tangled with the Pole Pawel Waloszek (white), who got up to win the re-run. Anders Michanek, wearing No.4 (above), also fell and was excluded from a race that had to be re-started three times!

thought anyway – I never set out to be the most popular speedway rider in the world.

If you believe in something very strongly, you have to say your piece, and I don't mean just about track conditions either. I had a big row with Reg Fearman's first wife, Joan, one night when we were riding at the old Reading track at Tilehurst, which he also promoted. It had been a wet meeting and, after it had finished, I went into the shower and there was no water. Can you imagine getting sweaty and mucky after riding in a speedway meeting and then finding out you couldn't get cleaned up before going home.

The speedway office was just next to the shower block, so I wrapped a towel around my bathing shorts and went in there to sort it out. Reg's wife, Joan, was in there and I told her how angry we all were. If the showers had been tested before the meeting, it could have been sorted out. "It's not good enough," I told her. "It stinks – and not only that, but I do too!"

The next morning Reg phoned me and went beserk. He accused me of storming into his office, naked! I pointed out that I had, in fact, been wearing bathing shorts, a towel and flip-flops, and reiterated how disgraceful I thought it was that we all had to drive all the way home stinking like pigs and not being able to stop for anything to eat because we were filthy. I was really wound up, but I told him that I hadn't been rude to Joan, I was just forcefully telling her something I felt strongly about. That's how I was. Everyone else was whinging about it, but none of them said a word.

The 1972 World Final was the only one to feature both me and Nigel. It was also the last time either of us took to the track for the big night. My only two points came in my final ride when I finished behind Ole Olsen after passing Alexander Pavlov on the last lap.

I had gone down with a tummy bug the night before and I was as sick as a dog before the meeting, although I suppose that's a good excuse if you haven't done well – two points in a World Final is terrible. There were 3,000 Halifax fans there and I was more disappointed for them than I was for myself. They had spent a lot of money to get there – I was being paid to ride, but what a plonker I was.

The talking point of that World Final – won by Ivan Mauger, incidentally – was the unusual number of crashes. The Wembley track was diabolical. I tangled with Pawel Waloszek in the first heat which was started FOUR times. The start was okay but the middle of the first corner was so wet it was like a swimming pool. It caught me out and the bike did a full 360 degree turn, and that sort of thing just shouldn't happen in a World Final.

Four heats later, Briggo lost a finger in a bad crash with Bernt Persson, and you didn't often see Barry crash. Yet again the SCB came in for more criticism as they were in charge of track preparation, or rather the lack of it.

I left the World Final feeling disappointed, and I wasn't too happy as I made my way back home from my first taste of long-track racing either. Three long-track meetings took place on an adapted trotting track at Motherwell in 1972 and, being as eager as I was to have a go at all sorts of motorcycle sports, I jumped at the chance to be involved. It was a big 680-yard sand track and the meeting attracted some top speedway names.

Unfortunately, as I was going flat out in the first race in very heavy rain, my throttle jammed open. I suppose sand gets into places where shale doesn't, and I should have spent a bit more time on the preparation making sure it didn't happen. I must have been doing 80mph when I baled out. The bike bounced off the fence and caught me in the groin . . . and that brought an abrupt end to the day.

On a happier note, our travelling supporters finally had something to cheer in mid-August – at Exeter of all places. Halifax had gone 24 away matches without a win when we pulled of a 43-35 victory at the County Ground. They finished 11th in the British League and we ended up 12th, so it was a good scalp to claim. Mind you, it was always difficult to win there whether they were going good, bad or indifferent.

Once again I ended the year with an average above 10 points but I wasn't happy, and so began the winter of discontent. I was only 27 but I was so fed up of the puny rewards in speedway that I was seriously thinking of giving it all up. The job was 10 times better than working but the risks were much greater too and the pay – particularly for the big meetings – just didn't reflect that. Don't forget we are talking about a time when speedway promoters were making money – a lot of it.

I never begrudged anyone for taking a gamble on opening a track and putting the work in to promote it, but I didn't see why they shouldn't share some of the money with the people who helped them make it. I wasn't asking anything that speedway couldn't afford. When I started considering retirement it was born of frustration, I suppose. It was the winter and I wasn't racing, so I had more time to think about it.

Once again, though, I agreed a deal with Reg and I was back in the No.1 racejacket at The Shay when the 1973 season started. Eric Boothroyd decided to eliminate the limestone mixture from the track and laid a new granite surface. Shale became sticky when wet and didn't drain as well, so he decided to make a change. The track

record had gone unbeaten throughout 1972 so he wanted to add a bit of bite to it.

The advantage granite had over shale was that it was readily available and was the same composition whether you bought it in March or September. That was important because you could never guarantee the quality of red shale – some has a lot of clay in it and other mixtures had very little.

Eric was right about the drainage too. Granite drained very well and, even if you'd had a wet day, you could get away with racing on it. From a rider's perspective,

Making my point to the FIM officials after my exclusion in the British-Nordic Final at Coventry.

though, I didn't really notice any difference. It was still two straights and two corners and you had to get round them.

There were changes to the team as well as the track in 1973 – big changes in fact. Dave Younghusband had hung up his leathers after breaking his leg at Poole the previous season while Greg Kentwell, Alan Jay, Chris Bailey and Malcolm Mackay were all missing from the team too. Back came Les Sharpe from Australia, with Bill Andrew – who used to double up as a jump jockey - Per Hansen and Charlie Monk joining him on the list of new arrivals.

Poor Les was soon in the wars, though, and he broke his leg at Cradley with the season just five matches old. The team shake-up seemed to do the trick and in June of 1973 Halifax stood proudly at the top of the British League table for the first time since we had won the title in 1966.

The British Final was held at Sheffield for the first time that year and, although I qualified for the British-Nordic Final at Coventry with nine points and sixth place, that was as far as I progressed in the World Championship. I won't ever forget the circumstances in which I bowed out – how could I?

I was at the centre of the biggest TV row speedway had ever known.

It was a difficult meeting to progress from because there was a high-class field of riders chasing eight qualifying places for the European Final in Germany. One last place was enough to really put you up against it, and that's where I finished in my first race after having clutch problems. I went out for my second ride along with John Boulger, Peter Collins and Bernt Persson and there was some movement at the tapes. Veikko Halme, the Finnish referee, excluded Persson for breaking the tapes, only to change his mind when he saw a rerun of heat seven on the TV monitor. The meeting was being filmed by ITV and Dave Lanning was up in the referee's box with Barry Briggs as his summariser. When Briggo showed the referee the replay, suddenly I was the one who had been excluded – and, as far as I was concerned, that wasn't fair. I had worked all year to try and get through to a World Final and that decision effectively ended my hopes of getting any further

At the time I didn't know he had used TV evidence to exclude me, but I was convinced he should have stuck by his original decision.

I rode up to the start line to get onto the telephone there and state my case. Peter Morrish, the announcer, answered and I asked him to put the referee on, but he said there was no point in doing that because he didn't speak a word of English!

Brilliant! As far as I was concerned, I'd been unfairly thrown out of a race and I couldn't even talk to the bloke responsible! So I asked to speak to the clerk of the course instead and, while I was still on the phone, the two-minute warning went for the rerun. The three remaining riders were coming up to the start and I still hadn't managed to get my point across, but I wasn't giving up . . .

I was determined to speak to someone before the race was restarted, so I parked by bike across the track. There was no point in me trying to protest if the race was starting without me! When the riders saw my bike across the track they did what I would have done and went back to the pits – there was no way it was going to start with a bike on the track, was it?

The clerk of the course spoke to someone in the referee's box – who clearly wasn't the ref himself – then came back on to me and explained there was nothing he could do. I was livid. I flung my body colour up into the air as far as it would go and, when it came down I stood on it and kicked it as hard as I could. I stormed off into the pits and refused to take any further part in the meeting. I acted like an imbecile but I was fuming – the fans loved it and I was a TV celeb for a while anyway.

When it all simmered down I was charged by the SCB with bringing the sport into disrepute by placing my machine transverse to the tapes, failing to notify the referee I had withdrawn from the meeting, holding up the meeting for six minutes and ungentlemanly conduct. Not a bad list of charges, eh? I finished up having to answer the charges at the SCB offices in London in October, by which time I had broken my arm at Newport, which I will come to later on.

Shortly before the tribunal I went up to Dave Younghusband's in Consett for the weekend because he was riding in a trial. I took the rulebook with me and, while I was there, I read it from cover to cover. It's surprising what you can learn if you read the rulebook properly. I was determined not to let this matter lie so, when I got home, I wrote some notes and passed them to my Auntie Muriel to type up and copy.

Reg Fearman, who was chairman of the BSPA as well as being my boss at Halifax, came with me to Belgrave Square, where the tribunal was taking place. When we arrived I addressed the room and said: "Gentlemen, before we start may I please present my paper on this matter?" The chairman agreed there was no problem with that so I passed around copies of what my Auntie Muriel had typed up to everyone in the room. There was a deathly silence while everybody read my typed notes. It seemed to go on forever but I had no intention of interrupting them.

Eventually we started discussing the charges and I explained that the only way I could tell the other riders I was still on the telephone was by placing my machine across the tapes. I wasn't impeding anyone because the race hadn't started, so all the riders had done was turn round and go back to the pits.

When it came to leaving the meeting without the permission of the referee, I pointed out that I had never actually left the meeting. I was so incensed about what had happened that I didn't take any further part, but I never left the meeting. I stood in the paddock with the rest of the riders and watched the rest of the meeting. And in any case, had I asked, how could I have got permission to leave , when the Finnish referee didn't speak a word of English?

It rumbled on, and all the time the tribunal were asking questions about the notes I had given them. I thought it was all going well but I feared I was in big trouble when they announced that they would be calling Norman Dixon, the clerk of the course, to give evidence after lunch. To be fair, I had been abusive – to him and anyone else who got in my way – so I was dreading what he might say. I had no idea he was going to be called, but he just happened to be in London on business that day.

After a lovely pub lunch – all paid for by the SCB, by the way – we started again. The clerk of the course duly arrived and was asked to tell the tribunal my reaction to being excluded at Coventry. Despite fearing his view of events, it turned out that

Norman was as amazed as I'd been that a referee who couldn't speak a word of English had been appointed to officiate at such a big meeting: "I think it's fair to say Eric was not amused," he told the tribunal. "He was very cross and I think he had every right to be."

Yippee – this was going better than I'd imagined! The clerk of the course confirmed that all I was trying to do by placing my bike across the track was gain some time because the race was about to start without me. He was asked what my conduct was like, and replied that it had been quite admirable given the volatile situation. "There was a lot of pressure," he said, "and I'm sure everyone in this room would have been just as angry at the actions of a Finnish referee who had to watch a TV monitor to make a decision."

At the end Reg and I were asked to go into the room next door and come back in when we were called to hear the tribunal's verdict. Soon afterwards the call came – and I was cleared of every single charge. I thanked them for making what I considered to be the correct decisions, although I admitted it wasn't very becoming of me to get so angry, but that I was a professional and had always taken my job very seriously.

I still hadn't finished, though. I pointed out that I had been injured in August and that I would be lucky to be fit for the start of the season in March. That was seven months without being able to work, I told them, so I asked for some expenses to cover my costs of attending. Reg couldn't believe it and kicked me under the table, but the chairman agreed to give me £15 to cover my train fare!

Since that sorry saga at Coventry in August 1973, no FIM non-English speaking referee has been appointed to take charge of a World Championship meeting, so at least my stance against stupidity did a bit of good.

Reg had warned me the charges were so serious that I could have been suspended. I really had no idea what the outcome might be but do you know what? I didn't care one way or the other. I just enjoyed playing Perry Mason and I fought the charges with the same rulebook that had been used to bring them in the first place.

Interestingly, when I arrived at King's Cross for my train home, who should I bump into when I was looking for a seat, but Norman Dixon. I bought him a couple of beers on the journey back to Yorkshire!

I got more publicity out of that fiasco than I ever did for 10 years of being well-behaved! Even today people remember that extraordinary incident.

Unfortunately for me, just 10 days after the incident at Brandon, I was in the news again. And this time it hurt.

No prizes for guessing the cause of the stoppage at Coventry.

8

RUSSELL HOBBS

I'D had some good meetings at Newport, including a 15-point maximum against Sweden in a Test match one year, but it was never my favourite track. I could ride it well enough but I just didn't like the place and I had even less affection for it after the events of August 10, 1973. That was the day I had my worst ever speedway crash while riding in a British League match for Halifax at Somerton Park.

I had finished third in my first race before being excluded for touching the tapes at the start of what should have been my second ride. In the very next race I was brought out as a tactical substitute to partner Bill Andrew against Reidar Eide – who no longer wanted to kill me by this time – and Geoff Mudge.

There was a D-shape across the first and second bends where the tractor used to park after work had been carried out on the track. Before the race the tractor had done a full lap, gone right round again, then turned in just before the second bend. What we didn't know was that, on the track, it had left a big pile of dirt which had fallen off the blade.

When the race started, Bill Andrew was on my inside and, as he came out of the second bend, he hit the pile of dirt. The bike stood up on one wheel and was coming across the corner at me. Automatically I went wide to try and miss him and hit the top of the fence along the straight.

There was a two-inch scaffold pole growing off the fence but there were no lights on it, no telephone, nothing and I have no idea at all what it was doing there. I had been thrown over the handlebars and when my right arm hit the pole . . . crunch! My arm was smashed and two bones were sticking out of my leathers.

Funnily enough, it didn't hurt at the time and I remember telling the medical staff not to cut my leathers off or, if they had to, at least cut up the seam where the zip was so they could be repaired easily.

All I could think about was my bike and how badly damaged it might be.

I walked to the ambulance room, which was halfway down the back straight behind the changing rooms, and then I was put in the ambulance to go to hospital. The night staff at the hospital in Newport manipulated the bones back together and put them back end to end before plastering me up from my shoulder to my wrist.

I arrived home the next morning and the pain was horrendous. I rang up Bernard, my mechanic, and asked him to come over. My four fingers and thumb were

A friendly word in the pits with Reg Fearman, with Mike Hiftle and Bill Andrew looking on. Bill was involved in the crash that caused the worst injury of my career at Newport.

sticking out at the end of the plaster and they were so swollen they looked like King Edward cigars. There wasn't a ripple of skin on them.

The pain was so intense that I could have happily cut my arm off, so Bernard brought over a big pair of cutters and began cutting the plaster off. It took ages to do because it was still wet but, when it was off, my arm swelled up by about three inches. Diane put some bandages on and I rang Dr Carlo Biagi at home.

Carlo was based in Galashiels, Scotland and was often the first port of call for injured speedway riders. I told him I had broken my arm and that I was in agony and he said that if I set off immediately, I could see him there and then. "Just tell the nurse to give me a ring at home when you get to the hospital in Galashiels," he said, "and I'll come straight away."

We set off and did what Carlo had asked me to when we arrived. The nurse thought it was a little irregular but I explained I was only doing what Dr Biagi has asked. I told her I was a speedway rider and there was no problem after that – they knew all about Carlo and his treatment of speedway riders so they were used to it.

I gave Carlo the x-rays I had brought with me from Newport, but he did some more anyway – and discovered that, on top of my other injuries, my elbow was broken in four places. He explained he would have to screw my elbow together and, while he was at it, he may as well pin and plate my broken arm too. I told him I didn't mind what he did to me as long as he got me back on a bike.

The following morning I was first into the operating theatre. When I came round I was all bandaged up and the job was done. I thought: "Lovely, I'll be racing again in another month." I was convinced I would be, too. Diane stayed for a couple of nights at a bed and breakfast in Galashiels and then, after that, she stayed at Dave

Younghusband's for a while and drove up every day to see me. After about a week I came home.

It didn't hurt once Carlo had operated on me but I was desperate to get back on a bike. In fact, I rode in the mechanics' race at Halifax at the end of the season in full plaster! I rode under the name of Russell Hobbs – have a look on your kettle and you might discover where I got the name from! I daren't ride under my own name because I had no insurance. One or two people in the pits knew it was me, but nobody else. I had blue overalls on and my arm was locked in an L-shape because of the plaster. It was a bit uncomfortable but I was still sliding the bike, although at the end of the race I couldn't stop! It took me ages to slow down and get my hand off the throttle.

Every month from then on I went up to Galashiels for a check up. Each time the pot was changed, it gave me the opportunity to give my arm a good scrub with carbolic soap. On every visit I would ask Carlo if I was ready to start riding again, but it was a slow process and it turned out to be February before I could even think of using my arm again.

I would sit at home with a knitting needle to scratch inside the plaster and, if was in the garage, I would get the air-line and blast all the dust out of the other end.

Being in plaster for six months didn't prevent me driving or from working on the house throughout that winter, though. In fact I completely slated my workshop roof because the bloke who was supposed to be doing it did one side and then never came back once I had paid him. All the Yorkshire stone slates were sitting in the garden so I thought I would do it myself. I had watched him do it before he disappeared, so I knew what to do. The slates were heavy but they fitted nicely in the apex of the plaster. I mixed all the concrete too, so my plastered arm became well and truly plastered.

It never crossed my mind that I wouldn't be fit for the start of the next season. I always used to inform Reg Fearman whenever I was going for a check-up at Carlo's and he was interested in my progress because I was his No 1 rider. Whenever I had the plaster taken off, I washed my arm and went off to have it x-rayed. While I was waiting for the results I would sit in Carlo's office while he looked at them.

On one occasion Carlo was on the phone and I distinctly heard him say: "I don't think he'll ever ride again." I asked Carlo who had been talking to and he told me it had been Reg. I didn't let on that I'd heard what he had told him but wasn't best pleased at the prospect of my career being over and I thought: 'Right, I'll show you.' It was another spur.

When the plaster did eventually come off I told Carlo I was planning to ride again in March and asked him what he thought. He explained that it might ache but, if I could stand the pain, there was no reason why I shouldn't be riding at the start of the season. That's when I came clean about what I had heard him say to Reg, but Carlo knew all along that I'd heard. "I only said that because I knew you were next door listening," he revealed. It was a psychological boost and, when you're in a situation like that, mental strength is half the battle.

I had a lot of time for Carlo. He knew when he treated a speedway rider that his patient's No.1 priority was to get fit and ride again as soon as possible. He would rather treat ten speedway riders than one NHS patient because all his regular patients wanted was an operation and a sick note for as long as possible – we wanted him to patch us up and get us back out on a bike as quickly as possible.

I was so sad to hear that he had passed away earlier this year because not only was he a marvellous surgeon and a great motivator, but he was a true friend to British speedway and in particularly the Northern tracks. Many riders like me, who were fortunate enough to have Carlo as our private guru, were saddened at his passing.

There is a lot to be said for mind over matter but I made a vow that there was NO WAY I would ride at Newport the following year. I stuck to my vow as well. I had criticised the place since the day it opened and almost lost my career there and I didn't care if the BSPA fined me £100 or whatever, I wasn't going back to Somerton Park. Not long after I broke my arm Malcolm Simmons was due there with King's Lynn, but he didn't go. When I talked to him about it, he said he realised if I could go there and injur myself so badly after years of riding speedway without barely a scratch, then there had to be something wrong with the track. He didn't like it either.

> "On one occasion Carlo was on the phone and I distinctly heard him say: 'I don't think he'll ever ride again.' I thought: I'll show you"

Strangely, I didn't get any help from the Speedway Riders' Benevolent Fund throughout the winter while I was plastered up and unable to work. Charles Foot was in charge of it at the time but he didn't seem to think I was a worthy cause. The ironic thing was that he was my accountant! I had to make do with about £15 a week in insurance money, which was hard work, but I wasn't bitter about it because I've never been bitter about anything in speedway.

To make it worse, the way it worked was that you didn't see any of it until after your last sick note went in and you were signed off and declared fit to work again. It was a nice cheque when you got it, but it wasn't too easy in between times. Diane had a part-time job, which was just as well, and we had to be very careful with our money until I was passed fit, especially as we had started off renovating our old barn.

When the plaster finally came off I had terrible trouble trying to get some movement back in my arm and I couldn't even fasten my own shirt. I had a stroke of luck, though, when I nearly electrocuted myself! I went into my workshop and plugged in my soldering iron but it must have been very damp in there because, as I turned it on, there was this huge flash. As I jumped in shock, my arm jerked backwards at the joint. It hurt so much it brought tears to my eyes – but after that I had another two inches of movement. I was so excited I ran in to show Diane. All the muscles had been set in one place for six months so it was always bound to be difficult to get it moving again.

Even today my arm is broken and the plates are still there to hold it together. For some reason they have never knitted together, and I'm not sure even Carlo ever knew why. But I can ride my trials bike for two days and, apart from a bit of an ache, I can't feel anything. But if I rode one lap of a speedway bike, it would hurt like hell.

The power of the new four-valve engines took some getting used to!

9

THERE TO MAKE THE NUMBERS UP

ONLY a few weeks before the start of the 1974 season, I finally got the go-ahead to get back on a bike. I had hoped to ride in Auckland, New Zealand, in January to prepare me for the British League campaign but I was still not fit so I had to cancel the trip. As you can imagine, I was enormously relieved to be given the all-clear to resume riding for Halifax.

When the tapes went up, though, I found myself in unfamiliar territory – at reserve! Reg Fearman received special dispensation from the BSPA to ride me there for six matches to see whether I was fit after the crash. I had restricted movement and still have today but I had no fears about riding again. What frightened me more was riding at reserve – wild isn't the word for it.

All the other reserves were ambitious and, all of a sudden they were lining up in heat two with Eric Boocock at the side of them. I had the reputation of being a good rider so they all wanted to beat me. It wasn't long before I demanded to go back to No.1 and, when Reg asked why, I told him it was because it would be twice as safe!

Because I broke my elbow I couldn't straighten my arm, and I still can't today, so I was riding with an arm I didn't have full movement in. The biggest problem was the twisting of the throttle because all the weight was on my broken arm and, when you ride a speedway bike, it's your right arm that does all the work. I tried cold water bandages, heat pads, all sorts. Wearing bandages restricted my movement even more. It wasn't painful in the way that a toothache is, but it got harder and harder with every lap.

I thought about altering the handlebars to get them into a better position, but that would only have been more restrictive. I had ridden with the handlebars in the same place throughout my career so I didn't want to have to learn to ride all over again. I wanted to ride because I wanted to earn some money and make up for the past seven months, and maybe that was the incentive to get back in the saddle – after all I couldn't do anything else, I'd always been a speedway rider. I enjoyed making my comeback because I proved to myself that I could ride again. Despite my injury, I was still at the top end of the Halifax points chart and I went unbeaten at home against Newport in my first match back at No.1 – I even equalled the track record.

On the World Championship front, I finished the British Semi-final at Sheffield on eight points, the same as Nigel, Bobby Beaton and Barry Thomas. All of us, along with everyone else in the stadium, expected a run-off to decide the final two

Welcoming the Flying Dutchman, Henny Kroeze, to The Shay in 1974.

qualifiers for the British Final – well, everyone except the referee that is. Instead of a run-off, he announced that Beaton and I had qualified on the basis of better race finishes during the night. We were absolutely certain that the referee was wrong but he would have none of it and off we went home.

Then, some time later, we were notified by letter that we were all required back at Owlerton the following Thursday to contest, you've guessed it, a run-off. The referee had got it wrong.

The problem Nigel and I had was that we'd booked to go over to the Isle of Man for the TT races that week and had planned to still be there at the time of the run-off. My good mate Mick Grant was a works Kawasaki road racer at the time and we had arranged to fly over there with John Cooper, another road racer, in his private aeroplane. Halifax and Coventry, who Nigel rode for, were both Saturday night tracks and neither of us had any midweek bookings, so it was a great opportunity for us to watch the TT. Having a week off in the season was unheard of so we were determined to make the most of it – I was adamant I wasn't coming back for the run-off. As far as I was concerned it was somebody else's cock-up, not ours so we should just let Bobby Beaton and Barry Thomas take the two places in the British Final. Nigel, however, didn't share my view and eventually persuaded me that it wasn't worth the risk of a ban or a fine, so we came back after a couple of days on the Isle of Man and took our places at Owlerton.

On the way home from the Isle of Man I told Nigel we had two options in the run-off. The first was that the two of us would cross the line ahead of the other two so that we got the two qualifying places. The second was to finish last. Third was not an option because whoever finished in that position would be reserve and therefore be required to turn up for the British Final without much hope of getting a ride. So

Leading a couple of old campaigners at Wimbledon – Trevor Hedge and Reg Luckhurst – in my last full season.

I made my mind up – when I was at the start-line, I would simply go whenever I was ready. If I broke the tapes, then I'd be last and wouldn't have to drive all the way to Coventry just to sit around all night. But if I made a lightning start, I could hold on and book my place in the British Final.

When we shook the balls for the gate positions I drew gate one, which was the best at Sheffield, and in fact still is. As soon as the green light came on I dumped the clutch and made a super start and disappeared off into the distance. I looked round and saw Nigel – who had drawn gate two - was in second so I just moved over a little bit. It was a wet and miserable night and I didn't want to fill him in with muck and, in any case, anyone behind us who wanted to get through at our expense would have to pass us both. I crossed the line first and Nigel was second so we clinched the two qualifying places. We were delighted to have qualified, although once again the incompetence of a referee in a big meeting had left us shaking our heads in dismay.

Victory in the run-off meant I would be back in the British Final at Coventry with a chance of making it a memorable World Championship qualifier there for the right reasons this time. But I didn't have the best preparation for what would turn out to be the most successful night of my speedway career, because I was in court on the morning of the meeting.

The effects of the fuel crisis were still being felt and 50mph speed limits had been enforced on motorways and dual carriageways. Some weeks earlier I had been caught speeding on my way to watch a meeting at Hull. I had a big Ford Granada and, to be fair, I was going fairly quick. I noticed a police car parked by the side of the road and it began following me so I slowed down to 50mph. It started to get nearer and nearer to me and eventually I was pulled over.

The policeman asked me if I was in a hurry and I admitted that I wasn't. He told

Holding off the challenge of Terry Betts at Coventry on British Final night.

me he had been watching me and calculated my speed by timing me with a stopwatch over a measured distance. To my utter amazement, he claimed I had been driving at 104mph! I told him straight: "This car would not do 104mph down a pit shaft with a sail up!" Those were my exact words – I couldn't believe what he was trying to tell me.

Why would I have been speeding AFTER I had seen the police car? It made no sense and I made sure the officer of the law knew that. I asked him when the last time his speedo had been checked and demanded to see inspection documents. Obviously he couldn't provide them and, despite my protests, I was issued with a notice to attend court – on the day of the British Final.

I pleaded not guilty but I was fined nonetheless. I think it was about £100 although I couldn't be sure. The hearing was in Hull so I had to get back to Wakefield to collect my bike and then head straight off to Coventry. I was running late, of course, and when I arrived home Bernard, my mechanic, was looking a little anxious. I told him we would only take one bike because I could fix that to the back of my car. If I'd taken two I would have to use the trailer and then I wouldn't be allowed to drive in the outside lane, in which case it was highly likely I would end up with another ticket and I certainly didn't want that.

At Coventry I was situated right round the corner of the pits – I was right out of the way and that suited me. And when it was time to race, I made a perfect start, holding off Ivan Mauger to open up with a win and it just went like clockwork for the rest of the night. Bernard asked me if I wanted to change my gear, but the set-up I had just seemed to suit the track and I stuck with it all night. I didn't touch a thing all night, I just went out and rode.

Two of my races were restarted which, given the problems my arm was giving me, was exactly what I didn't want. But I kept at it and having another crack at my third ride did me a favour because I was last on lap three when Reg Wilson fell off. I was on the outside gate, which wasn't the best, but in the re-run I came from behind to beat Martin Ashby and those three points kept me in the hunt.

Going into my last heat I needed a another win to take the title – I was on 10 points, the same as John Boulger and Terry Betts who were in the same race. Once again I made a great start and, although Bettsy was all over me, he couldn't get past and suddenly I was British Champion!

I was nowhere near the best rider in that meeting but I scored 13 points and, at the age of 29 with a smashed-up arm, I was British Champion. I think, the reason I won was because it was the reward for 10 years' hard work. After all, it was a gater's paradise at Brandon that night and every rider who was ahead at the first bend went on to win their race. I just happened to make better starts than the others, that's all.

I didn't do anything special to prepare for the British Final. In fact, I treated it just like a normal league match. I didn't particularly like the Coventry track and, as far as I was concerned, I had just gone there to make the numbers up. I hadn't even thought about qualifying, let alone winning it. Then, after I had done well in my first three rides, I realised I might score enough points to get through. I was getting pretty fed up with the restarts because I really didn't want to have to do it all over again, but I just kept at it.

> "I was nowhere near the best rider in that meeting but I scored 13 points and, at the age of 29 and with a smashed arm, I was British Champion"

I hadn't planned for this . . . the individual highlight of my career.

Winning the British Championship didn't change my life, but it was a nice reward for previous efforts.

I wasn't fully fit from the crash at Newport. I rode with a bandage around my wrist and movement in my arm was still restricted – I couldn't even comb my hair properly. In fact, after I had won the title in my last race, I did another half a lap at top speed because I didn't have the movement in my wrist to shut the throttle off.

Being British Champion was a decent achievement, but I didn't get carried away and even after being presented with the most prestigious trophy I'd ever won, I wasn't euphoric or anything like that. Nigel was more thrilled than I was. I didn't even ring Diane to tell her. In fact, I didn't even tell her when I came home and went to bed – and she's never forgiven me for that!

The following morning a few of the press lads rang to get my reaction and Diane remarked on the number of calls I was getting. I told her that I didn't know why so many people wanted to ring me either, although by saying that I wasn't being smart, I'm just like that. Not that it mattered anyway because, as it turned out, she already knew! She had pretended to be asleep when I got in, thinking I'd be all excited and eager to tell her, because Nigel's wife, Cynthia, had rung straight after the meeting to let her know.

Afterwards, when the penny had dropped, I realised that winning the British Final was poetic justice after what had happened the previous year, but even then I'm not sure I considered it to be the high point of my career. On paper it was the biggest title I had ever won and, let's face it, British titles were hard to win. Remember, there were Australian and New Zealand riders competing in those days too, so it was harder to win back then than it is now.

I probably won it at the wrong stage of my career to get excited about it. I was definitely winding down because my average had dipped - I think my experience got me to my nine-point average more than anything else that year. The tracks were getting slicker and slicker and backing the bike into corner at what seemed like 100mph wasn't speedway to me. I was getting demoralised by the whole game and I think that's why I couldn't get worked up about being British Champion.

What sticks in my mind more than winning the British Final was winning my first scratch race final and being presented with my first trophy at Edinburgh when I was 17. I had my very first trophy to display and that's when I knew I was on my way. By the time I won the British Final I had ridden for England, ridden abroad, beaten the best of them – and lost to them too!

After winning the British Final I took a two-week break from racing, which wasn't a decision I took lightly because riding a speedway bike was how I earned my living. But my broken arm was still giving me a lot of trouble and there was no point trying to ride if I wasn't up to it, or if it meant I did myself more damage and ended up back in hospital.

The crazy thing about my arm is that if I decided to do a tough two-day trial tomorrow, I could finish it without any problems. But, because it is still broken and only being held together my metal plates, it would be right back to how it was after the British Final if I did four laps on a speedway bike. The difference is that, when you're on a speedway bike, your right arm is pushing and pulling all the time, doing all the work. It's at a totally different angle to when you're on a trials bike, and it's twisting the bones all the time. So I knew that I needed to give it a rest – if I didn't there was a more than fair chance I would break something else and be out for a lot longer. I never chickened out of meetings, but missing two weeks was better than missing two months because you get in a bit of a state when you can't hang on!

I was back in action for the next round of the World Championship trail at Fredericia, the Anglo-American-Nordic Final, only this time my involvement was over almost as soon as it hard started. I was leading my first race in Denmark when, going into the fourth bend for the first time I crashed into the wooden safety fence. Scott Autrey was behind me and I think he was completely taken aback by the track. It was a disused running track with cinders on, but we had been out on parade so we all knew what it was like.

I had gone into the corner wide and Autrey came underneath me so fast and never turned, he just skated across. I pulled the bike round to the point where I was eventually going backwards and I backed straight into the fence. I hit a concrete post, unfortunately, and that is what did the damage.

I couldn't move and I couldn't feel my fingers or my toes which really frightened me. It was announced to the crowd that I had broken my leg but I've no idea where they got that from. I was taken to hospital and, when I arrived on the ward, they strapped a button to my wrist and told me to press it if I wanted anything. What good was that to me? I couldn't move, so I couldn't have pressed it if I'd wanted to!

At least the hospital staff brought me a TV – the meeting was being shown live in Denmark and I was able to watch the rest of the action. As the meeting wore on, more and more feeling came back into my fingers and toes which was a relief because I was genuinely very worried. I'm sure it would worry anyone, and it felt so good when the feeling started to come back, although the drawback was that I

My father with Nigel and me in the pits before my Testimonial meeting at The Shay..

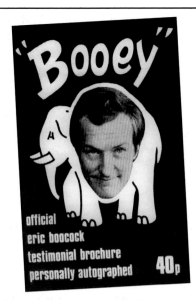

HALIFAX SPEEDWAY   N⁰   6819

Sunday, 14th July, at 3.30 p.m.

ERIC BOOCOCK
(Captain of Halifax & England)

TESTIMONIAL MEETING

PROGRAMME OF EVENTS
1. INTRODUCTION
2. GRAND PARADE
3. YORKSHIRE v. SUPER STARS

If for any reason meeting cancelled— No monies refunded

The front cover of my Testimonial brochure (left) and (above) a supporter's ticket from the big day itself.

"You couldn't park within a mile radius of the stadium and we sold out of programmes well before the start"

could also feel all the pain from the crash I'd had.

It was a long journey on the ferry back to England from Denmark and I knew the better option would be to fly, but I didn't have enough money for a ticket. So all the riders who had been competing in the meeting had a whip round and raised enough for the fare. Peter Collins arranged for his mechanic to pick me up at Manchester Airport and drive me home, then Alan Smith, my friend who played rugby league for Leeds, came straight round as soon as I got back. I still wasn't very mobile and I'd been wheeled on and off the plane in a wheelchair, so he picked me up and dumped me in the bath! He let me soak in that for half-an-hour, then lifted me out again. Yet again, Leeds RLFC came to my aid and gave me treatment to speed up my recovery. The rugby lads all thought I was mad for wanting to get back on a bike, but I had always thought that they were the crazy ones for being bashed about by an 18-stone forward for 80 minutes every week of the season.

In between those two World Championship rounds was a very special meeting for me – my testimonial. At the start of that year speedway had decided to follow football and rugby by awarding testimonials to long-serving riders and mine was the first ever. I'd spent 10 years with one club and 14 with the same promoter, so I suppose I was a deserving case, with Reg Fearman obtaining the necessary permission from the BSPA and SCB.

The crowd, I am convinced, was the biggest ever at The Shay for a speedway meeting. It was magic. The meeting was the first ever to take place at The Shay on a Sunday, and it was a red hot July afternoon and we had to put the start back because so many people turned up. You couldn't park within a mile radius of the stadium and we sold out of programmes well before the start. Before the meeting I stood out on the approach road with the policeman on duty, showing the fans where to park and reassuring them that they wouldn't miss the start.

As something different, we put a colour photograph of me in the centre of the

Above: My testimonial was a great family occasion. Back row, left to right: My mother Daisy, wife Diane, myself, sister Nina, father Carl, Nigel's wife Cynthia and Nigel. Front: Gary Younghusband (Dave's son), my son Ritchie, Darren Boocock (Nigel's son) and Mandy Boocock (Nigel's daughter).
Below left: The Masterchef and Diane go to work. Below right. With Joyce and Dougie Adams, who kindly provided the venue for a great barbecue.

testimonial brochure, and I signed every single one of them before they were put out on sale. Every mealtime there would be a pile of them waiting for me with a felt tip pen and I'd sign some before and after I had eaten. It was a thank-you to the fans for supporting me for so long – they were fantastic. A testimonial was a novelty then and fans from Sheffield, Belle Vue and other tracks came along as well as Halifax supporters, which was really nice.

The meeting took the form of an 18-heat challenge match between a Yorkshire side, led my myself, and a Superstars team. Nigel was due to be skipper of the Superstars but he couldn't ride because he had a broken collarbone, which was a shame for both of us, although he came along anyway as team manager. For the record, Yorkshire – made up of myself, Jimmy McMillan, Dougie Wyer, Reg Wilson, Rick France, Bobby Beaton, Tony Featherstone and Colin Meredith – were beaten 56-51 by a Superstars team comprising: Ivan Mauger, Ole Olsen, Peter Collins, Bob Valentine, Soren Sjosten and Henny Kroeze.

The one name I didn't have was Briggo, who was very disappointed not to have been invited. He had been a good mate for so long, but everybody was riding for nothing and I didn't want to drag him all the way up from his home in Southampton. I thought I would have put him under a lost of pressure if I'd asked him and I was worried that he might not be able to say "no" even if he had wanted to because of the good relationship he had with me and the rest of the family. I didn't want to embarrass him by putting him in an awkward position, so I didn't ask him. He went mad when he found out he hadn't been asked. I tried to explain that I had genuinely done it for what I thought were the right reasons and I think he accepted that eventually.

My testimonial day was rounded off beautifully with a surprise barbecue in Dougie and Joyce Adams' garden in Brighouse where all the riders and officials were able to tuck in, with me as Masterchef. Thankfully there were no reports of anyone falling ill afterwards!

After the testimonial it was back to the serious stuff and I scored my first maximum for four months in a home win over Oxford. Our final league position that season was seventh although the end of the season did bring its reasons to celebrate with the birth of our daughter, Sallie Ann, in September. Of course it was in the speedway season and my commitments were heavy at the time, so you can see what I mean about Diane having to put up with so much!

Mitch Graham was a rider with a talent and I was helping him out at the time. He was riding for Workington and Sallie was only a few days old when I ended up going to a meeting with him, which meant Diane wasn't very happy with me. She had a point, I guess, and I thought better of going down to the Division Two Riders' Championship at Wimbledon with Mitch, as I'd originally intended.

Whereas Ritchie, our son, took after me, Sallie was just like her mother in later life. She's got a right bubbly personality and qualified as a nurse before moving to Turkey where she now works as a travel rep. She lives in a lovely villa with her partner and they also own another one where friends and family can go and stay but, oh, for the time.

For the first time in my British League career, I ended the year with an average of less than 10 points – only just, though, as my final figure was 9.92. The season ended with another trip to hospital after a stone caught me in the eye during the final meeting. That match was at Belle Vue – a place I would soon be seeing a lot more of, especially with two good eyes.

Young Un and me are all smiles before the fireworks begin.

🔟
YOUNG UN

WHEN I first started racing speedway, my one aim was to be as good as my big brother Nigel – but he swore blind he would sell up and retire after I beat him for the first time! Nigel was a big influence on my career so, before we leave my riding days behind, I think it would be a good idea to give an insight into our relationship.

We had some terrific scraps after I joined Halifax, but the first time I ever got the better of him was when I was still with Middlesbrough and we entertained Coventry in an inter-league challenge match at Cleveland Park. I made the gate on him the first time we met on the track that night but, going down the back straight, he passed me.

He was the big star and I was the upstart so it was to be expected I suppose but, as he went by, he waved! I wasn't giving up though and back I came to beat him. The second time we met I made another good start but, once again, he passed me on the back straight and waved again, although once more it was me who crossed the line first. Exactly the same thing happened in the scratch race final – he waved as he went past, but I beat him to the chequered flag again so I was chuffed to bits.

He had said, in one of his moments of madness, that he would sell up the first time I beat him, so I was keen to remind him later that night. He was living in Rugby at the time because it was closer to his home track, but had arranged to stay at our mum and dad's overnight. So, when we got home, I said to him: "Right then, Young Un, you might as well go back home to Rugby and leave all your tackle here because it's mine now that I've beaten you." I reminded him what he had said about the first time I ever beat him but all he said was: "I knew that would make you go better!" And do you know what? He was most probably dead right.

As kids we were always keen to have the last laugh on each other too. One winter we were acting the goat, as usual, in the wood near the mill. We made a Tarzan rope, complete with a spade handle to hang on to, and the idea was that we would take it in turns to jump out of a big tree on the other side of the stream that ran along there and catch the rope.

It was Nigel's turn to go first but, when I threw him the rope, I did it too hard and it clattered into him. He told me not to throw it as hard so the next time it was miles away from him because I hadn't done it hard enough. They say practice makes perfect and my third throw was perfect – but Nigel jumped too late. His fingers seemed to be getting longer and longer but he still couldn't reach the rope. He

Coventry were a hard all round team, as this unfortunate King's Lynn opponent discovered when he challenged Nigel and his race partner and found no room on the inside.

missed it and looked like a big leopard out of control!

He went crashing down from about 12 foot off the ground and disappeared into the nettles and brambles below. He had broken his wrist and was clearly in pain, but I couldn't stop laughing and told him: "Tarzan never did owt like that!" Nigel was already riding for Coventry at the time and it was only about a month before the season started, so we had to keep his injury very quiet as his promoter, Mr Ochiltree, would not have been amused.

Some time later, though, it was payback time. Down at the mill there was a big barn and one summer our dad asked us if we could paint it. We agreed to do it so we bought the paint, a tar brush each and a ladder and set about the task. When we had finished we were stood on the roof admiring our work when Nigel spotted an area I had missed. We had a hip ladder which hooked over the apex of the roof and I started walking down to the area which needed painting so that I could finish the job. Normally I would have gone down backwards but I had to go down forwards, quite gingerly I should add, so that I could pick out the spot that had been missed.

All of a sudden the ladder hopped of the roof and both it and I started sliding down. Nigel thought it was great and I could hear him cheerily yelling "Geronimo" as I started my rapid descent! All I could think of as I went hurtling downwards was clearing the barbed wire fence at the bottom and luckily I managed to jump off the ladder just in time, and I landed in the potato field next to the barn yard. Nigel thought it was hilarious and couldn't stop laughing and I still don't know for certain that he didn't hook the ladder off the roof to send me flying! Whether he did or not, though, it was very reminiscent of the rope incident – only this time it was Nigel's turn to laugh.

I suppose we were no different to any other brothers in our rivalry, though, and being Nigel's brother certainly helped me launch my speedway career. It didn't open

Eric Boothroyd conducts the pre-race coin-tossing as the Boocock brothers are about to go head-to-head.

massive doors but it did open some. If Nigel asked a National League promoter if his younger brother could come along and have a ride after the meeting, it would be no problem. It's easier to break into speedway now than it has ever been, but in those days it was extremely difficult to get a ride so I was grateful for Nigel's help.

But for all that he was happy to do that, Nigel never, ever told me how to ride. His attitude was that I would make it if I was good enough, whether he told me what to do or not. He wasn't being nasty saying that – it seemed totally obvious to me. I was only 16 at the time and you think you know it all at that age. Who else takes any notice of their older brother when they are 16? At least I took notice of Dad who told me that if you are going to do a job, you need to get it right first time or you'll end up doing it again.

When I first started out there wasn't any particular on-track rivalry between us because Nigel was already established. He had qualified for his first World Final in 1956 and I was just a kid learning the ropes, but what he said about selling all his gear after I had beaten him stuck.

When I started going well I would have a look at the averages in Speedway Star and think: 'He's not that far ahead of me.' Then if he had a bad meeting I used to be even more keen to have a good one myself, to gain a little bit more on him. I'm sure that it worked both ways too and that, as my average started to increase, he would take a look himself and see that the gap was getting smaller.

The 1967 season was a particularly good one for because I was only unplaced six times throughout the campaign. My average was 10.38 and there was only one Englishman who had a better figure than me – and that was Nigel who finished that year with an average of 10.46. So although I was happy with my achievements that year, I would have been even more satisfied had I finished with a higher average than him!

Right from the time he moved away to Rugby, each of us always wanted to know how many points the other had scored in their previous meeting. "How many did you score last night, Young Un?" – that would be the question we would ask each other when we spoke. If I told him I'd scored 11, he would want to know if that was 11 points in total or whether I'd included bonus points. If I told him it was actually nine and two bonus, he'd say: "Well, you got nine then, didn't you, not 11!"

It all dated back to a few years earlier when he used to tell me how difficult I would find it once the two leagues amalgamated. It was good-natured but there was a lot of rivalry - Nigel wanted to be No.1 in the averages for Coventry and England and I wanted to be top man in the averages for Halifax and England.

For club and country.

When we were racing against each other, the old sibling rivalry thing always came out – he wanted to beat me and I wanted to beat him. It got a bit naughty sometimes and my mother used to play hell with us – she was convinced we were going to kill each other. Nigel was a hard rider and always gave 100 per cent – 110 per cent if he was racing against me, especially if he was behind me. For example, he ran over my foot and flattened my steel shoe one night when we were racing at Halifax so I had a right go at him in the pits afterwards. He was completely unmoved and just said: "Serves you right, Young Un, your foot shouldn't have been there.

Get out of the way next time!"

However, when we were in the same team we were as right as rain and I enjoyed riding with him. My World Pairs debut came in 1970 and I went all the way to the final at Malmo, in Sweden, with Nigel as my partner. In the Western Zone semi-final at Belle Vue, Nigel had a blinding meeting and scored 16 points while I finished on seven. Briggo

Nigel leading Ole Olsen in the 1971 British-Nordic Final at Glasgow.

and Ivan Mauger were partners for New Zealand and, when we came up against them I was at the back with Nigel chasing them. It was terrific to watch, he was inside them, then outside them looking for a way through. He didn't beat them, but what a race!

Nigel stayed at our parents' house that night and on the way home we stopped for fish and chips. We were munching away at our supper when he looked at me and said: "Young Un, you were crap tonight". Unfortunately he was right, so I had to agree

"It got a bit naughty sometimes and my mother used to play hell with us – she was convinced we were going to kill each other"

Before the same meeting at Hampden, Nigel and me are joined by Martin Ashby and Bob Kilby.

but in the final, where we finished third behind New Zealand and Sweden, I scored 13 and he only got six. So, when we got back to the hotel, it was my turn to taunt him. "Young Un," I said, "you were crap tonight!" You can imagine his response: "Who got us here in the first place?"

At that time, and for some while in fact, Nigel and I were the top two British riders in speedway. People have asked me if it felt strange being up there at the top with my brother, but I can't say that it did. It's not as if it happened overnight, it just sort of evolved. He had ridden hard to get to No 1 and my ambition was always to be as good as him. He was a lot better rider than I was but I think I always had better equipment than him and, while it was his brawn than got him where it did, I would like to think it was my brain that did it for me. I don't mean my brain in the sense that I was some sort of genius and had 50 'O' levels, but rather that I would think about what I was doing when I was racing.

I wasn't the only one who believed that, either. Ove Fundin had just won the World Final when I beat him from the back in the 1967 British League Riders' Championship at Belle Vue. He came up to me in the pits after the race and said to me: "If Nigel could think like you do, he would have been World Champion five times by now." Perhaps he was right – Nigel certainly had the ability. He was such a tenacious rider, like a terrier after a rat and he would never give up.

If you never saw Nigel ride, imagine Sean Wilson in his heyday at Sheffield. In fact I've watched Sean sometimes and thought it was Nigel. I can see Nigel all over Sean with his head down and backside up, going for it. But, of course, Nigel didn't know when to give up, whereas I did. He looked twice as exciting as me because he had a Devil-may-care style.

Nigel might well have had more success than me because of that – but he certainly tasted 50 times more hospital food than I ever did! Sometimes I would just know when it wasn't worth sticking my neck out, but Nigel didn't know when to give up. He was always breaking bones and I lost count of the amount of time he broke his collarbone. It was such a regular occurrence that he used to strap it up and carry on as though it were nothing more than a graze.

It was quite a strange experience when Nigel came to ride at Belle Vue with Coventry after I had been appointed manager at Hyde Road. I started riding after him but finished before him so, when he came to Belle Vue I was, in effect, his boss for the night because he was riding at my track. It never caused a problem and I used to pull his leg because he was at the veteran stage by then. "Come on Nigel," I'd say, "this meeting is going to finish at 11 o'clock if you don't get a move on." Nigel had been riding for 20 years by then, so it was nothing new to him and, even though he was in the twilight of his career, he could still turn it on around Belle Vue.

On bikes we were chalk and cheese but the ironic thing is that I supposedly had the brains and Nigel had none. Yet he has been retired for 15 years in Australia and I've had to keep on working – so who had the brains after all?

⑪
A LITTLE SUGAR SPOON

THOUGH we never rode for the same club side, Nigel and I were regulars for both England and Great Britain, when the top New Zealanders who rode over here gave the team an extra boost and turned us into a very decent team. Representing your country at any sport is a great honour and during my career I was selected to ride at full international level on more that 50 occasions.

My international debut in official competition was against Scotland at Halifax on May 11, 1966 when I scored 13 points from six rides as England won a pretty one-sided match 78-30. Nigel was an established international by then and was also riding, showing his class with an 18-point maximum.

To be fair, though, Scotland were nothing special and the scoreline reflects that. At that time Bert Harkins, Jimmy McMillan and Bobby Beaton were just starting out and, even though he was Australian, Glasgow's Charlie Monk was riding for the Scots. But you can only beat what's in front of you, and it was the start of a long and eventful international career for me.

A more challenging prospect came a few weeks after the match against Scotland when the Soviet Union arrived for a British tour. Once again I was in the England team and it was a great experience. We won the series 4-1 and the Soviets were really nice people – very genuine. They couldn't speak a word of English and, of course, I couldn't speak any Russian but there was something about the whole team that endeared them to the fans and anyone who rode against them. Even when I went abroad when I was England team manager years later, Igor Plechanov, Boris Samorodov and the like would go to the big meetings and come over to shake my hand. They enjoyed their racing and were so sporting.

The first Test match in that series was at Newcastle which turned out to be their only win of the tour. It was a big occasion because we had never had Soviet teams in this country at any sport. Mike Parker was the promoter there at the time and decided to give our Soviet visitors something on the pre-match presentation to mark their visit. It was a nice thought, but unfortunately all he gave them was an EPNS spoon that had 'Blackpool' inscribed on it. A little sugar spoon in a plastic case – that's all he gave them!

He lived in Blackpool and it seemed to me like he had picked them up at the last minute just so he had something to give them. It was a joke . . . you could win one

Signing autographs for fans while on England duty.

of those at a coconut shy!

My mother used to go to a lot of meetings and she was disgusted, so she went to the bank and ordered 10 Churchill crowns. She gave them to me and Nigel before the third Test at Wolverhampton and told us to hand them out to all the riders, the manager and the other officials at the presentation. We told the announcer, Peter Morrish, and, over the tannoy he told the crowd that the Boocock family were making the presentation as a token of friendship. Let's face it, Winston Churchill was very well known, even to anyone in the Soviet Union. They wouldn't have a clue where Blackpool was, but they would know who Churchill was!

It was a good series for me because, after scoring nine points at Newcastle, I top scored at Halifax and Wolverhampton in the next two Tests and that was enough to earn me a place in the Great Britain team that toured Poland shortly afterwards. And what a trip that turned out to be!

The schedule was for five matches in just six days and it was pretty much all one-way traffic as the Poles whitewashed us 4-0, with one meeting abandoned. It was a punishing schedule and, to be honest, it was a bit grim out there in those days. Briggo was the only Great Britain rider who could live with the Polish lads, and it's no coincidence that he was riding an ESO like they were, while the rest of us were on JAPs. Even then he had a 32mm carb because that's what we used in Britain, while the Poles all had 36mm carbs. Briggo was still slower than them and his big points total was down to track-craft rather than speed.

It was my first time behind the Iron Curtain but some of the other lads had been before and knew what to expect. Ivan Mauger was one of them and he took a suitcase full of Mars bars because he knew how grim the food was! He wouldn't sell

England line up to face the Russians at The Shay in July 1966. Left to right: Myself, Dave Younghusband, Nigel (on bike), Ron Mountford, Frank Varey (manager), Eric Boothroyd, Trevor Hedge and Bob Paulson.

the rest of us one, let alone let us have one!

Throughout the trip we travelled on a battered old bus with the bikes being towed on a trailer with a tarpaulin sheet over the top. Unfortunately, however, the roads were atrocious and on one journey, we lost the trailer! All of our luggage was at the back while we all sat at the front of the bus but, boy, those seats were uncomfortable! After a while I tried, without success, to get some sleep at the rear of the bus and then Ken McKinlay gave it a go as well, but he too found it no more comfortable. On his way back to the front, Ken casually remarked that the trailer was missing and, naturally, I assumed he was joking because it was certainly still attached the last time I'd looked out of the rear window. About 20 minutes later somebody else decided to try and get some rest at the back – and that's when we realised the trailer really was missing!

The bus driver had to make a U-turn and we drove back for about half-an-hour before we found the trailer, upside down in a field, about 100 yards from the road. We had coffee and some Coffee Mate with us, so we decided to have a brew while we were getting the bikes and the trailer sorted out. Coffee and Coffee Mate is no good without water, of course, so my brother Nigel and Ivan Mauger started up one of the bikes and rode off to a farmhouse we could see in the distance. A few minutes later they came roaring back up the road with Nigel riding the bike and Ivan sitting on the back clutching a pan of water! Just as they came riding down the road, up pulled a policeman to see what was going on. He didn't say a word to us but I think he was quite amused at seeing two blokes astride a speedway bike on a public road with a pan of water and, about 20 minutes after he'd left, another policeman arrived to have a look too.

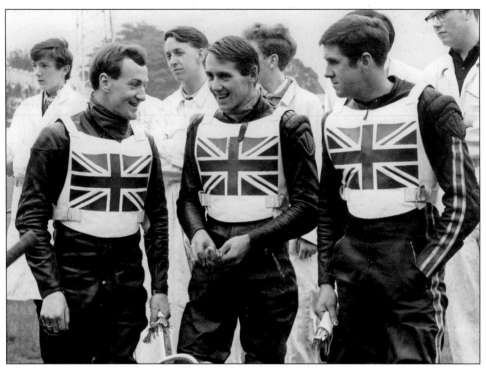

Enjoying a laugh with Martin Ashby and Barry Briggs.

We can laugh about it now, but the road was raised up quite a way so the trailer had careered down some banking before it overturned and a lot of the bikes were quite badly damaged.

Our guide on the trip was a Polish bloke called Charlie and none of us liked him – Briggo especially so. Charlie threatened to report us to the police for indecent exposure after we were late arriving to one meeting and had to get changed on the coach. Just as Nigel was about to pull on his leathers as we approached the stadium, Briggo lifted him up so the fans could see him in all his glory – and Charlie most definitely failed to see the funny side! In fact he was so angry that he told Briggo he was going to send him home. I'll never forget Briggo's reaction – he got down on his hands and knees in the centre aisle of the bus and pretended to plead! "Please don't send me home, Charlie," he said, "I love Poland and I want to stay here forever!"

One of the trips we went on during that tour was to Auschwitz, the former Nazi concentration camp. On the roof of this battered old coach we travelled everywhere in was a big plastic skylight measuring about 6ft by 3ft and, around three miles from Auschwitz, it lifted up and blew away. As if that weren't bad enough, within about a minute there was a massive cloudburst and the rain started pouring in. Quick as a flash, Briggo said to the guide: "Charlie – you'd better go and get our roof back." It was absolutely chucking it down with rain and Charlie didn't want to get his clothes wet, so he stripped down to his underpants and went running down the road looking for the roof. We all stood at the back of the bus, peering through the window and taking the mickey, and about 10 minutes later he reappeared with the skylight balanced on his head! He looked like a giant snail creeping along the road!

We eventually helped Charlie fix the skylight back on – although we wouldn't budge until the rain had stopped – and continued on to Auschwitz which was a harrowing experience. Everyone ought to go there if they are able, because it's a history lesson you won't forget in a hurry. It was an eerie sensation and you could just sense that something horrific had taken place there.

Another trip to Poland with the British Lions that sticks in my memory came in 1973 when Test matches were arranged on three separate Saturdays to avoid disrupting the British League fixture list. It seemed a sound idea but although it didn't disrupt the fixtures, it sure as anything disrupted me!

The first Test was in Wroclaw on the first Saturday in May, and I'd ridden at Halifax the night before in a Northern Riders' Championship qualifying round. This meant that, in order to get to Wroclaw in time, I had to spend two hours in the workshop working on my bike straight after the meeting and then dash down to Heathrow airport to catch a plane to Poland at four o'clock in the morning with the rest of the tour party. On top of that I had to strip the bike down when I got to the airport in order to get it on the plane, and then put it back together and ride it the following night.

These days riders race all over the place and jump on a plane like they're getting a bus, but they haven't got a bike to prepare when they get there because they've got someone to do it for them. But we had to do it all on our own back then. I couldn't be certain but I'm not even sure we even had our own mechanics with us – I think we may have had just one bloke between the seven of us.

Unfortunately it didn't get any better when the meeting started and I failed to score

After victory over Poland at Coventry in August 1966. Team manager Vic Gooden with (left to right): Ken McKinlay, Rick France, Cyril Maidment, myself, Jim Lightfoot, Bill Andrew, Barry Briggs and Our Nigel.

a point as the Poles gave us a 76-31 drubbing. I'd been due to ride in the other two Tests, at Rybnik and Gorzow, too but Halifax were riding the night before both of those matches too and I withdrew from the rest of the series because it wasn't worth the hassle.

Looking back now, what is interesting is that even in 1973, fixtures clashes were beginning to become a problem. The situation is so severe these days that no Elite League track can run on a Saturday night. I'm all for spreading the boundaries of speedway and it's fantastic that the sport has reached places like Latvia and Bulgaria, but the problem is that everybody wants the same riders and there are only so many to go round.

Having initially made my mark in 1966, I became a regular in the Great Britain side and I was in the side again when Sweden sent over a team for a five-match series in 1967. I missed just one Test in that series, and that was only because it was on a Saturday night and I was riding at Halifax. That was the series in which I scored my full house at international level – a 15+3 paid maximum at Glasgow. It's difficult now to remember how I felt at the time but I'm sure I was delighted, and I would have enjoyed riding with Briggo too because he was my hero. He was a great riding partner – so safe – and I've already described how he had a little word with Olle Nygren in that meeting.

After being paid for the lot against Sweden, I did even better against Poland the following month when I recorded my first 18-point maximum at international level on my home track. It was great to do it in front of my home supporters at The Shay and it was an important result because it clinched the series.

British speedway was looking strong and in 1968 we were kings of the world. I wasn't a member of the five-man team which won the World Team Cup but I did play my part in Great Britain's victory in something called the World League. The competition was designed to find the best seven-a-side team in the world and also contained Poland, the Soviet Union and Sweden.

My abiding memory of that series was the opening match against Sweden at Wimbledon, the only meeting in which I've deliberately dropped points. Sweden were nowhere near as strong as our side and, as a result, I scored just one point but I was paid for much more. It was pointed out to us by Ronnie Greene, the Wimbledon promoter, that it wasn't in the best interests of the competition if we were to go out and whitewash the opposition. Consequently I had a lot of mysterious engine failures that night and, coincidentally, so did some of the other lads as Sweden ran us unexpectedly close at 43-35. We were riding to order and paid a flat fee regardless of how many points we scored, and we won the meeting anyway so I suppose no harm was done.

I should point out, however, that this was the only time I have ever known this sort of thing to go on and I was genuinely surprised and amazed to be asked. Funnily enough, those mysterious bike problems had been cured by the time of our second match against Sweden at Halifax two days later – I scored a paid maximum as we won 51-27.

The Soviets, Swedes and Poles also rode a few Test matches while they were over and it was in one of those matches that I was handed the honour of captaining my country for the first time. Nigel had picked up one of his many injuries so I took over as England skipper for the second Test against the Soviets at Newport. It was a shame someone had to get injured for me to be chosen, especially when it was my own brother, but I was delighted to be asked. In fact I might have rung Nigel and asked him to get injured more often!

As you must have gathered by now, I always took meticulous care of my equipment and, if you ever saw me ride, you'll know that I never turned up for a meeting with a bike that was anything less than immaculate. It's the preparation and work I put in while I was in my workshop that helped me establish myself on both the domestic and international scene. I'd say that 90 per cent of speedway is down to what you have done in the workshop. If you have your bike perfectly prepared, all you have to do is turn up and ride it – but if you're worried about what might go wrong, you don't ride it properly.

So you can imagine my horror when the unthinkable happened – I broke down. It happened while I was leading a race in the second Test against Australia in 1969. It was my first retirement because of a mechanical problem for more than a year and the problem was the magneto, which was the only weak link on an ESO, or Jawa as they became known. Naturally I was frustrated at being denied a win but it didn't affect the outcome of the series which, incidentally, was the first in this country between England and Australia for 16 years. We won comfortably although the Aussies were always a different proposition on their home territory and I'll come to that soon.

> "I set off to Glasgow to ride in the first Test and when I returned at 4am she was stil sat on the bathroom floor with her head on the toilet seat"

Reg Fearman tosses the coin while a relaxed-looking Ove Fundin and me await the outcome.

Thje GB team that beat Sweden at Newport in June 1967. Back row: Terry Betts, Charlie Monk, Wally Mawdsley (team manager), Jon Erskine and Barry Briggs. Front: Roy Trigg, Nigel, Jimmy Gooch and myself.

The Aussies were back over the following year, although I was left out of the team for the first Test at Hackney. At the time I was quoted in the press as saying I was unhappy and that I reckoned I'd been left out of the team because I was too good – but that was just a good story for the papers really. After all, it says "Oxo" on the back of a bus but you can't buy it on a No.22!

No, the simple explanation was that we had so many good riders that we could afford to operate a horses-for-courses policy. What was the point in taking me all the way down to Hackney when we had, maybe, 10 riders good enough to make the team. I could easily be replaced by someone who lived much closer and could do the job just as well. Likewise there would have been no point in taking Colin Pratt all the way up to Halifax when Dave Younghusband could do the job. What a luxury. I bet Neil Middleditch wishes he had the same choice now.

As I've mentioned before, I never liked turning down a booking and I would always go the extra mile to honour a commitment – even when becoming a father for the first time fell slap, bang in between two Test matches on consecutive nights!

It was July 1970 and my wife Diane was heavily pregnant with Richie, our son. It was obvious she was not far off having the baby but, with her blessing, I set off to Glasgow to ride for Great Britain in the first Test against Sweden and when I returned home at about four o'clock in the morning, she was still sat on the bathroom floor with her head on the toilet seat. She was feeling absolutely terrible so I phoned the midwife who, despite being disturbed at such an early hour, came over and stayed until six o'clock. That was when the midwife phoned an ambulance to take Diane to the maternity hospital in Wakefield and eventually Ritchie was born – on Independence Day!

At about half-past eight I left the hospital and came back to the workshop to get ready for the second Test at Halifax that night. Despite just all of that, I took my place in the Test team, although I didn't do very well. I only scored three points but I don't think it was due to the euphoria of becoming a dad for the first time – it was down to the fact that I'd gone 48 hours without any sleep! I really wasn't happy that I'd had such a bad meeting but I think I got a bit of sympathy given the circumstances.

Ritchie was in the breach position when he was born and I've often joked that he's been upside down all his life! Diane has always reckoned that he's just like me – stubborn as a mule and cantankerous with it, so it was no surprise that he wanted to ride speedway like his dad when he was old enough.

Speedway is a hard life and to make it you have got to give it everything. A lot of riders start and only a few of them make any money out of it, so I didn't want to push him into a career like that. If anything went wrong, what would he have to fall back on? I'm 61 and I've been involved in speedway all this time so it's not a problem – but it sure would have been if I was 41 and didn't have a job in speedway any more.

I told Ritchie that although I wouldn't hinder him if that was what he wanted to do, I wouldn't help and that, if he was going to make it, he would make it on his own. My view was that he should get a job and learn a trade then, once he had got himself qualified, he could take a sabbatical and give speedway a go.

He did eventually have a bike put together and had a go but it all ended on the training track at Sheffield where he broke his ankle after another young upstart fell and went into him. As it turned out he got a good job with a forklift truck company and he's worked his way up to the point where he's got 16 blokes working under him.

Throughout his childhood Ritchie – and his mum and sister – had to put up with me coming and going at some rather odd times because speedway isn't a nine-to-five job and that's how I earned a living. He was only a few months old when I was off to Sweden for a Test series with Great Britain. Ivan Mauger was still riding for Belle Vue and was allowed to fly in and out for each Test while the rest of us had to take our cars and stay out there. It caused a bit of uneasiness among the lads because it wasn't fair really, but we got on with it and won the series 2-1.

He wasn't riding in this particular Test series, but one of the big name Swedes of that era was Torbjorn Harrysson. Have you ever seen a man run on crutches? Well Toby is the only bloke I know who could do that and, boy, could he shift! He'd shattered his leg but it didn't stop him from showing that he wasn't only quick on a speedway bike and, in fact, if running on crutches was an Olympic sport, he'd make sure that Sweden took the gold medal. I seem to remember it took him a long time to recover from that particular injury and I think that was because, even though he was on crutches, he liked a few beers every now and then and he kept falling over!

Throughout 1971 and 1972 I continued to be a regular in the Union Jack racejacket and did my bit when the authorities had another stab at staging a World Cup-type tournament. This time it was called the Inter Nations Championship and featured England, a joint Norway-Denmark team, Sweden, Australia and New Zealand. The competition took place throughout July 1972 and culminated in a last match decider at The Shay.

With manager Tore Kittilsen cunningly using Ole Olsen at reserve, the Norway-Denmark team had got the better of us at Poole, which meant we had to beat Australia on my home track to win the title. It didn't start well and we were behind after two heats but I chalked up nine points and Ray Wilson went through the card unbeaten as we triumphed 48-30.

The series was more successful than the World League in 1968 and returned bigger, better and slightly revamped under the banner of the Daily Mirror International Tournament in 1973. This time also including Poland and the Soviet Union who had declined an invitation to enter a year earlier, the competition also featured semi-finals at Belle Vue and Coventry plus what turned out to be a nail-biting final at Wembley.

England made a winning start to the tournament with a 40-38 victory over Sweden at Sheffield and it was my pleasure to be involved in what ITV commentator Dave Lanning described as the greatest speedway race he'd ever seen. Peter Collins and I needed a 4-2 over Anders Michanek and Tommy Jansson in the final race to make sure England took the honours and, after four spectacular laps, our mission was successfully completed. I reared on the start and I was hopelessly last but I carried on in the hope that somebody might stop. I was with the others but I wasn't really making up any ground when, on the second lap, PC went right round the outside of Michanek who had been leading the race.

That's when I knew I was right to keep on going and a lap later, in the same place, I went round Jansson to take third place and stayed there to give us the 4-2 we needed. I'd been watching from the back and, when I saw how the move had worked for PC, I thought it was worth trying it myself, and it certainly was!

The final at Wembley was as dramatic as you could ever imagine – and unlike that match with Sweden at Wimbledon I mentioned earlier in this chapter, this one wasn't stage-managed. With the final score dead level at 39-39 at the end of 13 heats, it needed a run-off between Peter Collins and Anders Michanek to decide the destiny of the trophy. PC was an emerging young talent at the time and had been quick to point out he'd never even seen Wembley before – but he coped admirably with the pressure and was awarded victory after he bit the dust as Michanek tried to find a way past on the pit turn. The Swedes weren't happy at the decision to exclude their man but it certainly looked the right verdict to me.

On a personal level, I failed to score in that tournament final at Wembley and it turned out to be my last international appearance. What a way to end my international career – I'd started it with a score of 13 points and ended it with a zero! I was included in the squad to face Sweden the following year but not used and I also had to withdraw from the England team to face Poland at The Shay because by that time I had broken my arm at Newport and was suffering from the effects of it.

Great Britain manager and Wimbledon supremo Ronnie Greene has a quiet word.

I would have loved to have ridden but if you're not fully fit for a Test match, you're not going to give 100 per cent so it made sense to give someone else a chance.

Riding for my country was a fantastic honour – one I'm immensely proud of – and, of course that was far from being my last involvement with the national side as I went on to become manager, which I'll come to in a later chapter.

As well as riding all over Britain and Europe with England and Great Britain, I was also a regular on the winter tours to Australia in the late 60s and they provided me with some more fantastic memories

"It was pointed out to us by Ronnie Greene that it wasn't in the best interests of the competition if we were to go out and whitewash the opposition"

Above: A chat in the pits with Ray Wilson, who took over from Nigel and me as England No.1 in the early 70s.
Below: My final appearance for England, after beating Sweden in the Daily Mirror International Tournament Final at Wembley in the summer of 1973. The final didn't go too well for me, but PC and I had done our bit in the thrilling last heat at Sheffield. Standing, left to right: Terry Betts, Martin Ashby, Len Silver (team manager), Malcolm Simmons and Peter Collins. Front: Myself, Ray Wilson and John Louis.

12

A POLICEMAN WITH A RADAR GUN

FOR four consecutive winters during my time at Halifax, I went out to Australia to race – and I loved every minute of it. Australia was – and still is – a fantastic place to be and I'm sure the reason it appealed to me so much was because throughout my childhood I spent as much time as I could playing in the woods near the mill, and that love of the great outdoors has never left me.

My first winter Down Under was in 1966-67 and I made the trip on the suggestion of Charlie Monk who had been staying with us. We flew out together and, when we arrived in Adelaide, I had my first surprise of the trip – when Charlie asked me to look after our bags while he went and made a phone call to check I had somewhere to stay! Call me presumptuous, but I had rather assumed that everything would be sorted by the time we arrived and the thought did cross my mind that I might end up sleeping on the beach that night! Fortunately, when Charlie came back the news was good and he had found somewhere for me to stay.

It was lovely accommodation too – our landlady was called Lorna Keys and she was a fantastic hostess and a wonderful cook. Charlie and I both stayed with her and she was like a mother to us. Her husband, Bill, was a typical pommie-bashing Aussie but we had some fantastic laughs with him.

Rowley Park was the local track and we only rode three races a week - four if we were lucky – because in those days the meetings consisted of sidecars, sprint cars, hot stocks and all manner of other races as well as solos. The meetings would start at 7.30 and not finish until midnight, although the solos were always on first which meant once we had finished and got loaded up, we could sit back on the banking and watch the rest of the meeting.

Rowley Park was set in a natural amphitheatre, very similar to Trelawny but not as big. It was a disued quarry with the track at the bottom and the fans – particularly those who followed the sidecars – often used to party right through the night after a meeting.

I'd never ridden handicap races until I went to Rowley Park, and what an experience that was! Sometimes there would be up to nine riders of varying ability in a race and, on one occasion my starting position was more than halfway down the back straight. In front of me were Ray Wilson, Charlie Monk and Johnny Boulger!

Handicap races were all right for about a lap, but that was when you caught up with the rookie who started at the front. The experiences guys like us were going far

Above: Flat out at Rowley Park, Adelaide on the inside of Chum Taylor and Roy Trigg.
Below: Relaxing at practice – me, Ray Wilson and Terry Betts.

faster so, as you can imagine, it got a bit hairy. Jim Airey had a great tactic when he rode in handicap races at Sydney. He was the star man and always off the back so, instead of waiting for the tapes to go up on the other side of the track, he just used to go when the grandstand lights were switched off! It probably gained him about 10 yards but, when you consider how big his handicap was, that wasn't much of an advantage.

It was while I was in Adelaide that I became particularly friendly with Rolfie Vonderbosch who I'd first met back home when he was Ivan Mauger's mechanic. Ivan wasn't riding in Australia that winter so he acted as my mechanic while I was out there. He became a great friend during that stay and I got along famously with his mum too – she made the best kangaroo tail soup I've ever tasted!

Rolfie's house was about four miles from where Charlie and I were staying and I was a regular visitor so, fairly early on, I realised I needed some sort of transport. Very quickly I realised how big Australia is and if anyone told me that somewhere was "just around the corner" that could mean anything up to a mile and a half away!

I finished up buying a Holden pick-up and after that my next task was to get a job. I didn't particularly need to but I was bored because Charlie worked all day and so did Rolfie which meant my day didn't start until the evening. I had a word with Kym Bonython who was the promoter at Rowley Park and, as luck would have it, he knew someone with a big engineering works about half a mile from the track where they made fire-fighting equipment. He offered me a job on semi-skilled wages and I took

The first meeting of the 1966-67 Aussie tour – Charlie Monk, Gote Nordin, Ray Wilson and me.

it – I even worked through the Christmas shutdown doing maintenance work.

The boss there became a good friend and some weekends we used to head off to his ranch a few miles up the river and have barbecues and go fishing. Other weekends Rolfie and I would head off into the bush – sometimes up to a couple of hundred miles away – and go fishing and shoot rabbits or wild ducks. At night we would sleep in the back of the pick-up with just a sheet each over us. We would make a fire and whatever we shot at Saturday tea-time we would cook and have for our evening meal.

On our way back from one weekend away Rolfie warned me that the road we were on was notorious for police speed traps. It was about six o'clock on a Sunday morning and I cockily told him we'd have nothing to worry about because there would be no traffic cops on duty that early in the day. Well, you can imagine what happened can't you?

I'd no sooner said that when a policeman with a radar gun jumped out from behind a bush and booked me for speeding. I was told to be in court four days after I was due back in England, so I took myself along to what was then the brand new courthouse in Adelaide to explain my position. I showed them my air ticket and the duty sergeant told me they couldn't reschedule my court appearance and advised me just to forget about it. When I flew back home at the end of my stay, I left the speeding ticket with Lorna, my landlady, and forgot all about it, just as I'd been told to. I'd been home about three weeks when I received a letter from Lorna saying the police had been round with a warrant for my arrest! She explained I'd gone back to England and we thought that was the end of it, but a year later I was back in Adelaide – and no sooner had I arrived in the Rowley Park pits when Kym Bonythan came up to me accompanied by two plain clothes policemen with a warrant for my arrest! I couldn't believe it – I thought Kym was joking until they showed me the warrant.

"He lifted up his shirt and there it was, in his pocket. Whether it was a starting pistol or not I don't know, but it was a big gun. I couldn't believe it"

The 1967-68 British touring team wearing our British League club colours. Left to right: Terry Betts, Nigel, Ken McKinlay (on bike), myself, Colin Pratt, Ray Wilson and Roy Trigg.

The fine was for 140 Aussie dollars and there was no way I could pay that on the spot, though thankfully Kym put his hand in his pocket and staved off the prospect of me being carted off to the local nick. I promised to pay him back as soon as I could and that night I scored an 18-point maximum. Ordinarily that would have earned me 144 dollars but when it came to getting my wages for the night I picked up the princely sum of four dollars – still it was better than spending the night behind bars! I can only assume that someone in the immigration office was a motorsport fan and had tipped off the police that I would be riding there. After all, Boocock is a distinctive name – if I'd been called Smith I might have got away with it!

The meeting in which I scored that 18-point maximum was an important one too. It was the fifth and deciding Test of the first official series between England and the Aussies for seven years and our 62-46 victory sealed a 3-2 series win. I remember that I started the meeting with a 59 rear sprocket and changed to a 58 for my next heat. I switched back to a 59 for my third race, then used a 58 for my fourth ride, then changed it around again for my last two. I just couldn't decide which one was best and for about two months after that Ken McKinlay, who was next to me in the pits, called me 'Sprocket'.

It was another fantastic tour and I think the fact I was enjoying myself so much was reflected in that I was the top scorer in that series and the only rider to record double figures in every Test.

The first Test of the series was at Sydney Showground, where we won by a single point – and the Aussies didn't like that one bit. After the meeting we went out on the victory parade and, because the track was so unbelievably narrow, we went out two to a bike. Colin Pratt and I were following Terry Betts and Roy Trigg when, all of a sudden, those two fell off onto the centre green grass. I thought it was really

Looking a bit apprehensive as I lead out Mike Broadbank and the rest of the touring Test team, with Aussie captain Jim Airey alongside me.

funny and nearly fell off myself where I was laughing so much – but then we realised what had happened. Some idiot in the crowd – which must have been about 40,000 strong by the way – had thrown a beer bottle which had struck Terry just above his left eye. It was a really deep cut, too, and there was blood everywhere. If it had hit him half an inch lower, he would have lost his eye.

I was furious, and then I heard someone shout: "That's him there – he did it." I looked into the crowd and I saw a guilty-looking bloke trying to run away. Because they had car racing there as well, there was wire mesh above the track fence at Sydney and I was climbing up it like a shot. I was going to get this thug, make no mistake.

Unfortunately negotiating the fence proved more of a problem than I'd expected, but someone else caught him anyway. One of the fans in the crowd was a big mate of Ken McKinlay's and he grabbed hold of him. I think it's fair to say he let him know what he thought of him before the police arrived!

Another incident at Sydney I'll never forget came after Garry Middleton approached me and offered to help me in the pits. Garry was quite a character and, during his time with Hackney, he used to ride on the continent on a Sunday. In order to do that in those days you needed to get your permit stamped by the SCB – it was a lot stricter than it is today. Garry couldn't be bothered with any of that so he nicked a stamp from the London Underground and stamped his permits himself! Just to be on the safe side, he then smudged them a little so you couldn't make out what they said. Another one of his tricks was to have a sign in his car saying "Doctor on Call," which he used to display in his window and then park wherever he wanted.

Although he was an Aussie, Garry didn't really get along with his compatriots and he had a particular dislike for Jim Airey. During practice for this particular Test match in Sydney, he told me he would like to come and mechanic for me that evening. He even offered me the use of his bike as a spare. I was happy to accept his offer and, sure enough, that evening he turned up. I thanked him for coming and he said to me: "No problem. And one thing is for sure, you won't be having any trouble from Jim Airey tonight or I'll blow him away!"

He had a gun! He lifted up his shirt and there it was, in his pocket. Whether it was a starting pistol or not I don't know, but it was a big gun. I couldn't believe it. "Are you trying to get us locked up?" I screamed at him "just put it in the car will you!" Thankfully he didn't use it . . .

The tracks that were used for the Test matches were always well prepared but we used to race against various state and select teams out in the bush too. Some of the facilities were a little spartan at those places – for example the after-match shower at Rockhampton consisted of standing under the water bowser, while the lights were so bad at Brooklyn that we all needed torches to work on our bikes in the pits. It all added to the charm of being Down Under, of course, and I was back the following year – 1968-69 – for another slice of the action.

It was during the 1968-69 series that I had a big crash with Les Bentzen in the fourth Test at Brisbane. I think I'm right in saying it was Les's first Test match and he was keen to impress. Unfortunately he came off gate one and he just never turned when he got to the first bend. He hooked up with me and we went into the wooden fence so hard it wrecked my bike and left me with concussion. Les was even worse off than me – he was unconscious for weeks and nearly died, although luckily he's all right now.

The Aussies weren't happy and, amazingly, I got blamed for the crash in the press, but how the hell could I have taken him into the fence when I was on the outside of him? Those accusations really annoyed me because there is no way I would have run someone into the fence and gone with him. I was a speedway rider not a kamikaze pilot!

Australia won the series 3-2 after beating us in the decider at Sydney but the Ashes were back in our possession the following winter. Tony Clarke was a revelation in 1969-70 – he wasn't the brightest spark, to be fair, but he rode exceptionally well on that tour and weighed in with 13 points on the night we won 58-49 at Sydney to ensure a series win. He was on a JAP too, while most of us were on Jawas, but it didn't seem to matter at all.

Once again the series went down to the wire and we settled it in the final meeting – but this time there were rumours that the fourth Test in Brisbane had been fixed to ensure the scores were level going into the final match. I said it then and I'll say it again now – there is no way that was the case. Australia won 56-52 in Brisbane but we wanted to win, make no mistake.

The Aussies used to throw everything but the kitchen sink at us when we were out there so, no matter what we had been offered, we would have refused it because we were desperate to beat them.

An example of what we were up against came in the final Test at Sydney when I was robbed of an 18-point maximum. As usual the Aussies were rolling like you wouldn't believe at the tapes and I ended up stranded at the start while they got away. But was the race restarted? No way! The Aussies weren't going to let an

Poised to pass top Aussie Jim Airey to win the New South Wales Championship at Sydney Showground in 1968.

opportunity like that pass and I finished up at the back – I didn't have a hope of making up 50 yards on a 680-yard track.

Sydney wasn't unusual in being such a big track, but the biggest of them all was Claremont in Perth. That track was huge and I absolutely loved it – the speeds you could get up to were tremendous. Because of the size of the circuits out there, some races – even in Test matches – were run over three laps, and I remember after one winter Down Under I stopped after three laps in my first meeting back at Halifax!

By the time that deciding Test took place, my brother Nigel had joined us after missing the start of the tour because he was recovering from a fractured skull, and his absence had meant I was captain of the Lions side. With a full strength squad we headed out to New Zealand from Sydney – and were very nearly back down to one Boocock straight away!

We arrived in Auckland for the opening Test against the Kiwis to be told that, despite the track being soaking wet and the rain still lashing down, we were to go out and practise so that some publicity photographs could be taken.

I was livid. I'd taken my bike out of its packing case and put it together, but I was so incensed at the promoter's crazy demands that I took it apart again, screwed the lid on the packing case and demanded to know when the next plane home left! Eventually it was sorted out though and we went on to win comfortably, just as we did in the other two Tests as well. Apart from Ivan Mauger and Ronnie Moore, the New Zealanders weren't a lot of good and picking up our wages at the end of the night was like taking money off the blind.

The Auckland racing strip had a cycle track running round the outside instead of a safety fence, and Nigel made a name for himself there riding it like a wall of death. If you went round the outside you struggled to turn because it was so deep, and one night Nigel got it totally wrong going into the corner that he ended up on the cycle track. The banking was so steep that after he had swept round there, about a third of the way up, he went back onto the straight so fast that I thought he was going to end up in Wellington!

Above: The 1968-69 touring Lions – left to right: Ken McKinlay, Jimmy McMillan, myself, Nigel, Dave Younghusband, Mike Broadbank and Bob Kilby. Below: My Halifax team-mate Greg Kentwell joins Nigel, Terry Betts and myself during practice at the Sydney Showground.

Nigel made the headlines on another occasion at Auckland when he went on the tannoy to complain at what were clearly biased refereeing decisions. England riders had clearly won the first two races, no doubt about it, but the referee awarded them both to New Zealand. Nigel, who had taken over the captaincy from me on joining the touring party, marched onto the centre green where the officials sat at a table by the starting gate. He took the microphone and began addressing the crowd, telling them that they were very much mistaken if they thought we had travelled 13,000 miles to be robbed by stupid, blind officials! "We're not going to be

Displaying our BL club colours again – this time on the Lions tour of 1969-70. Left to right: Jimmy McMillan, Arnie Haley, Tony Clarke, myself, Ray Wilson, Ken McKinlay and Martin Ashby.

pissed around any more," he told them, before going over to the officials' table and suggesting they all had their eyes tested! A little later, during the interval, two policemen came into the pits and told Nigel they had received a complaint because he had sworn over the tannoy. They ordered him to make an apology so, after the interval, we went back out onto the centre green and picked up the microphone for a second time. He explained that the Police had received a complaint and told the crowd how sorry he was if he had offended anyone… then added: "But it doesn't alter the fact that we haven't come 13,000 miles to be pissed about!" I think the local constabulary realised they weren't going to get any joy after that and the crowd thought it was great, too, so we didn't have any more trouble.

That tour was my last Down Under as a rider because, for four years, speedway had become a 12-month, 52-week-a-year occupation. We used to head off straight after the end of the British season and be there in early October, not returning home again until February, just before the start of the next season. By then I had done my stint in Australia and, although she might not believe me, I was beginning to think that it was a bit unfair on Diane who always stayed at home throughout the winter while I went swanning off to Australia. It wasn't all fun and games either. You're living out of a suitcase and driving 800 miles or so across the desert from Perth to Adelaide isn't a great deal of fun. It was things like that I wasn't unhappy to see the back of, but I had some wonderful times Down Under and made some friends I still have today and have been to visit numerous times since.

⑬
WHO MENTIONED RIDING?

IN December 1974 I decided I'd had enough. I retired from racing speedway. Reg Fearman phoned me up with details of the first Halifax practice session of 1975 expecting me to take part – but I just told him I would just go along and watch. He still believed I would be part of his team the following year but eventually the penny dropped.

Funnily enough, that was when he decided that I had maybe been at Halifax too long and that a season out on loan would do me the world of good! He told me he had contacted Danny Dunton at Oxford – which was a track where I went well – and that he would love me to join them. Sure enough, Danny rang me a few days later but I told him exactly the same as I had told Reg – I had retired. He offered me a brilliant deal – far better than I had ever had at Halifax, but my mind was made up.

I'd had enough of the same old routine, the driving, cleaning my bikes, being away from home for nights on end, slick tracks. I didn't want to do it any more. The effects of my broken arm made it a lot more difficult to earn a living by riding speedway, although I was still averaging nearly 10 points a match and I was British Champion, so I could still do it. But by this time I was nearly 30 and I had started riding at 16. I'd had four winters in Australia, I'd ridden on the continent, I'd done ice racing – it had been a fantastic run. I was very lucky too because the only bad accident I'd ever had was the one at Newport, so I was able to walk away from it pretty much unscathed.

When I retired I received a few sarcastic comments about the timing of my decision. Some people thought it was wrong that I should hang up my leathers so soon after my testimonial meeting, but my sentiment was that my testimonial had been awarded for the 10 years' service I had given to the club, and that it was not an incentive to do another 10! I was very grateful for a testimonial because I think that if anyone deserved it, I did, but I was also comfortable with my decision to call it quits.

It was very hard to get spare parts in those days so I decided to open a speedway and grass track shop after I retired from riding. Diane and I bought some premises about 800 yards walk from home and we put a lot of energy into building up the business over the winter. Eastbourne promoter Bob Dugard was a big help as he was involved in Weslake, who were just coming onto the scene at the time. There were very few Weslake dealers, but I was granted a Weslake agency which was good because a lot of riders were changing over to them. It was all coming together and we had envisaged building the business up. But then, right out of the blue, I got a call from Jack Fearnley, the promoter at Belle Vue.

Jack asked me to go over and have lunch with him, but I told him I was too busy with the business. In any case, I told him, I had finished with riding so I wasn't interesting in joining them. "Who mentioned riding?" he asked, which got me wondering what on earth he wanted from me. He was adamant he wanted to invite me over for lunch and asked me to name a day. In all honesty I could have gone there and then but I wanted to make it appear as though I was flat out, so I agreed to meet him a few days later.

I drove over to Manchester, which was less than an hour away, and met Jack for lunch. That was when he dropped the bombshell that Frank Varey, who was caretaker manager of the Aces after Dent Oliver had died, was stepping down. He was 65 and he'd had enough of the journey from Sheffield every working day, and I, apparently, was the man to replace him. My name was known in speedway, Frank had recommended me and Jack was sure I could do a good job.

We discussed a salary and a company car, but I told Jack I couldn't make a decision there and then. I needed to talk to Diane about it, and she was happy with that. He wanted me to take up the job in March, before the start of the new season, but I explained that would not be possible because I had agreed to take a training school in Italy for a month. Briggo had been approached to do it but wasn't able to so he put my name forward instead and I didn't want to let them down. Again, that was no problem, according to Jack. "Start when you come back," he said.

I was dead keen to take the job and I told Diane that as soon as I got home,

The other side of the fence . . . Frank Varey and I leading out the two teams at Belle Vue before the Soren Sjosten Testimonial meeting in 1975.

The Belle Vue team I managed in 1976. Left to right: Chris Morton, Peter Collins, Kristian Praestbro, Paul Tyrer, Alan Wilkinson, Les Collins, Geoff Pusey and Russ Hodgson.

although I was concerned about the effect it would have on the business we had just started. We had only set it up a couple of months earlier, but it wasn't as if it was a corner shop selling bread and tea cakes. We didn't need to sit in there all day, and a lot of the enquiries came in the evenings anyway because many of the riders worked during the day, so it was something we could work around.

I gladly accepted the job offer and, when I was at Hyde Road, Diane ran the shop. She picked it up very quickly. She knew about speedway and, although she didn't have a clue about engines, it didn't matter. We had a lot of enlarged drawings so, if anybody came in asking for something, they could point it out and she would go and fetch it. Diane learned very quickly what all the parts were and where they fitted.

Compared to the risks of riding, it was a good deal I had been offered – £3,000 a year plus a car and expenses. If I had ridden that season I would have expected to earn between £6-7,000 gross, if I was lucky. That was before any money had been shelled out on bikes, running costs, petrol, depreciation on the car and everything like that, so I was happy with the deal.

After I jumped the fence and became a promoter, I found it a real eye-opener. Some people have the impression that all a promoter does is turn up at lunchtime on race night, opens the gates, takes the money and goes home. Nothing can be further from the truth. If you want to do it properly, it's a full-time job and I certainly had more leisure time as a rider than I did as a promoter. Riders were given a booking slip telling them where they had to be on which day and at what time.

For the rest of the week you could do whatever you wanted. As a team manager, I suddenly had seven riders to look after, some of them going well and some of them not so good.

I adapted to my new role quickly because I had a lot of help from the people around me. Throughout my management career I tried to put back the little things that I missed when I was riding – things like a pat on the back after a good ride, a phone call in the week to say "You went well at the weekend" or "You weren't feeling so well, are you OK now?" It's a team sport and I always felt it was important to make sure the riders knew they were part of the team. It's hard to pinpoint everything, but I wanted the riders to know they were appreciated. I hope they appreciated me too and I think they did because, to the best of my knowledge, no-one ever asked for a transfer because they couldn't stick me.

I enjoyed every minute of it at Belle Vue. It was an old-fashioned speedway, run exactly the way it should be, and I had as much pleasure working there as I did riding for Halifax.

Belle Vue was owned by Trust House Forte until Stuart Bamforth bought it in 1982. That meant because it was part of the THF leisure group, everything had to be done by the book. We had a yearly budget which was broken down into an eight-month budget to cover the season and then, in turn, into a monthly budget. As much as we could, we had to stick to that budget strictly. It was like working for ICI or some other massive company, in total contrast to, say, Chris van Straaten at Redcar today. He is totally responsible for that speedway and can take decisions or authorise expenditure accordingly. If I wanted to spend any money at Belle Vue, I had to put a request in writing.

We had a budget for shale but occasionally there were two stock car meetings in a calendar month instead of the usual one, and that really threw us out of synch. A lot of shale was needed to put the track right after a stock car meeting so, if we bought extra, that would be the following month's shale budget gone. Fortunately Belle Vue had a good accountant, Peter Powney, who worked on site. He had a good grasp of book-keeping and would use what he called a drag-back, by not putting through the additional spending until a month later, so that avoided one potential problem.

Because we were part of such a big organisation, there was a department for everything – 28 in all. So if I wanted a small electrical job doing I would have to fill in a form and send it to the electricians' department. If the cleaners discovered a seat was broken and needing repairing, I'd have to fill in another form and send it to the joiners' department. If any building work needing doing, the form would have to go to the building department and so on, and that would then be taken out of our budget.

Unfortunately THF were less than willing to invest in Belle Vue. They simply wouldn't spend any money and the state of the place was so bad that it would be closed down and condemned if they tried to stage speedway there today – there is no way the stadium would meet the health and safety or fire regulations. The electricity wires in the stands used to run to old-fashioned pots and, on a wet, windy day, there were so many sparks it looked like a firework display. The whole place was made of timber and we all know what happened to Bradford City.

Around the first and second bends was a big stand which had a curved roof. Well, one winter that roof was blown away by the wind and almost ended up on Hyde Road. If it hadn't hit the wall, it would have landed on the road so, as you can see, the place was falling down.

THF were making a profit every year but they had seen their profits get less and less so they were determined not to spend anything and, beyond applying the occasional lick of paint, they never had a proper plan of maintenance. Just after the war the leisure park was booming, but in those days very few people had their own cars which meant they went there by train and made a day of it. As more and more people were able to afford cars it lost its appeal as they discovered new places to go.

But, even though the place in general was shabby, the racing at Hyde Road was some of the best you would see anywhere in the world.

My office was a meeting place for all the Trust House Forte bigwigs after every meeting. They would always be at Hyde Road on racenights and sit, suited and booted, in the directors' box. They would then come into my office where there was a drinks cabinet, stocked with booze bought by THF.

Stock car racing took place at Hyde Road once a month and I was in charge of that side of the operation as well as the speedway. That said, I think I only ever saw about three stock car meetings during the whole time I was involved there because I was usually with the speedway team at an away meeting at the time. I was fortunate to have some fantastic staff at Belle Vue and Roy Carter, the track curator, was one of them. He knew all about stock cars and I used to leave him in charge along with Renee Fenner, my secretary, for both the bikes and the cars.

Track manager Roy Carter seems to be bemoaning the stock car damage to PC.

I thought the stock cars were a pain in the neck. There is a place for everything in motorsport and, as far as I'm concerned, the place for stock car racing is not around a speedway track. But the way of the world is live and let live and if you have to run stock cars to maximise the profit, then so be it. The stock car crowds were big so it was a good earner – but a nightmare for us because the cars really used to mess the track up.

The track was Roy's baby. If you walked on the circuit after 5.30pm on a race night he would shout at you to get off it! At 7pm there would be four blokes on speedway bikes racing round it so we weren't doing a right lot of harm, but he was passionate and wanted the best.

It was a big track – 418 yards – so it was some area to prepare after the stock cars had been on it. Every now and then the size of the task would get to him and he

Despite all our hard work, as Malcolm Simmons, his mechanic Ken Beckett (right) and I discovered later, the cover sheeting kept off most of the rain but did nothing to enhance the racing on BLRC night.

would storm into the office, slam his keys on the table and say he wasn't coming back. He'd always be back the next morning, though, sheepishly coming into the office to retrieve his keys and get on with the job.

Belle Vue's big event of the year was the BLRC and it was usual that, if the weather hadn't been so good, Roy and his assistant, Dave Pemberton, would stay at the stadium all weekend to work on the track. One year the weather was particularly bad but the BBC had been planning to televise the meeting and were desperately keen for it to go ahead. They paid for some plastic sheeting which we laid over every inch of the track in an attempt to stop it getting waterlogged.

> "The state of the place was so bad that it would be closed down and condemned if they tried to stage speedway there today"

The big problem was how to keep in there, so we went round the whole zoological park in a tractor with a trailer and collected every stone, rock, piece of wood and in fact anything that wasn't bolted down. We brought back three tons in total and then drove round the track and used it to hold the sheeting down. Unfortunately it didn't work because the track was wet when we put it down and it didn't overlap properly in places.

The next dilemma was when to take it up because it was still raining on the day of the meeting. When we did eventually take it up the track was rubbish. It saved the meeting but there wasn't much in the way of good racing and it wasn't worth all the effort.

We had some laughs on BLRC day too. Because I used to work all day at the track before a meeting, I would hang up my smart clothes in the changing rooms while I had my overalls on. I arrived in the changing rooms to get ready before one BLRC and discovered someone had cut all the buttons off my shirt! It wouldn't have been so bad if they had just pulled them off but whoever did it had cut big holes where the buttons should be and I had a terrible job trying to look presentable that evening. It took me a few days but I eventually discovered the culprit was Malcolm Simmons.

Another problem we had with the track surfaced one Easter weekend. It was beautifully hot and sunny and we were due to race Sheffield – but we'd had a problem for about three weeks in the middle of the radius on the pit bend. There was a big patch there which just wouldn't dry. David Battye was the referee due to officiate at that night's meeting and, when he arrived for the track inspection, I voiced my concern at the problem. I told him we could move the white line out to get over the problem but he wasn't convinced. His argument was that riders would still go through the wet patch, so I suggested that he made it clear they would be excluded if they did, but he was still having none of it.

The meeting was due to start at 3pm and by 2.30 there was a big crowd inside the stadium with the hot sun beating down on their backs, looking forward to the racing. A postponement was the last thing on their minds but the referee was adamant that he would have to call it off because of that wet patch. I told him if that was the case it should be him who stood on the centre green and made the announcement but he was having none of it. "You'll have to call it off," he said, "but make sure I'm out of the stadium before you tell anyone!"

The crowd went wild when the announcement was made and fans started piling over the fence to have a look at the wet patch. I got back into the office and all hell was breaking loose outside – there were people trying to break the door down. I eventually managed to escape after my mate phoned and offered to drive round and

get me. He stopped outside the office door and I made a dash for it when it had started to simmer down. I was able to dive into the back where I laid flat so that no-one could see me, and he drove off. Believe me, it was quite ugly for a while.

We went off for a meal and came back later that night to see Jack. He was very cross and told us to be in the following morning to get it sorted. We needed a JCB to get to the root of the problem and he made sure we had one the next day. We used the JCB to dig a series of trenches and found an old cast iron water pipe which had broken and caused the wet patch on the track. We contacted the plumbing department who had master copies of all the pipes and it transpired the pipe that had been causing us all those problems didn't even lead anywhere so they just switched it off.

Jack Fearnley with our top two –
Chris Morton and Peter Collins.

We filled in all the trenches with clean limestone and built the track back up on top. You could notice it a bit the following week but it didn't cause any problems. People said I should have realised there was a problem and got to the bottom of it straight away but it was always so difficult getting THF to spend any money. But once we lost a meeting they were keen enough to spend money – they didn't want that happening again.

We didn't have a great deal of equipment at Belle Vue. I think that was because we didn't realise how little we had and in any case, had we asked for more, we wouldn't have been given permission to buy it. But Roy and David Pemberton always managed to produce a good race track although the pit corner on the third and fourth bends was always tricky to work on because the situation of the main stand meant the sun used to shine on the first and second turns and make it dry twice as quickly.

I had a wonderful relationship with Jack Fearnley throughout my time at Belle Vue and if ever I wanted to sign a rider, I had the authority to go out and get him. Jack was the sort of boss who arrived for work every day in a collar and tie and never got his hands mucky. One of his demands was that the fence had to be whitened before every meeting – he didn't care what the track was like, as long as the fence was gleaming! It used to drive Roy mad because sometimes he would still be putting the finishing touches to it as late as Saturday morning. Jack was right though – you would never stage a boxing match without ropes around the ring, so it was important to make the arena look good and we never had a fence that wasn't whitened, whatever the state of the track.

We had a very happy camp at Belle Vue and two other members of our team were Peter and Allan Morrey. Peter was the start-line marshal and Allan was clerk of the course. They were totally reliable and I didn't have to tell either of them how to do their job because the whole operation ran like clockwork. The track was in a huge leisure complex with a big funfair which was booming at the time. THF were determined to keep it that way and tempt as many speedway fans into the fairground as they could. They reckoned that for every five minutes after 9pm a meeting finished on a Saturday night, they lost £1,000. That meant we had to start every meeting at seven o'clock on the dot and finish at nine o'clock or before. Allan was concerned that if either the riders or the

Peter and Allan Morrey.

referee were to drag their heels, we would finish late – so he fitted an override switch for the two-minute warning buzzer in a cupboard in the pits. If he thought that the ref or the riders were taking too long, he would press the button to hurry the meeting along. No referee ever complained – after all, Allan had got the riders out on the track for him!

Jack was always adamant that we should start at 7 o'cock no matter what, in order to finish in time. If Belle Vue were racing against Halifax or Sheffield, a big crowd was guaranteed and there would be queues of fans at the turnstiles still waiting to get in at start-time. If I ever suggested to Jack that we should wait until they were all in before starting, I was told to forget it. His argument was that if we held the start back once, the fans would think they could turn up late every week and still be in time for the first race. He was quite right too – the fans who missed two races one week would make sure they arrived on time the next. You wouldn't see promoters do that today because they certainly need to keep every supporter they've got.

Renee Fenner, the secretary, was another key member of the team. She had been the secretary at Rochdale too and must have been used to working with awkward buggers because Dent Oliver had been her boss! She could cope with pressure and was brilliant at her job. If I was away for two or three days with the team, I could leave her to run the show in my absence.

Every year they had a big circus at the funfair and, at the end of the season, everyone involved with the speedway would be invited along free of charge. One year Peter Collins and Chris Morton amazed everyone by going into the ring and walking the high wire. It was incredible! They were 20ft off the ground and did it perfectly. They had practised a bit in the week, but they didn't tell anyone that.

PC and Mort were the two big fans' favourites at Hyde Road and it didn't take me long to realise how badly the supporters craved success. To be honest, they were awful sometimes! If you had won 40-38 in a meeting that produced the best racing there all season, some of them would tell you it was rubbish and be calling for heads to roll. If we had scored 60 points and left the opposition for dead every time, they would say it was terrific!

I'm not sure of the circumstances now, but at one point a petition was passed round calling for the resignation of both Jack and I. Jack came across the fans responsible outside my office, which was the central point of the stadium, near the starting gate under the stand. He gave them a stern lecture and told them to go home and not come back if they didn't have anything better to do. He tore the petition up and threw it into the bin – although by then I had signed it, to let those responsible know that I'd seen it!

That just goes to show how fickle some fans can be. They don't seem to realise that you, as a promoter or a manager, work your socks off all week but, once the riders are out of that pit gate, it's down to them. It's the same as in football – once the players cross the white line and start kicking the ball about, they are the only ones who can win a match. I think the only difference is that if all of us who have been speedway promoters had been football managers instead, we would have been sacked about 100 times!

A member of the BSPA (second from left) at their annual winter conference in sunny Tenerife.

One of the fans who used to come to Hyde Road was a bloke called Tony Gamley who was better known as 'Soldier Boy', from his days in the Army. He was a fanatical Ray Wilson fan at Leicester but, one season, he decided to attach himself to Belle Vue and shout for PC in particular. He was speedway daft and he didn't need a tannoy system to make himself heard because he used to stand at the front and the way he got the crowd going was fantastic.

"The crowd went wild when the announcement was made...I got back into the office and all hell was breaking loose outside"

Unfortunately he used to get a bit carried away and his language became a bit colourful. I had to take him to one side and ban him after one meeting because of his bad language. He was the easiest person in the world to ban because he was so loud that everyone knew him and you would easily find out if he had sneaked in. He phoned me up and was extremely apologetic, so the ban lasted for a week and then I let him back in. He was great fun and I wish we'd had 1,000 like him.

⑭
AN IMPORTANT JOB TO DO

THE season had started by the time I had arrived back from my six-week stint at Lonigo, although I had still been part of building the Belle Vue team for 1975.

I'd spent a few days at Hyde Road before going to Italy and, on my first day, I discovered a plaque with my name on it had been put on my office door. I was a bit embarrassed about it but Jack Fearnley insisted it was necessary so that any visitors would be able to find me. One of my most pressing jobs was to sort out which seven riders would be wearing an Aces racejacket in 1975. On one of my first visits I had a meeting with Frank Varey, who had been caretaker manager, to discuss the team. He read out the retained list and the first thing he said was: "What are we going to do about Geoff Pusey?" I asked him what he meant by that and he said: "He's useless!"

I'd come across Geoff in the past and he'd never struck me as being any good, but there weren't any alternatives so I told Frank we'd be riding him. He turned out all right too – maybe other people hadn't been handling him right, I don't know.

One of the riders on the retained list was Soren Sjosten who, being Swedish, couldn't pronounce the letter J. We had a workshop inside the stadium which the foreign riders used to use and I found him in there one Sunday trying to fix a problem he'd had the night before. I asked him if he had found the problem and he said: "Yes, my carburettor was full of gelly". Of course, he meant jelly but couldn't say it. He never rode a JAP, it was always a YAP – and if he flew anywhere it would be on a Yumbo Yet!

Peter Collins, Paul Tyrer and Alan Wilkinson had all come through the ranks at Rochdale who had a team in the Second Division which continued where the old Belle Vue Colts left off in terms of producing good youngsters who could progress. But the costs at Rochdale had become too prohibitive and it closed at the end of 1971, so I didn't have the benefit of what was effectively a training track for the Aces. If I wanted new riders, I had to go out and sign them.

One of the transfer moves I made before the start of my first season in charge at Hyde Road was to sign Russ Hodgson for £500 from Middlesbrough. The signing raised a few eyebrows because he was seen as a tail-end Charlie coming in from a second division club, but he started the season with an average of two and ended it with an average of five, so it turned out to be a good move for both of us.

Happy days . . . Russ Hodgson (left) brought a smile to the place, as you can tell from this shot of him with Chris Morton, Geoff Pusey, Peter Collins and myself.

The signing came about because Russ was a member of the SRA. I was chairman up until I retired from riding so we'd had quite a bit of contact. He rang me one day and said he'd had a fall-out with Ron Wilson, who was promoter at Cleveland Park at the time. Russ wanted 10p a point more than Wilson was prepared to pay him and neither of them were prepared to shift. I advised Russ that he didn't have much choice – he could either accept the offer or ask for a transfer. "If I ask for a transfer, who will buy me?" he asked. "I will," I told him, "you can come to Belle Vue."

Russ had an infectious laugh and an infectious smile, which were qualities I wanted in the Belle Vue team. Even when he was mad, and he used to get cross with himself if he thought he was letting the team down, he would still be laughing. He was very highly thought of by the lads in the team and I saw potential in him due to his enthusiasm. We became firm friends and our friendship is still going strong today.

I also brought in Peter's younger brother, Les Collins, who had second division outings at Crewe – and not just because he was a Collins. I never signed any rider because of his name, only for his potential, and that is still the key today. If you sign a rider with a nine-point average, there's only one way that he's going to go and that's down. If you sign someone on a four-point average, there's potential for it to go up a long way.

Belle Vue had a good relationship with Ellesmere Port and we signed a number of riders from them, most notably Chris Morton. Since the closure of Rochdale, they had become something of a feeder track, although the conversations I had with Joe Shaw, my Thornton Road counterpart, weren't always amicable. I'd had a big bust up with him over transfer fees. I felt he was always asking too much money simply because we were Belle Vue – we might have been a big and famous club but we didn't have pots of money to throw around. That left Jack and Ernie Park, the promoter at Ellesmere Port, to get their heads together and smooth things over for any potential deal to go ahead. Even though Joe and I would fall out every now and then, it was soon forgotten because he was just doing his job and I was doing mine.

I settled into the job easily because I had been chairman of the SRA for a while, which meant I'd had a lot of dealings with the promoters on an official capacity. They always got their way! I think every rider knew every promoter, but not on a personal level as I did through the SRA.

When I first spoke to Belle Vue about the job there, I was told that the Aces had the best name in speedway – which, to be fair, was true – and that they wanted the glory days to come back. Talk about a tall order for your first job in management! But 1975 was a good year to be involved with Belle Vue. Peter Collins won the BLRC, we finished second in the British League and beat Leicester in the KO Cup final, so I guess that's the sort of success they wanted.

I never once missed riding after going into management and it never crossed my mind that I wanted to ride again. In fact, it seemed a funny way of earning a living once I had stopped. Of course sometimes I would see a rider do something on the track and think that, if only he had done something else, he could have won the race, but I suppose that's only natural. I never went into it with the attitude of saying to a rider "I would have done this" or "I would have done that because I'm better than you". I saw my role as passing on advice based on the experience I'd had.

Soren Sjosten explaining the 'gelly'.

I had no hang-up about going back to Halifax as manager of Belle Vue, although it did seem to be a problem to certain members of the Dukes management. Dougie Adams was the announcer at The Shay and he told me that, on the night I took Belle Vue there for the first time in 1975, the management had instructed him to make no mention of former Halifax riders over the tannoy system. So the Belle Vue Aces, from over the hills, were given a warm welcome, but there was no mention of the fact that they were led by Halifax's former inspirational captain who had won the British Final as a Dukes rider the previous season and ridden for them for 10 years – nine of those with an average of more than 10 points a meeting.

That was so stupid, but I didn't get angry about it, I just thought it was really childish. I was going there to do my job, just as I had for ten years when I rode a speedway bike for a living. Reg Fearman and Eric Boothroyd had both been riders before they had gone into promoting, so why wasn't I entitled to do something else as well? The fans were great, however, and the people I had spoken to week in, week out, for a decade gave me a warm welcome and were chuffed to bits that I was still involved with speedway. To cap a fine night for me, Belle Vue won a cracker of a meeting.

It felt good to come from one side of the fence to the other and have a fairly successful first year, but it was the seven riders out on the track who deserved credit for that. Having someone like Peter Collins as No.1 was a fantastic position to be in – PC was such a great rider and so easy to get on with. In fact, we had a team full of riders who had the right attitude and all got on well together.

In 1976 we were second in the table again. This time Ipswich were the champions and also our conquerors in the KO Cup. The Witches were a good team, highly motivated by John Berry –

PC fully deserved the World Championship winged wheel in 1976 and was cruelly robbed in his defence of the title the following year.

to the point of being obnoxious sometimes. There was a lot of needle in our matches with Ipswich in those days. You can have a lot of good battles with your rivals and enjoy them – for example the matches I had against Coventry when Nigel was riding were competitive but I enjoyed them. That's not something I can say about our fixtures with Ipswich.

Before you even met them you knew there would be some aggro because that's the way Berry set it up. It was part and parcel of his make-up – upset them early and get them off on the wrong foot. If you arrived at Foxhall Heath early, you couldn't get through the pit gate. There were people inside the stadium but you, as the visiting team, were made to wait outside.

They would sweep the pits out at the last minute and leave the visiting team's side all wet. It wasn't a happy place to go to and the majority of their staff seemed abrupt.

We used to make everybody welcome at Belle Vue – and in fact Berry once reported us to the BSPA because we had the audacity to give the referee a cup of tea before the meeting! To me, offering a bloke who has driven a couple of hours to your track and arrived early is being a good host. He seemed to think it was an attempt to influence the referee.

What a load of rubbish. The referee was hardly going to decide against excluding Peter Collins just because his boss had made him a cup of tea. Good job I didn't give him a biscuit too!

Team-wise, we didn't win any silverware in 1976, having to settle for second spot behind champions Ipswich again for the second time in 12 months, but we did provide the World Champion. PC won the ultimate prize in Katowice, and what a worthy winner he was too.

To say he wasn't the world's greatest gater is an understatement but, funnily enough, if the referee was a bit slack he could cheat with the best of them at the start. He could soon weigh a referee up and, if he was allowing rolling to go on at the tapes, Peter could do it himself with aplomb, and he was astute enough to know when he could get away with it.

Slow gating was a common problem within the Belle Vue team, but you didn't have to gate well at Hyde Road to go well there. There were so many lines and you could go fast virtually anywhere you wanted. PC and Mort were my top two there and the fact that neither of them could gate certainly made for some exciting racing. It's why the crowd adored them so much – they loved to see them win races from the back.

Gating is the be all and end all at tight tracks where it's as slick as a board and there is nowhere to get past, but that was never the case at Belle Vue. Sometimes during the week we would spend all day out on the track with PC making start after start after start, trying to get it right. Chris Morton and some of the other lads would be

I briefly came out of retirement in 1978 to face PC in a jubilee match-race series.

Mucking in with the lads – Mort, PC and Dave Trownson.

there too. Being able to get out on the track whenever we wanted was one of the advantages of owning our own track and Ivan Mauger used to do a bit of behind-the-scenes testing there too, even though he didn't ride for Belle Vue after 1972 and had since moved on to Exeter and then Hull.

PC's success came with the power of a Weslake engine – he certainly didn't have to buy much that season in the way of equipment! The Weslake, manufactured in Rye, Sussex, soon became very popular with riders. A year before Weslake started to emerge as a force, Phil Crump rode a four-valve Neil Street-Jawa conversion and, at the end of the season, he won virtually every open meeting with it.

The purpose-built four-valve Weslake revved higher than a two-valve Jawa and success wasn't long in coming. Jawa weren't far behind in producing their own four-valve engine, of course, and then Don Godden followed suit. In fact Shawn Moran won the World Long-track Final on a four-valve Godden. The Godden was probably a better engine than the Weslake – it was certainly stronger – but for some reason it didn't hold the same favour among the riders. Perhaps it had something to do with what they thought of Don. Simon Wigg made the point that you could tell Don exactly what you thought his engine needed but he wouldn't listen.

I was with Peter in the pits when he won the title on that glorious night in Poland. I don't think he really needed anyone with him and he was never highly-strung, but at least I was able to give some moral support because it helps to have someone to talk to and make you laugh when you're in a high pressure situation.

I told him I'd bring my overalls and muck in while I was in the pits, and he was happy to have me along. Because he was never a good gater, I told him I would work

Frank Varey presents me with the Chopper Bike Championship trophy – it was another fun night out with the lads. The riders are (left to right): Kristian Praestbro, Chris Morton, Geoff Pusey (on bike), Chris Turner, Derek Richardson, Paul Tyrer and Phil Collins.

on the clutch after every race. In truth it wouldn't have made a scrap of difference but I thought that it might help him, mentally, as it would reassure him that the clutch was in tip-top condition. After every race he would come back into the pits and I would whip off the clutch, clean the plates and put it back together. It was dead easy and only took about five minutes, but it gave PC some peace of mind.

I had no doubt he would be World Champion that year. Katowice was a big, fast track which suited him – and he was going so quick that he broke the track record in his first two races. He was beaten by Ivan Mauger in his final race but that was his only defeat all afternoon, and I'm still sure that Peter could have won that race too if he had really wanted to. He rode a blinder of a meeting and I was delighted for him.

PC reminded me a lot of my brother because they both had the same never-say-die attitude. He loved winning and, if there was someone in front of him, he just had to pass them. He was a born racer. By and large, he had a really laid back style but he could get cross and, when he did, he was a stickler for his point. If he was having an argument he would fight his corner because he had his principles. But, generally, nothing was a problem – not even all the commuting he did onto the continent to ride on the grass-tracks and sand-tracks. Steve Hartley, who had been a good grass tracker until he got injured, was his manager and we had a deal. As soon as PC was offered a booking, Steve would ring me to see if it clashed with any Belle Vue commitments. Usually we could work around it if there was a problem but sometimes I had to try and change a fixture. I didn't like doing that but the promoters loved Peter Collins because he was a big draw.

Belle Vue didn't win the league during my seven seasons in charge – we finished second three times and third once – but they were the draw and, whenever we went away, the home track had their best crowd of the year. At the back end of the year, whenever they held the Benevolent Fund collection, Belle Vue were always walking round stadiums with buckets collecting. The track we visited wanted to make sure they raised as much money as possible so they chose the meeting that would have the biggest gate, which is fine, but it was a bit unfair on the Aces riders.

Peter had a great sense of humour and he gave a good example of that in the showers one evening after the meeting. One of the riders was shampooing his hair and couldn't understand why the lather wouldn't go away. It was because as fast as he was rinsing it, PC was sneaking up behind him and pouring more shampoo on.

Another memory I have of PC was when we were travelling down to Eastbourne one Saturday night after a home meeting. We were at Arlington on the Sunday so we travelled down on the Saturday night to stay in some accommodation Bob Dugard had sorted out, which meant we could have a lie-in. PC and Alan Wilkinson both had three-litre BMWs and we went down in convoy. PC discovered his battery wasn't charging so he followed behind me and Wilkie with just his sidelights on, even though it was pitch black. Eventually he flashed us and we pulled over.

The engine had started missing, which was bound to happen because the ignition was off the battery too. We were going to tow him for the rest of the journey until Wilkie came up with a brilliant idea. "Why don't we just swap batteries?" he said. It seemed the perfect solution – PC would have a fully charged battery and the one Wilkie received in return would soon charge quick enough. So we switched the batteries and Peter's car started no problem. He said we would catch him up and he roared away from the hard shoulder.

But when Wilkie tried to start his car, he couldn't because of the flat battery. PC's tail lights were disappearing into the distance

> "I had no hang-up about going back to Halifax as manager of Belle Vue, although it did seem a problem for certain people at The Shay"

PC on his way to the world title in Poland in 1976, with Scott Autrey and Phil Crump leading the chase.

and we were stuck at the side of the road. Fortunately Paul Tyrer was also in the convoy and we managed to get Wilkie's car going again with the aid of a bump start.

Anyone who remembers 1976 will recall the drought we had that year. It was a blazing hot summer with virtually no rain and, as a result, there were severe restrictions on water usage and hosepipe bans were in force all over the country. That, of course, caused a lot of problems when you had a speedway track to water, but fortunately at Belle Vue we had a disused boating lake within the grounds of the leisure complex. That meant we could drive the tractor round to the lake and suck up the water into our bowser, then take it round the track.

On one occasion somebody reported us because they had see us watering the track and wrongly assumed we were flouting the hosepipe ban. I don't know who made the complaint, but it was obviously a snitch living nearby who didn't like speedway. We were paid a visit by an environmental official who wanted to know where we were getting our water from – and it was perfect timing because, just as he arrived, Roy was pumping some water out of the lake.

What the snitch who reported us never got to find out, though, was that we were a bit crafty on one occasion. Going to the lake, pumping out the water and bringing it back was a long-winded process and, with every lap you did, you were tyre-packing the track, so on one particularly hot weekend during the heatwave, I came up with a plan. All around Belle Vue there were big, old-fashioned fire hydrants, and I decided to use them to completely flood the track one Friday night.

At about 10 o'clock that night, we opened all the cupboards where the fire hydrants were and unravelled the big four-inch hoses that were in there. We completely flooded the track like you've never seen. It looked like the boating lake we'd been using to fill the bowser! We could have got into big trouble for doing that but, when we had finished, we rolled the hoses up and carefully put them back so that nobody knew what we had done. I went back to the track the following morning and it was impossible to tell we had put any water down at all. It had soaked in, though, so it made it easier for us that day.

The time we were reported for watering the track wasn't the only run-in we had with the do-gooders living near the track. Over the back of the stadium there were rows and rows of Coronation Street-style houses which were built well after the track so, if anybody moved in there, they knew full well they would be living next to a speedway track. But somebody who lived in one of those houses was unhappy at the noise on a Saturday night and started up a petition. Manchester City Council made an appointment to come along and do some noise testing and it was the best thing that could have happened to us. They sent us the results which showed that, to anyone living in those houses, the sound of a bus driving away from the bus stop outside the stadium was louder than the noise coming from a speedway race. It did us a great favour because we kept the report on file and, if anyone else had complained abut the noise, we would have just shown them that.

The start of the 1977 season saw silencers being used on speedway bikes for the first time, and I had a lot to do with their introduction. I wasn't exactly welcomed with open arms to my first ever promoters' meeting in 1975. There was quite a commotion because I had only just retired and, it was assumed, I would be riding again in the very near future. It was embarrassing more than offensive but I had to point out that, unless I ever changed by mind and rode again, I had as much right as anyone else to be in that meeting because I held a promoters' licence. Eventually I was accepted and, before I left, I was given the task of looking into the development of silencers for speedway bikes. I had just finished riding so I was quite well up with engines and the technical side of things, which made me the ideal candidate. So, in the space of one meeting, I had gone from being not welcome to being part of the association with an important job to do!

There was a company in the Midlands who made silencers for cars and I was asked to hold exploratory talks with them about making a prototype for speedway bikes. They weren't interested because it simply wouldn't have been cost effective for them but, after that fell through, I had a call from a Dr Roe who was a professor at Manchester University. He had done a lot of work for BMW in Germany and was into bikes big style, so I started working very closely with him.

Unfortunately, he was eventually and affectionately nicknamed Dr Slow but he kept bringing his creations along and we tried them out. He was a nice bloke to work with – just one of the lads really – and PC did a lot of testing for us. However the silencers he produced were mainly designed for Weslakes and Ole Olsen was a works Jawa rider and the Czech company had their own silencer designed for their own bike. Coventry promoter Charles Ochiltree, who was revered in speedway, fought a strong case for Olsen because he was a Bees rider. According to Ochiltree, Olsen was at a disadvantage and the BSPA agreed.

What they should have done was told him that they had made the rules and it was up to Jawa to design their engine to work with our silencer. But they didn't. So Jawa silencers were approved for use as well – and everybody knew that they worked better, even on a Weslake. It meant that virtually all the Weslake riders were using Jawa silencers.

Even more unfortunate was the fact that a large number of the Roe silencers had been produced but were no longer required. The last I heard of them, they were all stacked up in boxes at Hackney Stadium. It was a shame because, once again, we missed the opportunity to equalise the bikes. Nobody wanted a silencer but they had to have one whether they liked it or not. If everyone had used a Roe silencer it would have stopped the development of the bikes but, by doing that, it would have got us all back on an even keel.

But because the minority didn't like something, it didn't happen. Nobody looked at the welfare of the sport. It's no good tuning an engine for 100 BHP if the silencer restricted it to 80 BHP – so you might as well have had 80 BHP, but we didn't do that.

To many people 1977 will be remembered as the year of The Queen's Silver Jubilee celebrations and when the Sex Pistols spearheaded the new punk rock fashion. But for anyone connected with Belle Vue, it will be remembered for one of the most astonishing acts of bravery ever seen on a speedway track.

Peter Collins was the reigning World Champion and among the favourites to win

Above: PC did astonishingly well to finish second in the 1977 World Final at a very wet Gothenburg. With him on the rostrum are winer Ivan Mauger, third place man Ole Olsen and the fourth placed Michael Lee.
Below: Having a word with Peter before he faced Ole Olsen in the 1977 BLRC.

the prize again in the final at Gothenburg – until he suffered a serious leg injury in a crash at Hyde Road just six days before the big night. Because we watered the track with hoses, there were manholes right near the edge of the track. They were all in a bit of a state from where the stock cars used to run over them and one of them was situated just as you came out of the second bend.

The hosepipe must have clipped the cover of that particular manhole while the track was being watered, and displaced it, to leave it sticking out a bit. In those days the referee didn't do a pre-meeting track inspection so nobody spotted it before the meeting began.

Unfortunately, during the second half of the meeting when he was trying out his World Final bike, PC caught his front wheel on the corner of that manhole cover as he chopped back coming out of the bend. It tipped the cover straight up, sending it crashing against his shin. He did another half a lap then pulled over onto the centre green and fell over – we didn't know what on earth had happened. His boot was shredded and so was his shin – he was a right mess, and with the World Final just days away.

The muscle in his leg had been severely damaged and he had also broken his fibula. He was livid about the crash and described it as like being struck on the leg with an axe, but to his enormous credit he didn't go on and on about it.

It shouldn't have happened – we all knew that – and today there would be one hell of a claim making its way through the legal channels, but PC didn't make a fuss.

It was so unfortunate because he was riding better than ever that year and I feel sure that, had he been fully fit, he would have been World Champion again. He had a three-hour operation and needed more than 200 stitches in his leg, internally and externally, but, despite his injuries, he was determined to ride in the World Final so there was a mad panic to get him there.

Jack Fearnley was a big mate of Sir Charles Forte, the big boss of Trust House Forte, and he made his private Lear jet available for us to fly out to Sweden from Manchester Airport. We pushed PC through the airport on a luggage trolley and got him onto the plane, then took a taxi to the track.

When we arrived at the stadium we put him on a stretcher and I wheeled him round so he could take a look at it. He could stand up, just about, but wasn't able to put any weight on his injured leg which was hardly the ideal state to be in when you're defending your world title.

The biggest problem he was faced with was how he was going to ride with all the strapping around his leg, so I contacted a firm in Leicester who made a special boot which would fit around it. They added a steel strip down the middle too so, if he had banged it again, that would take the impact.

The weather was awful in Sweden and, had it been a Grand Prix today, it would have certainly been called off – but I told Peter it was quite simply shit or bust. If he got out in front he had a better chance of staying there than if it were dry, which seemed a funny thing to say to a bad gater, but he made four superb starts that night. In the other race Ole Olsen just got to the corner first and I think PC just knocked it off a bit to be on the safe side. If it hadn't been for that, he could have won it.

Ivan Mauger went on to win the title, although not without a bit of luck. He was back in third in his last race when it was stopped because John Boulger and Ole Olsen fell in the muck – and he went out and won the rerun.

But Peter did amazingly well just to ride – to finish second to Mauger was unbelievable. It was a mark of his dedication, and he still went into the meeting firmly believing he could win it. I don't know how he did it. We lifted him on the bike and we lifted him of it after every race and sat him in a deckchair. He didn't move again until his next race and he had ice packs on his leg when he wasn't riding.

I was chuffed to bits that he had finished second because he'd had a good World Final. But I was disappointed for myself because I knew that the freak accident which had caused his injuries – at my speedway track – should never have happened. It probably cost him the title, although we'll never know.

Alongside PC and Mort, one of the most popular riders at Belle Vue was Alan Wilkinson, the captain. Tragically, though, his career was brought to an early end in July 1978 when he broke his neck in a crash against Swindon at Hyde Road. It wasn't even a bad crash and I think 999 times out of 1,000 you would see a rider get up and walk away from a fall like that.

He tangled with Geoff Bouchard as they came away from the start but their bikes had locked together so they lost all their speed. The bikes parted but then came together again as they went into the corner. They went across the track until they got to the fence where they fell down.

I was stood in the pits at the other end of the track, and I fully expected both riders to get straight back up – after all, Wilkie was the hardest man in speedway. He never stayed down after a fall so, when he didn't get up after three or four minutes, I started to get a little concerned and realised he must be hurt.

I started trotting across the track to see him although I didn't rush because I genuinely expected him to get up. But, when I reached him, he still hadn't got up and he was being put on a stretcher I asked him what was up and he said: "I've broken my f****** neck."

I told him not to be silly – of course, he couldn't have broken his neck. He told me he couldn't move or feel anything but I reminded him of my crash in Denmark, when I was paralysed for about five hours.

Sadly, however, I was wrong. Wilkie knew it. And I think that, if he'd been able to get up, he would have swiped me one. As they took him off to hospital he said to me: "Now get this meeting won without me."

The rules then were that you could use an estate car to take injured riders off the track while the ambulance was away – things were certainly a lot less strict in those days – so we carried on racing and did as Wilkie had asked, by winning the meeting, 47-31.

After the racing had finished, the track doctor came into the office and phoned the hospital, to be told that the initial prognosis was definitely a broken neck. As you can imagine we were all devastated and the mood in the room just plummeted. I rang Diane and told her Wilkie had been involved in a bad crash and then went straight to the hospital where I spoke to the team looking after him. They wouldn't

A year before his career-emding crash, Alan Wilkinson with Chris Pusey, who moved from Belle Vue to Halifax when I arrived at Hyde Road in 1975.

let me see him but they confirmed what had been said to our doctor.

It was gone 2am when I arrived back home and Diane was still up because she thought the world of Wilkie and his lovely wife Jean. I told her what had happened, that he'd broken his neck, and then I just burst into tears. It upset me so much because we were close and I had a lot of time for Wilkie.

The following morning Diane and I went straight back to Manchester to see him in hospital. Back then they just didn't seem to know how to treat people with that sort of injury and, when we walked into his room, all we could see was a mattress on his bed. Then we noticed Wilkie was strapped to the bed facing the floor – and Jean was underneath reading the Sunday paper to him. That's the way they treated someone with injuries like his in those days, turning them over every so often.

Diane and I went and joined Jean under the bed and started chatting. It was quite a while before they could move him but, when they did, he was transferred to the spinal injuries unit in Southport, which was closer to his home in Barrow. The ambulance even had a police escort for the journey.

Wilkie's injury put a big downer on us all because he was very popular with the team and the fans. I think it's fair to say that he was as popular as Peter Collins, although for different reasons. If there was any trouble, Wilkie was the first to go and sort it out. If anyone ever asked his opinion, they would always get a straight answer – and on one night he and I fell out.

It was red hot and Roy had been watering the track all day. Then, at 5pm it suddenly clouded over and there was no sun anywhere. Whereas before the track was drying as soon as we'd watered it, it was now too wet and it stayed that way all evening.

Wilkie went out for his first race and got totally obliterated with shale. He wasn't happy and he had a fair point because I wasn't either. He went absolutely mad, but I told him all I could do was apologise. I couldn't go round with a giant sheet of blotting paper trying to soak all the water up and, if it was any consolation, at least it would get better as the night went on.

He went out for his second ride and finished stone last once again. He arrived back in the pits covered in muck again and didn't even stop – he rode straight to his car with the intention of packing up and going home. I went to see him and he was spewing mad. All I could see was his eyes because the rest of him was covered in red shale, but I told him that if he walked out of the meeting and went home, he would never ride for Belle Vue again.

I reminded him that we were not a team of quitters and, when the going got tough, we got going because we were tough. I apologised again for the track conditions, but it was too late to do anything about it. The choice was his – he could muck in with the rest of the lads and ride without doing anything stupid, or he could go home and not come back.

He bulldozed his way back into the pits, won his next two races and won the second half scratch race final and the matter was never mentioned again. He must have been going well to win the second half final because in those days it was virtually unheard of for anyone but PC or Mort to take the honours.

One of the funniest memories I have of Wilkie is when we were staying in a plush hotel in London one Sunday night after a meeting at White City. We were riding at Exeter the following evening and Jack Fearnley had arranged for us to stay in a very nice Trust House Forte hotel the previous evening. I had gone to bed but a few of the lads stayed up and had a couple of beers. They decided to have a competition to see how far they could walk along the corridor on their hands and they were all acting the goat when an irate American tourist came over to complain that his sleep was being interrupted.

Wilkie calmly told him that was the way we always went to bed in England. It made perfect sense – 'we were all on our feet all day, so we needed to rest them.' And in any case, being professional sportsmen, they had been told the only way to relax at night was by doing some handstands before going to bed.

Wilkie was a great bloke to have in your team and he lived for Belle Vue Speedway, but I never treated him any differently to the other lads. He had a reputation and, if ever he needed to live up to it, he could do easily. He wasn't a trouble-causer, although I do remember him doing something a bit over the top to Leicester's Alan Cowland going into one of the turns at Belle Vue. When he came into the pits I asked him about it and he told me straight: "I've got a long memory – he's had that coming to him for the past two years, so we're straight now." Remember what I mentioned earlier about little black books?

Emil Sova (centre) has PC and me smiling about his 'little man with the hammer'.

The track doctor was the son of his predecessor who had been at Belle Vue for years and, just like his father and everyone who had done the job before him, he sat in the directors' box during the meeting. He always maintained that his job was to treat the riders once they had been taken to the ambulance room by the paramedics, and there was a lot of aggro from the riders about that because he didn't go out onto the track after Wilkie's crash – not that it would have mattered a jot, because the damage had already been done.

The riders argued that the doctor should have been standing out on the centre green so that he could have got to him straight away. But even if we'd had an operating theatre at the side of the track, it couldn't have undone what had happened. It was very hard to put a case for the doctor, even though I knew what I was saying was right, when one of my best friends had been badly injured.

Feelings were running high and the doctor was upset by it, so much so that he saw the season out and then found us a replacement. But guess where the new bloke watched the meetings from? That's right, the directors' box! I should point out that, although the directors' box might sound all la-di-dah and posh, it was in fact about four rows up from the starting gate with just a small fence separating it from the rest of the seats where the fans sat. It wasn't as if he was right up in the roof of the stand in a box with double glazing and central heating – if he was a good jumper, the doctor could have leapt straight from his seat onto the track!

When we came to terms with losing Wilkie midway through the 1978 season, we wanted to win the league for him, but in the end we finished two points behind Coventry. It was an improvement on our fifth place the year before but it was a

> "I told Diane what had happened, that he'd broken his neck, and then I just burst into tears. It upset me so much because we were so close"

With two new signings in 1980, Mike Lohmann (left) and Larry Kosta.

shame we couldn't finish top because I know that if we'd had Wilkie in the team for the last three months of the season, we would have won it by a mile. The lads gave it everything but we were without our third heat leader and that was always going to make it a very tall order. We actually won more away matches than Coventry but home defeats by Bristol and Ipswich, very late in the season, proved too costly.

For the following season I dipped into the transfer market and signed Czech rider Emil Sova. Unfortunately by the time he arrived at the track for what was supposed to have been his debut, the second half scratch race was just about to finish. He had no idea where Belle Vue was and, when he had asked someone, they told him it was in Poole – so that's where he had been! He found the speedway track all right, but it wasn't the one he was supposed to be riding at!

Despite getting off on the wrong foot, I soon discovered Emil was a terrific bloke. He had a Lada and used to drive home once a month – 880 miles there and 880 miles back. Halfway through the journey it would often start running on three cylinders, but he just used to take the plugs out, clean them, and be on his way again. He didn't have a particularly good grasp of English but joined in with everything straight away.

After one race, in which his bike hadn't been going very well, he came back into the pits and tipped it onto the footrest. He was revving it up and listening to it, so I went across to ask what the problem was. "I have problem," he said in his broken English, "man with little hammer in my engine". What a fantastic way of trying to explain that his engine was knocking because the big end had gone!

Coventry retained the league title in 1979, while we finished 10th, the lowest in my seven seasons at Hyde Road. Reading denied them a hat-trick in 1980, though, and we had a better season, finishing third in the table and reaching the KO Cup final against Cradley Heath. One of the reasons for our success was the fantastic team spirit we had. We all got on so well and liked a good time but the best bit was that everyone used to know when to stop. They knew where the line was drawn and, although it was stretched once or twice, it was never crossed. Nobody ever did anything that would embarrass themselves or Belle Vue Speedway. After all, none of us dared to with Jack Fearnley around.

We always especially enjoyed our trips to Poole because we would always stay overnight in Bailie House, the big guest house run by Ken and Bridget Middleditch – Neil's mum and dad. It was one big house of fun and Bridget's party piece was to dress up as a character she called Ruth. Everyone would be in the lounge when there would be a knock on the window. The guests would look round and see this woman who looked like a witch at the window. "She's harmless," Ken would explain, "just ignore her – she used to go to the speedway and likes to come and be nosey when we've got guests." Then there would be another knock and she would appear at another window. Eventually she would knock on the front door and Ken would reluctantly let her in.

As you can imagine, no-one quite knew where to look when confronted by this bedraggled figure with big teeth in a pack-a-mac and a headscarf. "Don't worry," Ken would reassure everyone, "she might nick things from you but we always turn her pockets out before she leaves so you'll get everything back."

'Ruth' would pick on one of the good looking members of the team and sit on his lap, stroking his hair. Just as Ken warned us, she would pick up various items and try to sneak off with them. She certainly had me fooled and the first time I saw her I asked Ken if she had a broomstick! After about 20 minutes Ken would turf her out and retrieve everything she had pinched. Then, just as she went to walk out of the door, off came the headscarf, out came the teeth and she would reveal herself as Bridget! I don't think anyone ever guessed it was her. Because you were embarrassed and daren't stare, you never got a good look at her. The teeth, it turned out, were her mother's that she had found after she died!

The Middleditches were fantastic people and they were so good to everyone who stayed with them. It was always great fun whenever we stayed there and as far as I know a lot of other teams had a good time down there too.

On another occasion we were there I was laying in bed reading the programme from that evening's meeting while Diane was reading a book, when suddenly the wardrobe door flew open and Peter Collins jumped out! He had been hiding in there until we had got settled and he frightened the life out of us.

I made a few changes before the 1980 season and one of the new arrivals was American Larry Kosta who was doing well in California and I had been tipped off that he was a good prospect. He was a good lad but very highly strung. He used to get so worked up about his racing that the word was he visited a psychiatrist to get his head right. I don't know if it is true but it was certainly mentioned at the time.

Two other new signings for the start of the 1980 season were Louis and Peter Carr from Ellesmere Port. Neither of them pulled up any trees for Belle Vue, but I think the problem is that we remember them now as much better riders than they were when they were at Hyde Road because they hadn't yet made their mark. Both certainly went on to be very good riders and, when we signed them, they were both

PC in more serious mood here, but not when he leapt out of our wardrobe.

young lads coming through. But because they didn't show the same promise as PC, Mort or Les Collins, they weren't considered by many as good, although they both did a decent job.

When they signed, the only transport they had was a Vauxhall Viva van. The night before we were due down at Eastbourne that season we had a home meeting and they had started to encounter a few mechanical problems with their van on the way, but they assured me they would make it down to the south coast.

They were true to their word and, when they arrived at Arlington, I asked they how they had managed to do it. It transpired that the bloke who lived opposite them in Preston owned an identical Viva van. They had limped home in their van after our home meeting and knocked the poor bloke up. They asked him if they could borrow the engine out of his van and, when he agreed, they set about taking it out and putting it into their own vehicle. When they got back home they put the engine back in their neighbour's van and repaired their own.

The Carrs' grandad used to travel with them to a lot of meetings but on one occasion, after yet another breakdown, he started to get cold in the back so they put some methanol in a tin and lit it. That worked well until the tin was knocked over and set the car on fire!

⑮
ABRUPT AND STRAIGHT TO THE POINT

HAVING Chris Morton and Peter Collins leading the Aces was a team manager's dream. Mort was in PC's shadow much of the time, which was a shame because anywhere else he would have been an outstanding No.1. His contribution was absolutely enormous and to have him in a team with PC was a dream.

I never rated Chris any less highly than I rated Peter. They were both my No1 and, if ever you needed two boys to pull a 5-1 out of the bag when the chips were down, they were the pair to do it.

Mort was dyed-in-the-wool Belle Vue and a great team member. The deal he was on wasn't good – neither was PC's because in those days nobody was on a good deal – but he just wanted to ride for the Aces. If you said the wrong thing to Mort he would bite and respond, but that didn't work with PC. If you wanted to get Peter going you would have to ask him questions like: "Is your bike OK tonight?" or "Have you lost some compression?" Talking to him like that, and making him think, could really have an effect.

That is a part of trying to build a successful team – all the riders are different and respond in different ways. Some would want a shoulder to cry on, others would want a kick up the arse!

In 1981, however, the dynamic duo looked like they had ridden their last meeting together in Belle Vue colours. At the very end of 1980, PC crashed heavily in the KO Cup final at Cradley and damaged his shoulder really badly. He managed just a handful of meetings the following year and then announced his retirement.

He was back in 1982, but he was certainly serious about calling it quits. Even today we haven't got to the bottom of how that cup final was given the go-ahead to take place. It was right at the end of the season so the weather wasn't so good and on the morning of the meeting I had a call from Cradley to say the meeting was off because the track was too bad.

I then phoned our riders and passed on the news. Then, at about one o'clock, I had another phone call to say the meeting was back on. I wasn't happy because I had already told everyone the meeting was off but there were no spare dates and it was right at the end of the season, so I agreed to ring round all the riders and tell them it was back on. Unfortunately, one of them had made alternative arrangements and couldn't make it so I had no alternative but to go with a weakened team.

If I knew then what I know now I would have refused, but I was trying to be sporting and doing what I thought was best for speedway. When we got there the Dudley Wood track was terrible and PC crashed heavily, injuring his shoulder. In fact he did it so badly that it's still not right today.

What we still can't get an answer to, even to this day, is who authorised the meeting to be called off? And, more to the point, who authorised it to be back on again once it had already been called off? It shouldn't have gone ahead – the conditions were terrible and, in hindsight, I realised I should have been firm and refused to go. Just to add insult to PC's injury, Cradley won the cup.

Peter declared that he wouldn't be able to ride the following year and announced his retirement, although he subsequently made a comeback when he felt fit enough – and went on to reach another World Final. But when he told me to plan the team without him, it left me with the difficult task of replacing him. How on earth do you replace Peter Collins?

The rider I chose to take his place – probably the only option at the time, to be honest – was New Zealand star Larry Ross, who we bought from Wimbledon for £18,000. He had always gone well at Belle Vue and was looking for a move, so I spoke to Jack Fearnley and a deal was struck. Everything was signed, sealed and delivered, and Larry was all set to make his debut at Belle Vue the following Saturday.

The only thing we didn't have was £18,000! Jack had to go down on the train from Manchester to London to meet the directors of Trust House Forte to ask them to sanction the spending of £18,000 – little did they know that the contracts had already been signed and that we had effectively spent the money before we had even got it! Jack was very nervous because the club could easily have folded if they had turned down our request for the money to buy a new No.1. Fortunately they agreed and Larry turned out to be a good signing. He was easy going and got on with his job – I enjoyed having him there.

By this time I was also a member of the BSPA management committee. It was amazing to think that, when I had first switched to the other side of the fence I was made unwelcome and seen as a man who was suddenly going to start riding again after a couple of seasons, knowing all the secrets of the BSPA's inner sanctum. Then they realised I wasn't as bad as they first feared I might be and invited me to serve on their management committee. I stayed on the management committee for a number of years and I did so because I wanted to do what I thought was best for the sport. If you are going to change anything, you need to be in a position where your views can be heard.

It was quite an honour to be voted on and in a few short years I had gone from being a rider to team manager, to co-promoter and now management committee member. But my time at Belle Vue was running out.

There had been rumours that THF wanted to sell Belle Vue for some time and Stuart Bamforth emerged as a prospective buyer. There were other suitors but both Jack and I felt that Bamforth was the best option. He had been world stock car champion, which may not be the greatest accolade, but it showed he had been involved in sport and was successful at a high level.

Jack and I knew more about Belle Vue Speedway than anyone at THF headquarters in London – we had all the gate figures, programme sales and everything else from every meeting we had run there. Jack gave them to Bamforth quite openly so that he knew what he was letting himself in for and, to be fair, THF London hadn't a clue about speedway, only the Belle Vue Zoological Gardens operation as a whole.

> "He turned very nasty and demanded to know where I thought he was going to get that money from. I told him straight – I didn't care"

In November of that year the deal went through. Everyone who worked for Belle Vue was actually made redundant by THF because Bamforth didn't want to get involved in any of the pay-offs, but Roy Carter and I were both employed by him straight away in our existing jobs so we were never out of work.

My job throughout the winter was to deal with season ticket sales and get on with all the usual close season jobs. But throughout that time I hardly heard from Bamforth at all. Whenever he phoned he was very abrupt and straight to the point. If a conversation could last a minute it would last a minute, not 65 seconds.

He never asked me how things were going, whether we had sold many season tickets, if I wanted a hand with anything – nothing at all. If I had been in his position I would have been so grateful that someone was doing the spadework and want to know how things were progressing, but Bammy was too busy selling scrap from his yard to raise the money for his Belle Vue purchase.

My first suspicions that my working relationship with Bamforth would not be a good one came after he asked me to build up three bikes over the winter while he decided which riders would be on which deals. I still had the shop with Diane so it wasn't a problem for me to do that of an evening. It was fine . . . until I gave him the bill.

He turned very nasty and demanded to know where I thought he was going to get that sort of money from. I told him straight – I didn't care. He had placed the order with me and I had spent my own money on buying the parts to build the bikes up – surely it was only fair that he paid me what I was owed. Eventually, about three or four weeks later, he paid me, and only then did he get the bikes.

I found Stuart Bamforth difficult to talk to and our relationship soon deteriorated further. I used to write up all

Mort, big money signing Larry Ross and the late Stuart Bamforth – the reason why I left Belle Vue.

my own programme notes and, as the start of the 1982 season approached, I took my contribution for the first meeting into his office, which was in one of two cabins we had at the track. He was in there with some of his workers eating lunch and, no sooner had I given him the notes than someone had knocked soup all over them.

"Never mind," said Bamforth, "you can write them again." This annoyed me because there wasn't a hint of an apology and a complete disregard for the time and effort it would take for me to type them up a second time.

The final straw came on the night of the opening meeting. Bamforth decided that he didn't want any freeloaders getting in to meetings for nothing so he made virtually everybody pay to get in – the St John Ambulance Brigade included. Taffy Owen had the track shop and, even though he paid a rent to be there, he had to pay too. He ended up passing money through the fence to the St John people so that they could get into the stadium.

I'd seen a system in Australia where everyone, even the competitors, had to pay at the gate but, once you had signed in at the office, you got your money back. It's a great foolproof system to clamp down on people getting in for nothing when they shouldn't and you can't knock it. Bamforth wanted to apply the same principle – only he didn't tell anyone what he was planning to do and the first they knew of it was when they arrived at the stadium for the opening meeting of the season.

He banned all NUJ passes so respected national newspaper journalists like Richard Frost and Dick Bott, who had given Belle Vue such good – and free – publicity, had to pay to get in and do their job. He upset so many people that night, I couldn't believe it. We had always worn a collar and tie on the centre green during meetings, but there he was in a check fleece, jeans and boots smoking a big, long cigar.

That was when I realised I'd had enough. I had just enjoyed seven fantastic seasons and I simply didn't want to put up with it. So after the meeting, when it had quietened down a bit, I went over to see him in his office. I said to him: "Stuart, you have fulfilled your ambition by buying Belle Vue Speedway but after one meeting it's plain to see that me and you are chalk and cheese. We're not going to get on."

He was the boss so things weren't going to change. It was never going to get any better for me so I told him I was leaving with immediate effect. The only thing I wanted out of my office was my England file so I went across, picked it up, and walked out. It was a poor end to a lovely relationship with Belle Vue. It was 38 miles there and 38 miles back but I absolutely loved going to work there and I could quite happily have gone in seven days a week.

I didn't mention a word to Diane about what I had done until I arrived home later that night. We were sitting down having a cup of tea when I casually mentioned I had told Bamforth to stick his job where the sun doesn't shine! She couldn't believe it but I told her not to worry. "We're not going to die because I haven't got a job," I told her.

The following day Bamforth phoned me and asked if I had simmered down. I told him that I had, but that my decision stood – I wouldn't be going back. He made it clear that he wanted me to stay but that was the nicest thing he had said to me since November and, as such, was a bit late.

Ian Thomas turned out to be my successor as team boss and he went on to win the league that season. That was the Aces team I had put together, of course, and Ian went on record as saying his success had come with a side he'd inherited from me, which was nice of him.

Bamforth was a grafter, there's no doubt about it, but he had to work because all the money he had in the world had gone into Belle Vue Speedway. But there is a right way and a wrong way of doing it. Being polite and civil is the right way – treating people like dirt is the wrong way. Peter Morrey and a lot of the track staff left soon after I did, so it obviously wasn't just me who felt that was about Bamforth.

Having bought the stadium for a reported £350,000 in 1982, Bamforth then sold it at the end of the 1987 season for £2.2m. It wasn't long before the bulldozers moved in, but he had no option really because he couldn't have gone on much longer with the stadium in the state it was in. It would have cost millions to put right. It would have been cheaper to demolish it and start again. He spent a lot of money on the toilet blocks but the whole place was very, very dilapidated and needed completely rewiring. Literally just across the road was another good stadium where he could base the team, so when he sold up I thought: 'Good luck to him.'

By the end of 1982 I was looking for work outside speedway. Because not only had I left Belle Vue, but I'd quit my position as England manager too.

16

A SHIP WITHOUT A RUDDER

ALL the time I was working for Belle Vue, Diane was running the shop single-handedly, and doing a very good job of it too I must add. About four years earlier we had moved about 10 miles closer to Belle Vue to cut down on my travelling time. Diane would take the kids to school in Wakefield, go to the shop and then pick them up after school to bring them home.

To be honest, after I left Belle Vue I lost a lot of interest and I'd turned into a bit of a recluse. I went through a fairly bad stage in my life, that winter particularly. Speedway had been my life and, although it was me who shot myself so to speak, it wasn't easy to find something else to do.

I didn't even have any interest in the shop. I was like a ship without a rudder for a while. In fact we had a very big garden and I became interested in gardening – we turned our garden into something really special. Diane pulled me through it. I really don't know how she has put up with me. I lived 100 per cent for speedway and nothing got in the way. She's had to put up with a lot over the years – I've forgotten birthdays, parties, all sorts of things, but I couldn't help it, it was just the way it was. How she's put up with me for 39 years I'll never know, but thank God she has – I wouldn't be a right lot of good without her.

I eventually found something to get my teeth into when I bought an electro-plating business with Steve Finch. I knew Steve well because we have grown up in the same village. I was looking for a job after leaving Belle Vue and he was looking for something to do after breaking his leg riding for Halifax. I was telling him one day that I had seen a business for sale in Halifax and he asked if he could come with me. I was more than happy and, when we had taken a look at it, we agreed to go half-and-half and buy it. The previous owners were a married couple and we thought we could build it up into something bigger – it looked like a good opportunity.

As it turned out, we were well and truly stitched up by the previous owner and to this day, he still owes us £5,000. When we bought the business he signed an agreement to say that he wouldn't enter into any electro-plating or polishing within a certain radius of Halifax. But we discovered that not only was he still doing polishing but that he was doing work which should have come to us. We found out where he was doing it and, when we went round there, we caught him red-handed.

We took the matter to court, where it was agreed that he was most definitely in the wrong and that he should pay us £5,000 compensation plus costs. Unfortunately, everything he had was in his wife's name, so to this day we have never received a penny. Not only that, we had to pay our legal costs – another grand – ourselves.

But we soon settled into the job, although it was hard graft, that's for sure. We were the only two who worked there, which meant doing absolutely everything ourselves. We barrel-plated nuts and bolts and it was a very, very long process. From bringing them into the shop to taking them out again there were 14 lifts. On one Saturday morning when we had a rush job for a good customer, we did more than a ton-and-a-half of nuts and bolts. Every single bolt had to be lifted 14 times so, as you can imagine, we were both fit as fiddles.

The business was situated in the basement of an old mill and, one winter, the landlord asked us if we would consider moving to an old garage across the road. We used a lot of acid in the job and the people who worked upstairs were getting sick of the smell! We were happy to agree and we made the move over the Christmas period. Unfortunately, some of the tanks had been stood in the same place for years and didn't take too kindly to being moved. But we knew a steel fabricator who made us some new ones and Steve's dad was an electrician so he rewired the place and we had a pretty nice, well-organised shop when we opened up in January.

The problem was, though, that we couldn't go forward because of the size of the place. What we should have gone into was chrome plating which is one of the top ends of the plating industry. But we would have needed different tanks to do that and we didn't have the room to expand, even though our new premises were bigger. All we seemed to do was slog our guts out to chase money from customers who were slow payers. We added another string to our bow when we petitioned one corner off and started doing polishing, but that was about as far forward as we could go.

Steve was a fantastic partner. He was still riding for Halifax so sometimes he had to dive off early to get to a meeting. But if he knew he could get to a meeting by leaving at four o'clock, that's what time he'd leave, not two o'clock. He would always make the time up too and, if we were behind, we would stay all night to get the job done.

But after a few years I came to realise that I couldn't see myself doing that job for the rest of my life. We were earning a living but we weren't going forward. We were standing still and working ourselves into the ground, so I told Steve that I wanted out. I think he was a bit miffed about that, but he didn't kick up a fuss. I suggested he could buy my share if he wanted but in the end we decided to sell up and we placed an advert in the local paper.

After about three months we had a visit from a lad who had been made redundant and wanted to run it with his wife. He put a lump sum down and then, every day for a month, he came along and we taught him everything we knew. After that he paid the rest and the business was his.

Steve went on to become a driving instructor and made more money at that than he ever would have done with the electro-plating business, and I ended up back in speedway.

In fact in May 1983, after more than eight years out of the saddle, I was back on a bike . . . as a member of the Halifax Dukes team again.

Former Halifax rider Steve Finch became my business partner.

⓱
BACK IN AN HOUR

IHAD never, ever given another thought to riding again. But, because he lived in Halifax, Eric Boothroyd used to regularly call in on Steve Finch and me and have a tea or coffee with us and one day he asked me if I fancied making a comeback.

I told him that I didn't, which was true. Eric kept asking me, though, and then Steve started trying to persuade me. He was still riding for Halifax and told me we could share a van and travel together – we could even pick up Dougie Wyer, who had transferred from Sheffield to Halifax by then.

Word got round that I could be riding again so I asked Diane what she reckoned. She wasn't against it, so I thought about giving it a go.

I explained to Eric that I didn't have a bike or any equipment at all. I'd sold my bike when I retired in 1974 and I gave away all the spares I had to young lads who were trying to make the grade. I told Eric that if I was going to make a comeback, he would have to set me up with equipment – but on the understanding that I would give it all back when I had finished with it. Eric knew me well enough so he could rest assured it would be in immaculate condition when he got it back.

My first comeback meeting was at home against Cradley on a Monday evening – and I had the final fitting for my leathers the night before. The only practice I'd had prior to my comeback was after Eric had called in one afternoon and said he was doing the track and asked if I'd like to nip over to The Shay for a spin round. Steve and I put a note on the shop door saying 'Back in an hour' and headed over. I got round all right but I couldn't get it into the corners flat out. Before that the only four laps I had done on a speedway bike were at Peter Collins' testimonial so I had every right to be a bit rusty, but I felt I was nearly there. Steve said he thought I'd gone better than he expected and Eric admitted he was surprised and reckoned I would probably get back on the pace.

What a pity all three of us were misguided!

I knew I needed to be quicker, though, and I had the added disadvantage of coming into the side two months into the season, when everyone else was well into the swing of things. Going out with three other riders in a race was a hell of a lot different to going round on my own.

It was a wet night when I made my comeback and I got covered in muck going into the first bend. I was a nervous wreck and did no good whatsoever, but it was early days and I felt I could improve. There was a good crowd there too, so the Halifax management must have more than compensated for the outlay they spent on my equipment.

When word started to get around that Boocock was on the comeback trail, Birmingham expressed an interest in me as well. As it turned out, one of my earliest meetings back was away to the Brummies at Perry Barr in the League Cup. I was excluded for touching the tapes in one of my races, so I decided to wind the referee up. I picked up the pits phone and gave him one big sob story. I said that I wasn't the only one nudging the tapes, and then I really went for it. "How can I earn money when you've excluded me?" I asked him. "You don't really think I want to ride again do you? I'm skint! My business has gone pear-shaped and I've had to come back and ride again just to feed my family!"

None of that was true, of course, and all the riders in the pits thought it was hilarious. They were all egging me on and creased up with laughter. The referee fell for it, though, and put me back in the race. For the first time ever, I made a referee change his mind!

Kenny Carter was the No.1 and Halifax hero during the early 80s. He wasn't everyone's cup of tea but he was certainly mine. He had some funny ways and he was no good as a partner because, if you were in a race with him, you were racing him as well as your two opponents. He was going to win, no matter what.

During my comeback year I also reached a scratch race final at Halifax and, as I lined up on gate two, Kenny was on my inside telling me to move over. I was having

**Too laid-back . . . just before going on parade in one of my comeback meetings,
with Dukes' team manager Dennis Gavros, Dougie Wyer and Steve Finch.**

Here we go again . . . back in the saddle for the Dukes in 1983.

none of it and we sat there shouting at each other. Then, just as the green light came on, I stamped on his foot with my steel shoe as hard as I could! I made a rocket start by he got past me after about a lap-and-a-half.

"What a trick that was," he said to me in the pits afterwards.

But Kenny and I got on really well and he used to come over to the shop regularly, often staying for a coffee and a chat.

I have to be honest, though, and say that after a month into my racing comeback I still wasn't enjoying it. I wasn't serious about it either, whereas before I'd been deadly serious about speedway. I hated being beaten before I'd retired but this time it didn't seem to matter. I was travelling with Steve, we were picking Dougie up and we were laughing and acting the goat on the way to meetings. I wasn't bothered and that was totally wrong. I was enjoying it too much and for the wrong reasons.

I wasn't finding it easy and when Halifax were at Hackney for a British League match one Friday, Les Silver wanted to know what a "has been" like me was doing riding again. I told him it was better to be a has-been than a never-was! But he was entitled to his opinion and I've got a lot of time for Len Silver, who has done a good job wherever he has been as a promoter. He says what he thinks and there is nothing wrong with that. In any case, he was right – I was a has-been.

One Saturday night, I got home from a meeting and had a chat to Diane. I told her that I wasn't enjoying it and that I was letting everyone down. My scores were low – twos, threes, fours and on several occasions zeros – and I realised it wasn't working out. I decided to do the decent thing and ring Eric Boothroyd to tell him it was time to call it quits.

Throughout our time at Halifax he was always known as Eric and I was Young

Eric. So I phoned him and said: "Hello Eric, it's Young Eric here." I told him I was letting myself and the team down. I said it had been a mistake coming back and that I wanted to quit. Eric told me he was pleased I'd called – because he was going to drop me anyway!

The writing was on the wall when I arrived for our meeting at Leicester and my name wasn't in the programme. I was livid. I knew it wasn't working out but a lot of effort had gone into coming back after such a long time out. Mine wasn't the only space left blank in the programme – the management were obviously weighing up a few options.

But I told Eric and Reg Fearman that if I wasn't good enough to have my name in the programme, I wasn't good enough to be there at all. And if it happened again, the space would stay blank – I wouldn't be riding. I was fully aware what was going on, having learnt all about the management side of things from being at Belle Vue.

When I contacted Eric about a week or so later to tell him I was calling it quits, he was lovely about it. There were no hard feelings and, even though the arrangement was that I had to give the bike back, he told me I could keep it.

Maybe it would have been different had I been asked a few months earlier and then I'd been able to enjoy the benefit of practising over the winter. But I knew I had let the team and myself down, although at least it convinced me never ever to ride speedway again.

The smile from this 'has-been' in the pits at Hackney disguised the fact that I wasn't enjoying it.

I think Eric had expected me to make a slow start but he didn't bring me back to score two or three points a meeting. He probably expected a bit more and I think everyone else did too. The hope was that, once I found that spark again, I would score six or seven points a meeting which would make me a pretty decent middle order man, but unfortunately I couldn't even achieve those figures.

Ironically, the best meeting I had was my last one against Eastbourne, when I scored seven. I was genuinely improving but I wasn't enjoying it and I was finding it hard. Maybe it was because I'd been a 10-point man throughout virtually all my time at Halifax in the 60s and 70s and now I was struggling for points and getting covered in muck every night.

All the time I still had the electro-plating business so, whatever time I got in from a meeting, I was still setting off for work at seven o'clock the next morning. I still had my bike to clean and repair too and, at 38, I was no spring chicken. But if I'd never tried a comeback, I'd never have known.

There are very few people in any sports who make a successful comeback. It was the same sport I had left eight years earlier – there were still four riders doing four laps and all turning left, but times change very quickly. The four-valve Weslake was so different to the two-valve Jawa and JAP

Getting used to the Weslake wasn't easy.

engines I'd always previously ridden. There was so much extra power that I struggled to get the thing off the start for ages.

By the end of August I was back to being what I'd been at the end of April – an ex-speedway rider.

"We sat there shouting at each other. Then, just as the green light came on, I stamped on his foot with my steel shoe as hard as I could"

18
DAYOH

I'VE made a couple of references to being England manager in earlier chapters of this book, so now is a good time to take a look at my role with the national team. My first involvement on the management side with England came in 1980 – and what a season it was too.

That year England completed the grand slam, with Michael Lee winning the individual World Final, PC and Dave Jessup winning the World Pairs and Mort, along with reserve John Davis, joining the aforementioned trio to win the World Team Cup. My involvement was coach – or coach driver, as I used to tell people – to work alongside manager Ian Thomas.

Ian was good on the administration side because he had done it all before, at Workington, Hull and Newcastle, and obviously I had the benefit of all those years riding. Ian knew the rulebook inside out – and still does as team manager at Belle Vue – but he couldn't offer any tactical advice because he had never been a rider.

With the FIM getting bigger and bigger and so many more international meetings added to the calendar, the BSPA decided it was getting too big a job for just one promoter. I threw my hat into the ring and I was delighted to get the nod, especially after the success we achieved.

Ian and I have always got along very well, right from my riding days. He's straight to the point and doesn't suffer fools gladly. I don't think there has ever been a better promoter in speedway when it comes to using the rule book, although I think the rule book is about 30 pages thicker because of him!

He was another one, like John Berry, who used to antagonise the visiting teams and, whenever you went to The Boulevard when he was promoting at Hull, you would always get a terrible parking space. Then you would find your side of the pits was flooded while the home side's was always bone dry. It was a packed earth surface in the pits so your toolbox and anything else you put down would be covered in muck.

When I realised it was being done deliberately I told the Belle Vue riders to arrive early for our next meeting there, which they all did, and we camped ourselves in the home area of the pits. We refused to move until they made our side usable and all hell broke loose.

Another stroke he pulled was to prevent me using a rider I wanted to track while I was in charge of Belle Vue. Ian and Bryan Larner, his partner at Hull, objected about 20 minutes before the start even though I'd put the team in a week before the meeting. It was quite probably a mistake on my part but, to wait until the last minute before pointing it out was a classic example of gamesmanship.

I couldn't use the rider I wanted to and ended up having to borrow a scrubber. I made a point of remembering that and a few weeks later I got my revenge. I was there watching, as I often was, and Hull were a rider short, so they announced they would be using Phil Kynman instead. I went straight into the office and pointed out he was my rider and that I was refusing permission for them to use him. Eventually I sold him back to Hull – he had been practising at Belle Vue and as he'd signed a contract with us, I made sure we received a fee for him.

Despite all of that, Ian and I got on very well and none of our disagreements were long-lasting. The first part of our World Championship trilogy – the World Pairs final - was held on a baking hot day in Krsko, Yugoslavia. The track was as slick as anything although the best gates were one and two – three and four were terrible. Usually in a pairs tournament your two riders would alternate between starting on the inside and on the outside. But because PC was a poor gater and Dave Jessup was quick out of the traps, I decided to change from normal policy.

It seemed biased because I was Peter's boss but I told Dave to go off the worst gates every time and Peter off the inside. That way, I felt we would have a better chance because it would give Peter the advantage. Dave was happy enough to go along with that and, in any case, I told them they could soon cross over and ride their preferred line. As it turned out, Peter made some reasonable gates and DJ made some terrific ones. They rode absolutely superbly – it was like they were on a piece of string after the first bend and they were rewarded with victory.

Michael Lee's World Final triumph at Gothenburg was another glorious night for British speedway although one Englishman who wasn't smiling too much was Don Godden. We had a furious row with him because Michael was riding Jawas while John Davis was on a Godden. John was going very well but it was obvious that, when they met late in the meeting, the one who had fewer points was going to help the other one out.

I told them not to mess it up for each other and pointed out to John that, if Michael was in front, he shouldn't try to pass him or they could both end up losing out.

Don didn't like that. He argued that, as John was an Englishman with an English engine, he shouldn't take any notice. My point was that we wanted an English World Champion – and it didn't matter if John was on a lawnmower! As it turned out Michael beat John but he was given a much harder race than expected.

Michael's second gold medal came in the World Team Cup in Wroclaw, Poland. Dave Jessup almost didn't get out of the country after the meeting though. He was having a sleep before the meeting when he woke up to find someone in his room stealing his wallet and his passport. He chased him down the corridor but couldn't catch him. Unfortunately, we had to leave him in the country when the rest of us flew home because, without a passport, he couldn't board the plane. At least the English press contingent stayed behind with him and the British Consulate eventually sorted it out but he wasn't very happy at staying behind.

In those days the food was still not great in that part of the world so, during practice, I was cooking baked beans to keep us all going. I poured some methanol

Michael Lee, Dave Jessup and Billy Sanders – top three in the world at Gothenburg in 1980.

in a Coke tin and lit it, then put a couple of bricks either side and balanced the bean can on top. We managed to get some fresh bread to eat with it and it went down a treat, although we did get some very funny looks.

The food after the meeting was much better, though, and in much plusher surroundings. We were invited to a big banquet in a huge mansion. All the bigwigs were there and our spirits were high. Michael, it has to be said, was very much the worse for wear, and disappeared for about half an hour. He reappeared just as the dignitaries on the top table had begun their speeches. The room was hushed as we all listened to what the man with the microphone had to say – until Michael burst in singing at the top of his voice! "Dayoh, dayoh, dayoh," was the chorus as he bounced from pillar to pillar on his way back to our table.

I was furious and told him to sit down and shut up, but he wanted to borrow £100. I gave him the money and said: "Now f*** off and don't come back!" I don't know what he wanted it for but I wasn't in the mood to ask. I think he got away with it because he was a young lad, he was World Champion and he had just helped England win the World Team Cup, but it was very embarrassing for the whole England contingent.

Michael's problems in later life have been well documented, of course, and I think he was already on the slippery slope then. It was the beginning of the end. When Michael became mixed up in drugs we all hoped it was just a fad and that he would quickly grow out of it. When those problems began to surface, it would have been naïve not to have realised he was getting involved in some way, although I think it's also fair to say that everyone makes mistakes. Remember, smoking wasn't the social stigma it is today, even though the government have now relaxed their laws on smoking cannabis. I should also point out that I never saw him take any drugs.

There were also a number of other riders we suspected were smoking cannabis, notably the Americans. No-one can ever prove that they were, of course, because they had enough sense not to do it in public.

The International Fours meeting at Reading is a meeting which should never have gone ahead – but the Yanks didn't care and it seemed pretty obvious why! The track was as slick as a board until halfway across where there was a big ridge of dirt and the surface was as rough as a ploughed field.

But did it bother the Americans? No way! They rode the outside like they were motoring down the main road. You only had to look in their eyes to know that most of them had enjoyed a few joints before the meeting.

Luckily that was just another problem in speedway which seems to have been and gone. The Yanks certainly wouldn't have got away with it today, and I would hate to be on the starting gate racing against someone who was out of their tree on drugs. What's ironic, of course, is that the Americans were so talented on a speedway bike that they didn't need anything at all to enhance their performance.

Len Silver took over management of the England team for 1981 but over the winter of 1981-82 I was asked to do the job again, this time in tandem with John Berry. I wasn't a fan of John's operational methods at Ipswich but I've always been able to get along with someone if I need to – even if I don't like them. In the event he didn't last long anyway because, part-way through the season, he quit. I don't know his reasons although, in fairness to him, he phoned to tell me before it was announced. I was happy to carry on if the BSPA gave the go-ahead and they did.

As an Englishman who had ridden for England and captained England, I was delighted to be England manager. You can't get a bigger honour than that because to manage your country at a professional sport is something to be proud of. A vote of thanks is due to the BSPA general council because they decide who the team manager is going to be. These days it seems to be a case of whoever wants the job can have it, but it wasn't like that back then.

The first Test series of my reign with John Berry was against the USA at Wimbledon and, although we won 63-45, there was a major issue to deal with. Michael Lee had turned up and was complaining he had a stomach bug – but I didn't believe it at all and I still don't believe it. He turned up looking terrible and said he had been feeling poorly, so I told him not to ride if he didn't want to and he didn't.

I class riding for England as a big honour and anyone who doesn't want to ride for their country should just say so. Michael was just beginning to get a reputation as a wild child and wanted to pick and choose where he rode. If he was on form he was like lightning, but if he turned up with his head up his backside, he couldn't care less.

I wasn't happy with Michael and I told the BSPA I wanted him dropped from the rest of the series, but the management committee insisted he kept his place. He was a big name and had been World Champion not long before so I didn't get the backing. But, looking back, I was right because he rode like a big tart. He scored two at Swindon, seven at Ipswich, where he finished last twice, and one at Poole in the decider, which we lost heavily.

Above: Two's company . . . Ian Thomas and me formed a successful partnership in 1980, when England completed a unique grand slam of World Championship honours. We also brought a bit of style to the job, by insisting all the England riders wore blazers, shirts and ties to all our international meetings.

Below: Coal Products Ltd were great friends to speedway in the 80s and early 90s. Collin Pratt and myself are pictured with two of CPL's big-wigs, John Taylor and Ron Baker, at the press conference to announce their sponsorship of the 1990 World Final at Bradford.

We've mentioned Michael's personal problems before and I think that by this time he was on the slippery slope. Michael was a smashing lad and still is, but you can't mix business and pleasure at that level. Maybe, just maybe, a jolt like being left out of a Test series could have done some good but at that time I doubt it.

The international season finished with a fours tournament against the United States, Denmark and Australia – and after that I resigned. It was an ill-conceived Mickey Mouse tournament and the riders just weren't taking it seriously. Australia managed just one point between them in the final match at Eastbourne – what does that tell you? Only a handful of the riders were giving it their best shot and, if you can't get them interested, what is the point?

There as no way I could have dropped into the same mode and gone about my job in a half-hearted way because I cared too much. I didn't want to be party to anything like that, so I wrote out a letter of resignation straight away and put it in the first post box I came across on my way home from Eastbourne.

At the time I was quoted in the press as saying I just wanted to get away from speedway and that I had no enthusiasm for the sport. I was disappointed and I felt as though I was flogging a dead horse, but I didn't really mean a lot of what I said because it was in the heat of the moment.

A few years later I was back for another stint in the England hot seat, this time as joint boss with Colin Pratt. We both felt that it was too big a job for one man who was trying to promote his own BL track as well as manage England. Also, two heads would be better than one. I could tell Colin a lot he didn't know about what had happening around the northern tracks and, likewise, he could tell me things about what had been going on at the southern tracks. We used to pool our ideas and share our responsibilities.

When Colin and I were appointed in 1986 we most definitely insisted upon some rules of engagement. One of them was that we had total control over team selection, which didn't go down too well, but we both had a lot of years' experience in speedway. What's the point in having a dog and barking yourself? The management used to select the Test teams in the old days but we wanted to win by our own bat and, if we lost, we would take the blame.

Look at the Michael Lee situation a few years earlier when I wanted to leave him out of a Test series but the BSPA wouldn't let me. We knew the business side of it and we weren't going to decimate somebody's business by picking four riders from one team to ride for England on a night when their club had a match, but it was totally unfair for a promoter to tell us not to pick his rider because they had a tough fixture.

That's the sort of thing that used to happen on a regular basis. Every other international team manager selected their best team, so why couldn't we? We genuinely made every effort to be sympathetic to the promoters but, when push came to shove, everybody knew that we were within our rights to select whoever we wanted. That said, there were still promoters who would ring up and ask us not to pick one of their riders because they needed him to ride for their club.

One such occasion was when Pratty and I called up Bradford's Paul Thorp to

With Paul Thorp (left) and Kelvin Tatum at the 1989 World Pairs Final in Leszno.

replace the injured Simon Cross to partner Kelvin Tatum in the 1989 World Pairs Final at Leszno. Thorpy had cost Bradford promoters Allan and Bobby Ham £20,000 from Belle Vue, so they naturally wanted to get the most out of their investment and we could see their point. But we had a duty to select the best pairing.

Thorpy has been underestimated since he was a kid and he was on fire. He was so laid back and, where the likes of Kelly and Shawn Moran went off the rails, Thorpy didn't because he was never on them in the first place! He was a great gater and an unbelievably good speedway rider who loved the big tracks. He rode exceptionally well at Leszno and even beat Hans Nielsen as we finished in the bronze medal position. It's funny, but he always seemed to get the better of Hans.

We always felt that a successful England team would be really good for the sport in this country. The press like to write about winners, so you get far more recognition if you are at the top of the tree. That was proved the year we did the grand slam when we had an enormous amount of publicity.

John Berry had been England manager just before us in '85 and that year he'd adopted a policy of appointing a team captain on the day of each Test. We decided to get back to having a permanent skipper for the national team . . . and chose Kenny Carter.

Kenny was such a little hothead but he was so immensely proud to be riding for England. When he had that Union Jack racejacket on, his chest stuck out another three feet, he was so incredibly proud. He was a winner and he didn't want to lose but, boy, did he upset some people.

Throughout his life he had been brought up to look after himself and that's exactly what he did. He would ride under, over or through anybody but we thought that giving him a title and the responsibility that went with it would steady him down and make him think a bit more.

Kenny wasn't greatly popular among the other lads because he wasn't a team player. So long as he was getting 18 points in a Test match, he didn't care about any of the other riders. He loved it when the team won, but he was more concerned at his own performance, which was hard for us to accept.

With the exception of Peter Collins, I don't think the others disliked him – they just saw him as a big-headed, clever-clogs. I had a lot of time for Kenny, though. I'd been close to him for a number of years and he was a regular customer at our shop. Unless he was in a desperate hurry he would always come to the house and we would sit chatting for hours.

Kenny had only been captain a few months in '86 when I had a telephone call to say that he had shot his wife, Pam, dead and then killed himself. It was quite late at night and I was in bed when the call came. I was astounded. At about midnight the phone rang again and it was a TV station in Australia who were asking me about it. I don't know how they got hold of my number, but I told them I could confirm what they had heard. It was so tragic. He was hot-headed but I don't think anyone expected him to do anything like that.

First and foremost Kenny's death was a tragedy, but from a professional point of view Kenny's death had left Colin and I, as England managers, with another problem. We had lost Michael Lee, while Peter Collins, Chris Morton, Dave Jessup, Malcolm Simmons and the like were all coming to the end of their careers, so we

The tragic Kenny Carter, who died soon after we made him England captain.

had to look at introducing some fresh blood to the England team.

Fortunately there were an exciting crop of youngsters emerging so we reintroduced the Young England side and staged a three-match Test series against Denmark. Gary Havelock, Andrew Silver, Martin Dugard, Paul Thorp and Andy Galvin were among the riders included as our young guns beat the Aussies 3-0.

By then we had already given Silver his full England debut against Denmark and he had also ridden against the USA. He was still only 17 and riding for Arena Essex in the National League but we gave him his full Test debut against Denmark at Wolverhampton. The Danes weren't happy – in fact they wanted him thrown out of the meeting because they felt he was riding dangerously.

He was a bit wild, to be fair, but he was young and that was how he rode, full of guts and determination. He frightened the Danes and he frightened me and Pratty too! He had so much talent but didn't make the most of it. He enjoyed having a good time and was probably too happy-go-lucky to make the step up from being a very good rider to being a great one.

The following year Thorp, Dugard and Havvy all followed him into the team for the Test series against Denmark. It looked like we were in for a bright future.

In fact Havvy was in our Sunbrite Lions party for a tour of Australia in the winter of 1987-88. Now that was an amazing trip. My brother Nigel, who lives in Australia, organised it from that end and I organised it from here and it turned out to be the best trip I've ever done in my life. It was so good that many a time we have spoken about having a reunion.

We won the official Test series 5-2 and also won all five of our unofficial internationals against an Australian Select – and one of those defeats was down to the fact that the lads were out partying all night before the meeting. I'd gone to bed and I wondered why they were wandering around like zombies the next day.

The party had a very strong Northern bias to it, with Neil Evitts, Peter Carr, Havvy, Andy Smith, Paul Thorp and Sean Wilson from up North and only Alun Rossiter from the South. Maybe that's why Roscoe had the micky taken out of him throughout the tour. He took some stick, but he gave as much back.

When we arrived at Sydney we went straight to Brisbane for the first Test. I loaded Nigel's big trailer up with all the bikes, spares and tyres and set off with five of the riders in the car. But the trailer was so heavy that I couldn't drive over 55mph and I almost turned the car over within an hour of leaving Sydney! Nigel had hired a big people carrier and had the rest of the party with him.

We drove through the night and stopped off at a roadhouse for breakfast. After we came out, I automatically stood on the tow bar and it went clonk! I did it again – another clonk! It wouldn't have lasted another five miles without ripping the back of the car off. We were so lucky that we spotted it in time and, even more fortunate was that there was a metal fabricator about three miles up the road who could fix it. We were miles from anywhere so the chances of finding someone like that must have been very slim.

We set off when the work had been completed, arriving at the roadhouse where we had arranged to meet Nigel and the other half of our party. But there was no sign of

Talking tactics with Ipswich's Jeremy Doncaster.

them. There had been a fork in the road some way before that and it didn't really matter which way you went, so we thought maybe Nigel had gone the other way to us.

We arrived at the track at tea-time but there was still no sign of him although the promoter, Clive Featherby's son, told us that Nigel had phoned because he'd had an accident. The Aussie promoter reassured us that they were all OK and we headed off to stay in a motel up the road.

We went to the track the following morning and some time after that Nigel and the other lads turned up. It transpired that Roscoe, who drove heavy goods vehicles for a living, was itching to have a go at driving the big people carrier they were in. Within half-an-hour of taking the wheel he had fallen asleep and tipped it into a ditch. The lads reckoned that before it had even ground to a halt, Nigel was out of the sun roof, in the middle of the road, flagging the next car down. It was quite a lucky escape.

Nigel rang the hire company and told them a horse had bolted out of a field and they ended up in a ditch after swerving to miss it! The company accepted his explanation and brought them a replacement.

Roscoe broke his collarbone in only the second meeting of that tour, a challenge match at Albany. I had an agreement to call up Sean Willmott as a replacement in case of injury because he lived in Sydney, but the lads made it absolutely clear they didn't want him in the team, although I've no idea why.

One thing Carlo Biagi had told me was that you should only rest a broken collarbone when it aches like mad so, when Alun asked me what I thought about

Colin and me study the programme while Neil Evitts awaits instructions during a Test against the Danes.

him riding, I told him it was important to keep it moving – in other words, give it a go. He was staying with the editor of a newspaper who had a big swimming pool in his garden and, every day for a week, he swam ever so slowly up and down to keep it moving. He passed himself fit to ride in an individual meeting at Claremont the following Saturday, which was just a week after breaking his collarbone, and finished third with 12 points – a great effort.

There was quite a bit of needle between the Aussies and us, so some of the Test matches got a bit out of hand. When the Aussies are in their own back yard you're not only racing eight riders but 8,000 people plus the referee, the tractor driver and the flag marshals! The Australian riders would zig-zag down the straights and push our lads wide, almost into the fence.

I was worried I'd end up having to visit a coroner's court by the end of the trip but Neil Evitts, who was captain, and Peter Carr told me to leave it to them. They stuck to their word and anything the Aussies could dish out, they could dish out too.

The final Test was at Mildura where Sean, who was riding at reserve, made the mistake of beating Phil Crump on his home circuit. Sean put his head down, backside up and went for it. It was just as though he had mirrors on his bike because if Crumpie went to go round him, Sean moved out, and if Crumpie went inside, that's where Sean went and he never looked round at all. Sean had led him a merry dance but he wasn't being dirty. He wasn't looking because he was only a kid.

When the race finished I spotted Crumpie waving his fist and pointing to Sean, so I warned Nigel there was going to be some aggro. Crumpie roared into the pits and, as Sean parked his bike, he hit it. All the bikes were in a line, so they all fell over.

The Sunbrite Lions has a younger look about it – apart from Pratty and me! Back row, left to right: Gary Havelock, Mark Loram, Andrew Silver, Dean Barker and Simon Cross. Front: Jeremy Doncaster, skipper Kelvin Tatum (on bike) and Marvyn Cox.

What a free-for-all followed. Everyone and their gran was involved. There were fists flying everywhere and toolboxes going up in the air – Nigel even gave me a black eye when he belted me by mistake in the melee. The big stewards came to break it up and eventually it all calmed down.

After the meeting we were invited into the clubhouse by the promoter and, although we weren't sure we should go because we were concerned there would be more trouble, we agreed to call in. Everything was fine until I went into the office to sort out the riders' money. We'd won the Test, and the series, and after his last race Peter Carr pulled a wheelie then did another lap.

> "I was furious and told him to sit down and shut up, but he wanted to borrow £100. I gave him the money and said: Now f*** off and don't come back!"

When I went to collect the wages the promoter told me that Peter had been fined £250 by the referee for ignoring the red lights – even though the race was over and there was no-one else on the track. Peter went to argue his case and ended up in a slanging match with the promoter who insisted he wasn't at liberty to pay him his full wages. Eventually we agreed to write the promoter a letter explaining that we were appealing against the fine and that we would pay it at the next meeting if it went against us. That way Peter got his money and the promoter was in the clear.

The next meeting was at Melbourne Showground where the referee was a mate of Nigel's. He had heard about the fine but agreed it was crazy so he told us to write whatever we wanted on the cheque but to make sure we gave it to him in a sealed envelope. So I wrote out a cheque for 150 cents, made it payable to Mickey Mouse . . . and signed it Donald Duck! I put it in a sealed envelope, handed it to the referee

When Simon Wigg was just focused on speedway, he was a great captain.

and never heard another thing about it.

Simon Wigg didn't go on that tour, but he was Kenny's replacement as captain and he was the perfect choice. He was good with the riders, good with the promotion, good with the fans and good with the media – the ideal captain.

It's fair to say it wasn't always easy keeping some of the riders on an even keel when we were away. They are young and in high spirits. You can remind them they need to get some sleep but can't order them to bed like schoolchildren. All you can do is tell them to behave themselves, but you don't know what is happening once you have gone to bed yourself.

On one occasion we were in Denmark for a big meeting. A lovely buffet was laid on for us the night before the meeting – even the mechanics were invited – and we all had a couple of drinks. It got to about midnight so Colin Pratt and I decided to turn in. As soon as we went to bed, the riders went off nightclubbing and didn't arrive back until about five o'clock the next morning. We had no idea they had gone out until it slipped out over breakfast the next morning. The problem is that you can't treat them like kindergarten kids. Surely they don't need telling that their career isn't going to be enhanced by going out clubbing until five o'clock on the morning of a meeting.

There were even bigger problems in Denmark when we went there for a pair of hastily arranged Test matches in 1988. No costings had been done for the trip so Colin and I had to work it out on the boat, in order that we could charge each BL track a proportion of the outlay. We were all booked in to stay at a holiday camp on the beach which hadn't yet opened. It was pitch black when we arrived and there was nothing in the fridges, so the riders decided to go into town that night.

Colin and I stayed behind because we still hadn't finished working out the costings and went to bed when we had finished. The next morning we realised something was up. The riders were saying things like "I wonder how she is" and "We'd better go and find out" so we sat down with Simon Wigg and demanded to know what had happened.

It transpired that they had all gone to a disco where one of the England riders was trying to chat up a girl. He'd had too much to drink and, when she said something he didn't like, he gave her a back-hander across the face. She cracked her head on the floor when she fell and had been taken to hospital.

As it turned out she was a big speedway fan, too. We had a collection and bought her a big bunch of flowers and a box of chocolates, which Wiggy delivered to her in hospital. He asked her if she wanted to see the rider responsible but she didn't. He told her how sorry all the riders were and, during a conversation with one of the nurses, he discovered that she would be off work for three days and therefore lose three days' pay. So we had another whip round to pay her the money she would be losing.

It was blackmail in a sense because we were paying her to keep quiet, but there was no way we could have this made public. You can imagine what the headlines would have been if she had said anything – 'England Test team in nightclub fracas'.

We hadn't been home long before the BSPA had caught wind of the incident, but by that time it had simmered down. We watered down the story and maintained it had all been blown out of proportion, but it should never have happened.

There was an incident after the 1990 World Team Cup Final at Pardubice in the Czech Republic when one member of the England party thought that televisions could fly! It wasn't the only thing that went out of his hotel window that night, and it was a long way up. But I never, ever got to the bottom of what happened, and I never got to the bottom of who paid for the damage. After all, team riders on tour don't break rank.

Wiggy had been a great captain, but that was when he wanted to ride speedway and wanted to ride for England. He was a big name on the long-track and grass-track scene and missed the final international of 1988 – the rescheduled third Test against Denmark at Oxford, his home track – because it clashed with the Ace of Aces grass track meeting. He could earn big money racing on the continent at weekends and also asked to be left out of England's first Test of 1989 – against the United States

Wiggy (far right) was back in World Team Cup contention here, with (left to right) Marvyn Cox, Jeremy Doncaster, Kelvin Tatum and Chris Morton.

at Cradley – because of his continental commitments. We had very good team sponsors at that time in Coal Products Ltd who also sponsored a number of riders individually – Wiggy included. It was Colin and I who clinched that deal and, as well as being a great boost to the sport, the CPL people were speedway through and through. I think their favourite rider was Wiggy and it was such a crying shame that, after all the help they had given him, he would rather fulfil a grass-track booking than ride for the England team.

It was awful for me and Colin because we could see exactly where Wiggy was coming from. Your career doesn't last forever and you have to run it as a business. I can't remember how many times we heard the mantra that if Wiggy had any pride he would have ridden for England in preference to any other booking. But who in their right mind is going to choose any other option when they can earn 10 times more for riding abroad?

We saw the problem loud and clear, but it didn't help us as England team managers. You can't pick and choose which Tests you want to ride in - if we had allowed him to do that, how do you think it would make his replacement feel, knowing he wasn't really good enough for the team and was only in it because Wiggy didn't want to ride?

We had a chat with Wiggy and, with the backing of the BSPA, we told him that we wouldn't be selecting him for England duty any more. We weren't trying to be smart, we were just trying to do the best job for England. We chose Kelvin Tatum to be his replacement as captain and he did a terrific job.

The one time we did recall Simon was for the World Team Cup Final at Bradford in September 1989. He was such a Bradford favourite and went so well there that he was an obvious choice if we were going to win the title. We asked him first, before announcing it, and he was delighted to accept.

Wiggy went on to score 11 points in that meeting and England ended the afternoon as World Champions for the first time in nine years – but that day will always be remembered for the heat one crash which ended the career of Erik Gundersen and very nearly cost him his life.

Erik's crash well and truly took the gloss of our victory. Speedway made the

Wiggy was good with youngsters like Andrew Silver, who was capped while still a National League rider.

headlines, but for the wrong reasons. The crash happened when Erik pulled a slight locker after going into the first turn at Odsal. He went in very hard and I think the track caught him out. It was very slick and, when he locked up too much, all the other riders went into him. Simon Cross was also taken to hospital while the other two, Sweden's Jimmy Nilsen and Lance King of the United States, were injured as well and none of them took any further part in the meeting.

"He wasn't popular among the other lads. He wasn't a team player. So long as he was getting 18 points, he didn't care about the other riders"

I've seen a lot worse crashes and they have all got up and walked away. It wasn't long before we knew Erik had been badly hurt, although we didn't know it was a life or death situation until later. The medical staff had to put a tracheotomy in to get him breathing and news of that filtered back to the pits.

We went on to win the meeting quite convincingly, with Kelvin Tatum, Wiggy, Jeremy Doncaster and reserve Paul Thorp all scoring double figures. I don't know what the mood was like afterwards, though, because I didn't stay around long enough to find out. Within 10 minutes of the finish Colin and I were on our way to Pinderfields Hospital in Wakefield where Erik had been taken. He rode for Colin at Cradley, so we headed straight off.

I was local and knew where to go, whereas Colin didn't have a clue, so I went along with him. Colin was my partner in crime and one of my best mates in speedway throughout our careers, and I knew he would have done the same for me.

When we went to Pinderfields we met up with Erik's wife, Helle, and we were sat in a small waiting room when the hospital secretary came out to see us. He asked us all who we were and, when we told him, he said: "I think I have to prepare you for the worst – he will be lucky to be alive in the morning."

That's when we knew how serious it was, but Erik was hanging on in there and where there was life there was hope. Also in Erik's favour was that he was in a brand new, state-of-the-art spinal injuries unit about 15 minutes away from where he'd had the crash. If he'd been anywhere else, I don't know if he would have survived.

Despite that initial prognosis, Erik thankfully did pull through and Helle stayed with Diane and I for about four months. She was very positive throughout it all and to start with she would get up, have some breakfast and then not come back until 9.30 at night. But, as he started to improve, she would sometimes come back in the afternoon for a bit. It was like a telephone exchange in the evenings with all the calls from people wanting to know how he was.

Erik used to play hell with me when I went to visit because I made him laugh and, whenever he did that to start with, it hurt. When he got out of intensive care and went into the gymnasium, he worked bloody hard. He pushed and pushed and pushed himself – and that typified the sort of sportsman he was.

Erik's improvement continued and we arranged to go and see Mick Grant and take a look at his racing bikes on the day he was allowed out of hospital for the first time. We stopped off to have a pint and something to eat at a pub but he became tired very quickly and we took him back to hospital without ever getting to Mick's. Even so, it was lovely to see he had improved to the extent that he was allowed out of hospital.

He stayed with us on his first night out of hospital too. He was a good friend and that is what the family of speedway is all about. I know that if it had happened to me in Denmark, he would have done exactly the same for me and Diane.

The following year we whitewashed the Danes 3-0 – the first time we had managed to do that since the series started in 1981. By this time Simon Cross had burst onto the scene and was our top scorer in each of the three meetings. But

We saw a lot of Erik and Helle Gundersen as the Dane recovered from his terrible injuries.

Denmark were without Erik, which cost them 15 points a meeting, and Tommy Knudsen too, so they were going through what we had been going through after we lost Kenny Carter, Wiggy, PC and the like.

One of the problems we encountered on the international scene was making sure that the machines made the minimum weight limit. There were all sorts of tricks to make sure the requirements were met – chains hidden in air filters or strapped underneath the seat and things like that. The FIM inspectors became quite astute, however, and started weighing the bikes at random during the meetings. They were fairly strict but nobody ever got pulled out of a meeting or had their points deducted.

Some of the FIM noise testing and machine examination was a complete joke, though. A case in point is the 1991 World Team Cup Final at Vjoens. The individual World Final had been at Gothenburg two weeks earlier so a lot of the bikes were taken straight to Denmark from Sweden. They had been inspected in Sweden and arrived marked up and stickered to say they had passed – but some of them were failed by the scrutineers at Vojens for being too noisy. They hadn't been used – in fact they hadn't been out of the van!

Jeremy Doncaster couldn't get his bike through the noise test and eventually we stuffed a carburettor rubber right up the exhaust pipe as far as we could get it to see if that did the trick. The procedure is that one official revs the bike while another holds the noise meter. Jeremy's bike was really quiet until the official with the meter asked his colleague to rev it higher. It gave a phut, the rubber flew out and the noise went right up.

We had about five or six bikes in the England squad that simply wouldn't pass the noise test. We were slackening tappets off, putting enormous main jets on, getting it red hot before the inspection, trying everything to get the noise down even though we knew there was nothing wrong with our silencers in the first place.

So, on the morning of the meeting, we went to see Ole Olsen, the Vojens boss, and told him that it needed sorting out. The situation was clear – if he didn't get it sorted, we wouldn't be riding. It wasn't a threat, it was a simple fact. We wouldn't be riding because we didn't have anything to ride, so unless he wanted the whole meeting messing up, he had to do something.

Ole told us to leave it with him and when it came to the final test on race day, they all sailed through even though they were completely untouched since the previous test.

Sam Ermolenko couldn't get his bike through the noise test at Gothenburg the week before and ended up running round to a tent behind the stadium just before the meeting and getting a silencer from one of the bikes that was on display there. They were still doing noise tests on the centre green while there was a band marching up and down shortly before the meeting started! How on earth can you get an accurate reading in a half-full stadium with air horns going off and a band marching up and down? Rules are there for a reason, but surely a piece of common sense should be applied.

> "I wrote out a cheque for 150 cents, made it payable to Mickey Mouse and signed it Donald Duck ...I handed it to the referee and never heard another thing"

There was certainly never a dull moment during my tenancy as England boss but all good things must come to an end and in the winter of 1993 Colin and I made way for James Easter and John Louis to take over. I talked to Colin about it and told him I felt we were getting stale. We'd given it our best shot and we told the BSPA it was time for someone else to have a go.

Pratty and I were back in charge of the England team again by Christmas 2000, although it didn't take us long to realise we had been a bit hasty in resuming the job. In fact the 2001 season hadn't even started when we handed in our notice.

We agreed to do it again because we wanted to give England a lift but, in the cold light of day when we'd had time to think about it, it didn't seem like the right move. I was working full-time for Hull, which was taking up more and more of my time, and we were both getting older. We'd had a great stint in charge of England before but we were both running tracks and we weren't really being fair to ourselves by agreeing to do it all over again. It's not that the England job is labour intensive, it's just that it's a distraction from your day job. You start thinking: 'Have I got those tickets booked? Is that van organised? Is the paperwork sorted?' – lots of little things. I phoned Colin to tell him I'd begun to think we'd been too hasty and he agreed we had. But we had been hasty because we were passionate about speedway and wanted to do what we thought was best. England didn't have any international fixtures for some time so we contacted the BSPA and told them we wanted to step down, although it wasn't a decision we took lightly. Neil Middleditch took over and he's younger than us for a start and he's a team manager – I was too, but all through my career since I stopped riding I've held a promoter's licence so I have run my own tracks on other folks' behalf.

Neil has more time on his hands – and I mean that in a nice way. He doesn't have to run Poole seven days a week like Colin does at Coventry and I did at Hull. Neil has been a great choice as England (sorry, Great Britain) manager and I'm pleased to see him doing a good job. He's been desperately unlucky with injuries and he's also had to cope with the fact that we just don't seem to have the quality there any more. But the Danes went through a bad spell until they regained the World Cup in 2006 and the Swedes haven't got many top class riders any more, so it happens to everyone. Hopefully Neil will keep at it and get his reward – he will certainly deserve it, too.

But even someone as enthusiastic as Middlo must think about throwing in the towel sometimes when he's faced with injury problems and a lack of out-and-out star quality riders to choose from.

⑲
HIYA DUDE

OVER the 1983-84 close season I had a telephone call from Derek Pugh, the promoter and owner at Cradley Heath, who wanted me to become his new speedway manager. I was chuffed to be asked, but I was trying to build up the electro-plating business with Steve Finch so I had to turn it down. I suggested, instead, that he contacted Colin Pratt who'd had a number of successful years at Rye House. I'm pleased to say that he took my advice and Colin did a very good job with the Heathens, right up until their closure in 1996.

Not long afterwards, though, I had a call from Maurice Ducker. I knew him because he was Shawn Moran's sponsor and he used to come to the shop to buy spares from him. He phoned one Sunday night, only this time it wasn't to order any parts – he wanted to tell me that he had done a deal with Ray Glover to buy Sheffield Speedway.

He had a meeting with the BSPA the following morning and he'd been informed that he needed a 'name' to act as an advisor. Any new promoter who comes in now has to have somebody with some experience to act as an overseer and, when he asked me if I would go with him the following day, I agreed straight away.

We agreed that we would thrash out a deal for me to work for him later on – the important thing was for me to be with him when he met the BSPA. Sheffield was close enough to home for me to be able to combine working there as speedway manager with the electro-plating business, so I was happy to be involved. It was the start of five happy years.

Officially it was a part-time position, although once again it managed to take over my life. I took regular phone calls while I was at work and I was always on the phone during the evening. I soon set to work building a team and two of my first signings were Les and Neil Collins. They had ridden for Leicester the previous year, but were left without a track when Blackbird Road was sold for housing redevelopment over the winter. Leicester had done a deal to sell them both to Exeter – only they didn't know about it! When they found out they made it clear they weren't going to ride for the Falcons and that's where I stepped in.

The deal was that the transfer fee had to be paid in full before they turned a wheel. We did that, although we were then hit with a demand for the proportion of the fee each of the Collins brothers were entitled to, as they hadn't asked for a move. We argued that it was part of the price and took in to the Control Board but they ruled against us.

I also brought in Jan O. Pedersen on loan from Cradley. He had joined the Heathens a year earlier but the points limit meant they couldn't fit him in for 1984, so Colin rang me and asked if I wanted him. Jan O. was just starting out in what turned out to be a very successful career and he soon became a favourite at Sheffield.

Throughout my five years at Owlerton, though, the biggest favourites on the terraces were the Moran brothers. Peter Collins, who I had worked with at Belle Vue and with England, had worked and worked to be an outstanding rider – but Kelly and Shawn Moran were two of the most naturally talented racers I've ever seen. They had talent like you wouldn't believe. Unfortunately, they didn't have the dedication to match their talent, but is that right or wrong?

Both of them could have been World Champion if they had applied their talent the right way, and indeed Shawn did win the World Longtrack Championship, but you only live once and, if that's the way they wanted to do it, who am I to judge them? Both of them enjoyed a drink, especially Kelly. If there were 24 hours in a day, they wanted to make sure they enjoyed 23-and-a-half of them.

The averages and the stats books will tell you that Shawn was the better of the two but there's no doubt that when Kelly had his head screwed on the right way, he was phenomenal. He was a better natural talent than Shawn, in my opinion, but he was also a lot sillier. Shawn was the better points scorer throughout his career because he took his speedway more seriously than Kelly.

Both the Morans were real party animals, especially Kelly, and I've had to keep the pair of them apart to stop them fighting each other on more than one occasion. Trouble was, whenever I did that, they would join forces and gang up on me!

Their powers of recovery after a drinking session were amazing, though. If I knocked back what they used to, it would take me about three days to recover, but both of them would just sleep it off and be right as rain the next morning.

The night before the 1986 World Pairs Final in Pocking, Germany, we heard a commotion outside the hotel and found one of the American mechanics climbing the outdoor steps with a clearly sozzled Kelly over his shoulder. He carried him up to his hotel room and chucked him onto his bed. The next morning when I went to see him, he was in exactly the same position on the bed – I thought he was dead! But he got himself showered and changed and we made our way to the track.

All the riders and officials were assembled in the pits as top FIM delegate Gunther Sorber gave his pre-meeting briefing. When Gunther asked if there were any questions Kelly, who was sat there cross-legged on the ground, said: "Yeah, where are the prostitutes?" It made everyone laugh, even Gunther.

I was sure that Kelly's partying the night before would have an effect on his racing but he had an outstanding meeting and he and Sam Ermolenko only missed out on the title after a run-off with Denmark.

Kelly lived next door to an old dear and between the two properties was a privet hedge. One night he got drunk after a meeting at Ipswich and when the lad who

Showing new Sheffield boss Maurice Ducker the ropes in 1984.

drove him home pulled up outside his house, he picked him up and hung him over the hedge like a sack of spuds. The old lady, who thought he was great, saw him there the next morning and covered him up with a blanket to stop him getting cold!

One of the craziest things he did after a few beers was to ask the Queen of Denmark for a dance. We were on our way home from a meeting in Denmark and she was on the same boat. Kelly had knocked back a few drinks and decided it would be a good idea to ask her for a dance. She was sat up on a platform in the ballroom, flanked by her bodyguards, but that didn't deter Kelly. As he approached her, the two big, burly bouncers asked him what he wanted. He told them he wanted to know if the Queen would like a dance. Of course, she declined, but she was very polite and thanked him very much for asking!

After a few more beers that night, the fun and games started. All the Yanks were in one cabin and decided to have a water fight. It started out as just a flick of water here and there, then cups and jugs of water were used and eventually the shower hose. From there it spread into the corridor where someone let off one of the fire extinguishers. And it didn't even stop there . . . someone went to the other end of the corridor, took the fire hose out of its cupboard and turned that on.

The next morning there was an army of cleaners all down the corridor armed with buckets, mops and sponges clearing up the mess. I had long gone to bed while the fun and games were going on, but announcement went out as we were having breakfast the following morning for the occupants of the cabin to report to the purser's office. I went to see what the fuss was about and the purser told me there had been quite a lot of damage done to Kelly's cabin and, if it wasn't paid for, the

Typically spectacular stuff from Shawn Moran, holding off Coventry's Tommy Knudsen.

occupants would be arrested on our arrival at Harwich.

He offered to show me the damage so I went with him to the cabin. We stepped over the lip under the door and the room was ankle deep in water. There were clothes swimming about in it, the mattresses were soaked through and the shower hose was off its hook. The purser was really laid-back, though – he had seen far worse damage caused by football hooligans, and said the cost to put it right would be £360.

I went back to see Kelly and explained the situation. Everyone involved had a whip round and the bill was paid.

By and large I didn't ever have a problem with either of the Morans, although I did threaten to send Kelly back to America once. We'd had a very wet summer and there had been a string of rain-offs, which forced us to run a number of double-headers at Sheffield. It was yet another wet night at Owlerton and we were desperate to get the meeting on but Kelly was in the visitors' pits telling everyone it should be called off.

Throughout my career as a promoter I never asked anyone to ride in conditions I wouldn't have ridden in myself, so I was furious. I told Kelly that if he didn't want to ride, that was up to him, but he shouldn't be roping in everyone else to do the same. I told him I'd had enough and ordered him to come to my office first thing next morning. "Your air ticket home will be waiting for you and you can f*** off back to America," I told him. Sure enough, next morning there was a knock on my office door. "Hiya dude!" beamed Kelly as I let him in. I told him we needed a serious talk and I really laid the law down. I hadn't organised any air tickets home, of course, but I warned him there would be no second chances.

One of the young lads coming through was Sean Wilson. He was doing well on the grass and practised hard at Owlerton so, on his 16th birthday, Maurice and I drove over to his house in York and gave him a contract to sign. The following Thursday he went into our second half junior team. We all had to have a four-man junior team at that time and Sean played a major part in us winning the junior league Knockout Cup Final against King's Lynn.

He was a little tiger, just as he was throughout his career. In the early days he used to fall off a lot, so Maurice and I used to joke that he'd be fine so long as he'd fallen on his head! He was good on the big tracks but he struggled around the tight Wolverhampton track in one of

Kelly Moran . . . the morning after the night before!

his early away meetings for the young, second-half side. He just couldn't turn at the first bend and, after starting from the inside gate, he sent the other three sprawling. When the yellow exclusion light came on he was horrified. "I'm the only one left racing," he protested. I explained that the other three blokes lying on the track were there because of him, but he still maintained he should be allowed to race on because he didn't do it deliberately.

It was quite amusing trying to explain what was obvious to me to a young, keen 16-year-old. Sean went through a daft stage when he was young and thought he couldn't get hurt, but on the whole he was a credit to speedway.

All in all we had a pretty exciting team for much of my time at Sheffield. Peter Carr was another crowd-pleaser and he was nicknamed the B52 because he used to dive underneath and pass right on the white line going into the first turn

I had five seasons at Sheffield in total and during that time we finished fifth, second, fourth twice on the trot and sixth in the British League, so we didn't do too badly. Sheffield was a club about to fold when Maurice bought it, so it was quite a turn-around.

It wasn't an easy stadium to work in because stock car racing also took place on the circuit, there was a dog track and, the first year I was there, they introduced rugby league too. That meant it restricted the times we could work on the track so it was a bit of a balancing act. But Maurice was a great boss to work for and gave me full authority to do anything I wanted.

"When Gunther asked if there were any questions, Kelly said: Yeah, where are the prostitutes? It made everyone laugh"

Neil Collins, Shawn Moran and the tigerish Sean Wilson – all genuine racers.

I was lucky enough to have some fantastic staff at Owlerton, and among them was my secretary, Betty Wilson, grandmother of Ben Wilson who races for the Tigers at the moment. Unfortunately Betty didn't know much about football as I discovered one Friday when Colin Pratt phoned over his Cradley team to appear in the following Thursday's programme. I was out on the track at the time but when I called into the office before I went home at the end of the day I couldn't believe my eyes when I saw the pad on which Betty had written down the names she was given.

Colin had decided to play a trick and, according to what he had told Betty, Glenn Hoddle, Chris Waddle and Bryan Robson were all going to be pulling on a Heathens racejacket the following week! I couldn't believe it, and neither could Betty because she had already rung the Sheffield Star newspaper and the local radio station with the teams! Fortunately, we managed to get the correct line-ups and rang them through in time, but Betty vowed she would get revenge.

As you can imagine there was a bit of banter flying around the following week when Pratty came into the office before the match. He was just about to go when he noticed his name was printed in the programme as Colin C Pratt. "What does the C stand for?" he asked Betty. Well, she told him straight and I'll leave you to work out which C word she meant! "That word fits you like a glove," she told him.

Another fantastic member of staff I had at Sheffield was the track curator, Graham Trollope. He hadn't long started when I went to Owlerton but we very quickly struck up a strong friendship which is still going today. He is very well regarded in speedway when it comes to track preparation and, wherever I have worked over the years, I have always asked Graham to come with me. In fact, if I had a track today I'd ask him to be involved.

He is the best in speedway at track watering – he can judge the weather, the temperature and how much water to put down. People don't realise the amount of work that goes into track preparation and I have a lot of respect for him. I must have travelled thousands of miles to meetings all over the country with Graham, and he was an absolutely fantastic driver. If he ever decided to get out of speedway the ideal job for him would be a chauffeur! He's never late, he never gets frustrated and he's always absolutely first class behind the wheel.

Maurice Ducker, meanwhile, used to drive Diane mad, because I'd call in to see him at about 5.30 or six o'clock after work and sometimes it would be midnight before I got home. We'd have a coffee, then a fag, then another coffee, then another fag. So it went on and all the time we'd be talking, talking, talking – often about rubbish! It was because he was tied up all day long with his haulage business and too busy to keep up with what was going on in speedway and this was his only opportunity. I enjoyed his company but Diane used to say: "Why don't you just go and live there?"

When Steve Finch and I sold the business in Halifax I went full-time at Sheffield and I was there every day. I was pleased to do that because I loved working in speedway but at the end of 1988 Sheffield closed.

The track's closure came as a surprise to everyone in speedway, except me. The stadium owner lived in the Isle of Man and, about a month before the start of the 1989 season, he decided he wanted more money from us. He doubled the car park charges, took back the reserved seats we'd had set aside in the grandstand so that the stadium could sell them themselves, and put up our rent by £350 a week. On top of that, he told us we had to build new pits and finance them ourselves, even though our lease clearly stated that our rent was for the stadium and all the amenities required to stage speedway.

Another Sheffield crowd-pleaser, Peter Carr, leading Bradford's Sean Willmott.

Brother Nigel's son, Darren, and me making fools of ourselves at the Sheffield fancy dress ball.

I'm convinced that the stadium owner assumed that Maurice Ducker would simply dig his hand deeper into his pocket, both because he was chairman of the BSPA at the time and also because it was February, and the start of the season was looming.

For about five or six days letters were going back and forth from our office to the stadium office – and they were only next door to each other! All the time we were going nowhere and, because the start of the season was getting ever closer, I said to Maurice that, if we weren't going to run, we really ought to be fair to our riders and let them know. We'd done the books for the year before and the club had lost £28,000 so we had to make a decision.

Maurice and I discussed the situation and came to the conclusion we wouldn't run. We sent a letter to the owner saying that, with immediate effect, the speedway promotion had ceased at Owlerton Stadium. Maurice owned a haulage business and, within 24 hours, had sent along two big wagons to take away everything belonging to us. In a way I talked myself out of having a job because I could have easily tried to persuade Maurice that we'd sort out our differences with the owner. But when you are running a business for someone and spending their money, you have to be answerable to the decisions you have made.

The rugby league club had moved to the Don Valley Stadium by the time we had gone and, by a quirk of coincidence, there was a problem with the renewal of the stadium's dog racing licence. So, for about three months of a beautifully hot summer, absolutely nothing went on in that stadium. They must have lost an absolute fortune – maybe poetic justice, eh?

20
LIGHT YEARS AHEAD

SPEEDWAY has been my life since I was 16, so the small matter of the track where I worked closing down wasn't going to keep me away from the sport.

I've always been eager to chip in wherever I can if it's for the good of speedway because I'm passionate about it. In fact back in 1985 I had a short spell helping out Scunthorpe in the National League. Steve Finch was riding for them at the time and it was fairly local so I used to go along to Ashby Ville on a Monday night as a spectator.

It was a bonny little place that was run on enthusiasm alone. Ted Hornsby, the promoter, ran a pub and, because crowds were a bit on the lean side, I'm sure he used to empty the one-armed bandits there to pay the riders some nights. Ted had asked me if I'd help out and I was happy to oblige, although the financial situation eventually took its toll in May 1985 and the track closed, by which time Tony Nicholls was the promoter.

When Scunthorpe closed Steve and Billy Burton both went up to Edinburgh to ride . . . so guess who ended up helping out on a Friday night? That's right, with the Monarchs! It started when I'd gone along to watch Steve ride for his new team at Long Eaton and they were losing after about eight heats. Tony Franchetti was the Edinburgh manager as well as promoter and I pointed out to him that, if he got his team sorted out, he could win.

He threw his programme at me and told me to manage the team for the rest of the night if I thought I could do a better job. I did, and we won! After that Tony asked me if I'd help out on a Friday night and I was happy to oblige. We still had the business in Halifax but I just travelled up with Steve – Maurice Ducker was happy enough for me to help out at Powderhall so long as it didn't interfere with my commitments with Sheffield.

Tony Franchitti was one of the most extrovert people I've ever met. When we were in the bar he would often hand over a £50 note to get a round of drinks in and tell you to keep the change. Billy Burton soon cottoned on to what Tony was like and would regularly ask him for the money to go to the bar with so that he could keep what was left over. He was unbelievably generous and I'm sure the riders would have bled him for millions given the chance.

On one occasion he came to stay with us and something went wrong with his car.

Trials riding is a great way to keep fit.

It was a Mercedes and the nearest dealership was over in Huddersfield. I was working so I couldn't take him over there but it was the school holidays so Richie, my son, went with him to show him where to go. When they came back Tony gave him £20 for helping out – not a bad little earner for a 14-year-old!

Having done my bit for Scunthorpe and Edinburgh, I was only too pleased to lend a hand when Bradford came calling the season after Sheffield closed down. Being just down the road, I was a regular visitor to Odsal and I was asked to help out when the season was a couple of months old. My role was team manager so it was very much just a Saturday night job, although it didn't last that long.

Allan and Bobby Ham had brought me in to run the team for them on race nights although, if I'm honest, it did feel as though they were looking over my shoulder for much of the time. If I wanted to make a tactical decision, such as bringing in a tac sub, they always appeared eager to let me know what they thought should be done. My understanding was that the team manager was appointed to make decisions like that. But that shouldn't detract from what was an enjoyable spell working with an exciting team at Bradford.

My spell at Odsal came to an end after I was offered a full-time job working for former road racing star Mick Grant, who was manager of the Heron Suzuki British Superbike Championship team.

I'd been friends with Mick right from leaving school and we're still great pals today. He lived in Middlestown, about half-a-mile from where I lived, and started road racing while I was riding for Middlesbrough. He had a rented garage in the village where he worked on his bike and one day I called in to see him. I joked that I didn't know how he could work in somewhere so small and pokey, and invited him to see where I prepared my bikes. "It's like an operating theatre," I told him, so he came to have a look and we have been friends ever since. I used to go and watch him race if I wasn't riding myself and he came to watch me sometimes too.

It was Mick who got me into trials riding, which is something we both still enjoy today. Whenever I used to pop over and see him he always seemed to have a trials bike he was working on and he told me I should give it a go. I said I didn't have the time, but he told me I should make time. So, when I stopped going to Australia to ride over the winter, I used to quite often buy a trials bike which I rode from November until February and then sold it so I could concentrate on speedway again.

When I started competing regularly in pre-65 trials, Mick was a great help in getting my first bike sorted out. He'd been messing about with trials bikes for 20-odd years and I didn't have a clue, so I was very grateful for his help. Mick would tell me where he was riding at a weekend and I'd tag along and have a go myself. I'd come home absolutely knackered – and then I'd find out I'd been competing in a British Championship round which was way above the standard I should have been riding in. But it did me good because I didn't know any better and I thought all trials were that tough.

The job working for him came about after I called in at his workshop one day and he was out. His mechanic was cleaning the bikes and I wasn't doing anything so I helped him. When Mick came back he couldn't believe how much work had been done, so he rang to ask if I wanted to come on board. He needed an extra pair of hands because there were quite a few bikes to look after, so he contacted Suzuki to get the all-clear to employ me. I worked on the chassis side, setting chassis, fitting gear ratios and things like that – a jack of all trades really. The team went all over the country and we went across to the Isle of Man and to the Ulster Grand Prix too.

The road racing scene was light years ahead of what speedway ever will be and the money in the paddock was phenomenal. The teams had 40 or 50 foot long artics with living quarters upstairs – they were in the multi-millionaire league. I used to say to the speedway promoters it would do them good to go along to a road race meeting one Sunday and take a look. A large proportion of the riders would be paying to ride as well. Speedway must be the only form of motorcycle sport where it's the other way round and the riders are paid to compete. Maybe that's part of the problem, I don't know.

I thoroughly enjoyed working for Mick and it was no problem combining it with my role as England manager. If there were any date clashes, I told Mick I had to be with the England team and it was no big deal.

"He would often hand over a £50 note. He was unbelievably generous and I'm sure the riders would have bled him for millions given the chance"

㉑
A PAIR OF LLAMAS

ALL the time I worked for Mick Grant's superbike team I was still joint manager of the England team with Colin Pratt and, when the offer of a full-time return to speedway came at the start of 1991, I couldn't refuse.

Long Eaton had won the National League (second division) in 1984 but then suffered a dramatic change in fortunes. They finished 18th out of 19 the following year and ended up either bottom or next to bottom in each of the next four seasons, which was when I was asked to become team manager and co-promoter.

The consortium in charge had lost a lot of money in 1989 and the Invaders looked like going under until Kidderminster businessman Tony Mole came to the rescue. Tony has the deserved reputation of being the saviour of British speedway after buying a string of clubs when they were on the verge of folding. Oxford was the most notable example because there is no doubt they would never have opened again had he not rescued them . . . and it was also his money and enthusiasm which prevented Long Eaton going to the wall at the time.

Tony rang me out of the blue that February and explained he was on the verge of a deal to buy Long Eaton. He was confident it would all go through and asked me if I fancied working for him at Station Road. He asked me to give him an answer in two or three days but I told him he had no need to wait – I agreed there and then. He suggested that I go to have a look at the stadium to be sure but again there was no need. I'd been going to Long Eaton since the 60s – it was a dump then and it was still a dump but it was a terrific race track and the people were lovely.

The previous consortium was headed by Steve Yorke and I made it clear that he should still be involved. While he was running the track he had an agreement with a local contractor who owned two big motorway scrapers. The deal was that the contractor parked his vehicles at the stadium when he wasn't using them and, in return, Steve could use them to work on the track. It was an arrangement which worked well and I was keen to see it continue. In addition Steve knew where the lights, water and power were – he knew everything about the stadium and, fortunately, he was delighted to remain on board.

I asked Tony which riders we had on the books and it didn't take long for him to go through the list because Gary O'Hare was the only name on it! I applied for my promoters' licence back and set to work finding another six to join him.

Putting a team together with less than a month before the start of the season wasn't as difficult as it seemed. The riders who were without a track at the time were looking for work so they were eager to come on board. It was easy to strike a deal too, because the truth of the situation was that the reason Long Eaton almost closed was because of its financial situation which explained why it couldn't pay top whack money. If a rider I spoke to said he was hoping for more money, I could just point out that the season was about to start and he didn't have a job so he could either accept my offer or stay out of work. I always had the reputation as a tight, skinflint Yorkshireman anyway, because I was dealing with other people's money. In this case it was Tony's and he was good to work for because he always gave me a free hand with all the transfer dealings and contract negotiations.

I felt it was important to be based at the track during the week so Tony put two portable buildings up on the banking and I travelled there and back every day, five days a week – a round trip of 148 miles. If we were riding somewhere down south for an away meeting, I would go to work first and then head off from there. I believed it was important for supporters to have a local telephone number to ring if they wanted any information and for someone to be at the track if they wanted to call in. Looking back, though, I don't think it made any difference.

I had the surprise of my life when I arrived at the track one day during my first season and found two camels outside my office. They were tethered up and happily grazing away at the grass on the banking – I thought it must have been a cheaper way to cut the grass! I walked though the gate on the first and second bends into the car park behind and there were a pair of llamas! It turned out that there was a circus at the stadium once a year but nobody had thought to tell us.

I had another surprise when I turned up in the rain one day. I always drove right up to the portable building I used as my office and parked my car outside, at the top of the banking. I drove a BMW Five Series at the time and it was pouring with rain when I arrived. I decided to make a dash for the door to try and get in without getting soaked through but, in the rush, I forgot to put the handbrake on. I looked round and saw my car disappear down the

Two wholehearted triers, Neil Collins and Martin Dixon.

banking. It went across the perimeter path, crashed through the concrete fence, rolled across the dog track and came to rest in the banking behind the speedway track. Rob Fortune, who ran the junior team, worked at a BMW dealership and, when he had finished laughing, helped me get it tidied up enough to drive home.

Despite doing £1,000 worth of damage to my car there, I found Long Eaton a smashing place to work and I had four very happy years there. Our sixth place finish in my first year at Station Road represented by far and away the Invaders' best season since winning the title in 1984 and, although we were ninth the next year, we ended up second in both 1993 and 1994.

Once again – and not for the last time either – I managed to turn around a team that had been struggling. I made a habit of it but I couldn't tell you what the secret was. What I do know, though, is that it's vitally import to know and understand people. I'd ridden for years so I knew all about that side of it, and I always made sure I was open and honest with everyone. I always made sure my riders felt part of a team as well, rather than being one of seven individuals who turned up every week.

One of the mainstays throughout my spell at Station Road was Jan Staechmann who dropped down from the British League with Wolverhampton to join us in 1991 and was our captain. He was a real professional - his bikes and his van were always immaculate and he was a big points scorer throughout his time at Long Eaton. In fact he started to make his mark on the international stage too and reached the last-ever one-off World Final at Vojens in 1994 which was a fantastic achievement for a National League rider.

Unfortunately, like a lot of overseas riders who come to ride over here, the better he got, the more he seemed to think he was bigger than the club. His World Championship ambitions became greater than his Long Eaton ambitions. For a while there was a bit of aggro between us because he would go back to Denmark and then phone to say he had been injured and wouldn't be fit for our next meeting. This happened more than once and the frequency was getting a bit much for my liking.

The rules were that I couldn't use rider replacement or a guest facility without a doctor's certificate but Jan wasn't happy when I asked for one because he thought I didn't believe him. In truth I didn't most of the time, but that was irrelevant because all I was doing was following the rules.

I felt a bit bad about it, because I liked Jan and I still do. The professionalism he showed rubbed off on the rest of the team and as he improved, so too did Long Eaton.

Although Jan was captain throughout his time at Long Eaton, another rider who had a voice worth listening to was Martin Dixon, who joined us in 1992. Dicko is a legend, there's no doubt about it. He was so laid back off the track but, when he was riding, his heart was 120 percent in speedway. There were no half measures with Dicko!

Carl Blackbird was another of those last minute signings who went on to serve me so well. I did a deal with John Campbell at Edinburgh to sign him and I also had his two brothers, Mark and Paul, at Station Road. When all three of them were together, their dad often had to step in as peace-maker. He had a more difficult job than Dr Kissinger! Carl was fairly placid but Mark was quite fiery and Paul was just starting off. It was worth being in the pits some nights just to witness the rows while their old man tried to keep all three of them happy!

Carl was a welder and eventually found he was earning far more money at that than he was at speedway. Eventually, during the 1993 season – the year of eight-man, 18-heat races in the National League – he decided to give up speedway and concentrate on his business. He was a very good rider, had a decent average and it was a shame to see him go, but I could understand his reasons.

He was difficult to replace because he loved the Long Eaton track and he could ride the white line on the pit turn better than anyone I've ever seen. So many times when we looked like having a 5-1 against us, Carl would rush into that pit turn and when he came out he would be in front.

Carl was a former England international who had been a £25,000 investment by Belle Vue some years earlier. Another former Aces and England rider I brought to Long Eaton was Neil Collins, who had ridden for me at Sheffield. Neil was a great rider but was always looking at ways of saving a few quid – not that there was anything wrong with that. He brought two bikes to every meeting, but one of them always stayed in his van because he didn't want to get his tyres mucky and he always insisted that he wouldn't need it anyway. I used to joke with him that he only brought his spare bike with him so that it could have a look out of his van window at the scenery. It used to annoy me a bit, though, because on the occasions when he did need his spare bike, it was stone cold in his van and he'd have to borrow one anyway!

Richard Hellsen was in his 40s when I tempted him out of retirement but he was a great asset too. He was a good old pro and had more brains in his head than ten riders put together. He was great with engines and if anyone asked his advice in the pits he was more than happy to help but, if nobody asked, he wouldn't interfere.

It wasn't just the riders I liked – the fans at Long Eaton were fantastic too. If we lost at home after a last heat decider they wouldn't whinge or complain – they would be delighted they had seen a good meeting. But one of the big problems there was that the track was used for stock car racing. In 1994, my final year there, there were more stock car meetings than speedway meetings and that played havoc with the track.

Over Easter they had four stock car meetings in as many days, and during that time there was also caravan racing and a big steel ramp on the back straight to make it more exciting, so you can imagine the carnage on the track after that.

Wherever I was involved, I always wanted to have the best possible track because fans could put up with a lot of things if the racing was good. But I used to cringe when I got to Station Road sometimes and found it in a hell of a state. We would find propshafts, brake callipers, discs, all sorts – it was like a scrapyard sometimes. The pillars for the stock car fence, which was behind the speedway fence, were old railway lines set in concrete and occasionally they would be bent over 45 degrees where a car had crashed into them. There was no way we could put our fence up in front of them if they were like that so we'd have a hell of a job to straighten them out.

The stadium was owned by Northern Promotions who leased it to Keith Barber, the stock car promoter, and we in turned leased it from him. Keith and I didn't get on well. I was a fanatic who wanted a good track, while he didn't mind if the track was bumpy and rutted because it didn't matter to the stock car lads. Sometimes we almost came to blows and, if it hadn't been for Steve and the motorway blade, I don't know what we would have done. He had a full-time job at a garden centre but he worked so hard on the track, it was unbelievable.

I brought in Graham Trollope and we used to go over on a Wednesday to finish the track off, by which time Steve had got it back after the stock cars had been on it. I fell out with Keith Barber after I made a comment in my programme notes which was something like: 'The RAF had refused to bomb the site because they felt it was derelict enough.' It was a light-hearted way of saying we made the best of what we'd got, but he took umbrage at it.

Round the outside of the speedway track was the greyhound circuit and there was a six-foot wide area of no man's land in between in the middle of the bends which used to get piled up with shale. One day Keith decided he wanted it clearing out so he took a big JCB to it, scooped all the shale up and dumped it on the speedway track. It would have been nice to know he was going to do it, but it wasn't a problem because Steve just took the motorway blade to it and flattened it out.

What was a problem, however, was that Keith accidentally ripped all the wiring out in the process and we didn't find out until the next racenight. We realised something was amiss when one of my riders was excluded for failing to beat the two-minute time allowance. We had a claxon in the pits and we certainly didn't hear it. I rang the referee who was adamant he had sounded the two-minute warning. He put it on again and, when we couldn't hear it, we realised what had happened.

I eventually left Long Eaton at the end of 1994 because I just couldn't do it any more. I was 50-years-old, I was travelling the best part of 150 miles two days a week by then and working every hour God sent on the track. I genuinely didn't know what to expect when I arrived at the track on a Wednesday after the stock cars had been on it. I'd told Keith Barber until I was blue in the face how important track conditions were for speedway but, even after four years, we weren't making any progress. I can't put into words the feeling inside me as I set off from home wondering what I would find because it was desperately hard work trying to get the track right after the stock cars had been on it.

That was when I phoned Tony Mole and told him I'd had enough. He made it clear that he didn't want me to leave, but I gave him 28 days' notice although he paid me until Christmas which was a very nice gesture. I told him he only needed to pick up the phone if he needed any help and he rang me about five or six times that winter. Some of the calls were to ask my opinion on the candidates who had applied for my old job and by far and away the best of the bunch was Graham Drury, which is how come he took my place. Graham, even to this day, still works for Tony at Workington.

㉒
A FEW STOREYS UP

AFTER leaving Long Eaton I wasn't involved in speedway again in an official capacity until I went to Hull in 1997, although I did have another stint at my old stamping ground at Cleveland Park.

The Boro Bears had lost heavily at home to Eastbourne fairly early on in the season and promoter Malcolm Wright brought me in to take a look at where they were going wrong and to offer some recommendations. I'd met Malcolm at promoters' meetings although I didn't know him particularly well at the time, so it was quite a surprise when he phoned. He explained that he'd got a reasonably good team but they just weren't getting the results they should have been. Middlesbrough was close to my heart because it was where I had started, so I was delighted to accept his invitation.

My role as team consultant began with a home match against Hull in the KO Cup and after the meeting Malcolm asked me what I thought. I told him that, as far as I could see, there were too many chiefs and just seven Indians on bikes. Too many people had a little job that they had turned into their own big job. I just stood in the pits during the meeting watching, and I noticed that they had joint team managers Dave Muxlow and Andy Wright both running around after the riders. Not only that, but Ken Knott, the co-promoter, was doing the same, so they had three people all telling the riders different things.

So before the start of the next home meeting, which was against Coventry in the Premier League, I went into the dressing room and told the riders that from then on, I was the boss. They were to take no notice of anyone else and, if there were any problems, I was the man to see. I asked them if they'd had any problems with being paid because that's often the cause of a team under-performing. It turned out that there were no problems on that front and I wasn't surprised because Malcolm has always been bulletproof when it comes to paying.

But the riders did say they weren't happy with the track – and that didn't surprise me either because I thought it was all wrong too. Tony Swales looked after it and he was fed up of being given different instructions from different people, so I told the riders that Tony would continue to do the track but he would do it how I instructed him to. Tony was sick of trying to please everyone but ending up pleasing no-one and, as a result, he

"We were sick of costs going up and the standard of racing going down as the gap between the haves and the have-nots grew ever greater"

Good mate Mick Grant and I getting exasperated at the missed opportunity with the petrol engine.

was ready to quit. I told him to make the track nice and slick coming in and then put some dirt on from midway round the corner – from halfway out to the fence. That way it would suit everyone. Scott Robson, Shane Parker and Toni Svab all liked riding at the bottom of the fence so there would be dirt there for them while David Walsh, who liked it slick and used to ride on the inside, had it his way too.

From then on we had an absolutely terrific run. It was the first year of amalgamation between the British League and National League and, although we were 16th in the final table, the performances were much better.

We had some good laughs that season and one of them came when Peterborough were the visitors in July. I always used to stop off at a Little Chef on the way for something to eat and, while I was in there on my way to this particular match, who should walk in but the majority of the Peterborough team with their promoter, Peter Oakes. Amazingly they didn't spot me so I sat there listening to their team-talk.

They were discussing how the track would ride, who would be the main dangermen, all sorts of things like that. I managed to sneak out without them seeing me, so Peter was very confused and surprised when he got to the stadium and I asked him how his meal was at the Little Chef and told him how much I had enjoyed listening to his team-talk!

That year turned out to be the last ever at Cleveland Park after the college next door bought the stadium, just to knock it down and build on the land. The sad thing was that the biggest crowd of the season was at the last ever meeting – you've no friends when you're alive but everyone turns up for your funeral. If all those people had turned up every week and signed a petition, maybe the stadium wouldn't have been sold.

With Cleveland Park shut, I wasn't involved in speedway again until I went to Hull for the first of my three spells at New Craven Park in 1998 - but by then I had already started a project I thought could revolutionise speedway. In fact, I still think it could have done the sport an enormous amount of good, but only if it received full backing from the promoters.

The project, which I instigated and headed along with my old mate Mick Grant who worked for Honda Great Britain at the time, was the development of a petrol-engined speedway bike. Mick had been a works Honda rider and knew all the right people so I think it's fair to say that without him, the project would have gone nowhere. Using his influence, we contacted Honda and they threw their weight behind it right from the start. We believed that, by getting Honda interested, it would open up enormous possibilities. Honda are a bit like Coca-Cola in that their brand is known all over the world so anyone who wants to be associated with them has a bit of clout. It would also open up all sorts of possibilities for the oil companies such as BP, Shell and Esso to get involved. Speedway bikes run on methanol which you can't buy at your local garage, but the engine we were using ran on the same unleaded petrol you put in your car. The engines were several hundred pounds cheaper than a Jawa or a GM and unleaded petrol was half the price of methanol, so we genuinely believed that we could do speedway a favour the world over.

We were sick of the costs going up and the standard of the racing going down as the gap between the haves and the have-nots grew ever greater. This was an ideal way to address it.

Had the concept been taken up, every rider in the Premier League – which became the second tier of British speedway following the creation of the Elite League in 1998 – would have one engine which would be factory-sealed. Every rider would have a passport with a serial number on it for their engine. If a seal came off while he was washing it or because he had crashed, he could give his passport to the referee who would note it.

We had sorted out all the logistics and we had planned to have some Honda registered dealers in place in different parts of the country. If a rider had a problem with his engine, he would send the whole thing to his nearest dealer and he would sort it, reseal it, stamp the rider's passport and send it back. In addition every track would have a spare engine which could be used in an emergency.

Neil Machin, the Sheffield promoter, was 100 percent behind the idea and we conducted test sessions at the Owlerton training track during 1997. Robbie Kessler was our test pilot – the ideal choice because he would ride anything with an engine in it – while Neil Collins and Martin Dugard were among the other riders who had a go.

The people who were against the idea were the ones who had invested in some good equipment which wouldn't have been any use to them if petrol engines were brought in. I didn't go along with that idea because I had started on a JAP, switched to a Jawa, and then a Weslake. Where did all of that end up? The tuners weren't happy either – they certainly didn't want a reliable engine that was going to stop them getting work!

We also met resistance from some of the promoters who questioned how we were going to get any passing if all the bikes were equal. That was just a joke – did they not expect a rider's ability to play a part in it? I was also very angry at suggestions from some promoters that I was only doing it because there would be a new car or some other sweetener in it for me from Honda. I was doing it because I honestly thought it could be the saviour of speedway and I never received so much as a hat or a T-shirt from Honda. The BSPA paid my expenses for attending the test meetings we ran, but that was all I got in return.

Honda told us that, if the idea was taken up, they could build a complete speedway engine within three years and the BSPA said they would give a decision one way or the other after we had conducted some tests.

To that end we agreed to stage a series of Honda Challenge matches at various tracks during 1998 and, to enable us to do that, Honda gave us nine road-going SLR 650 enduro bikes.

The reason we were only given nine was because that's all they had available – 650cc engines aren't exactly the things they have lying around on shelves! The reason we went for a 650cc engine was because we needed a flywheel effect to get the bike off the start and that did the job. It came with its own ignition and carburettor system so all we had to do was block up one jet in the carburettor. Obviously the only thing we could use was the engine itself, so we had to take all of the motors out and re-fit them into speedway bikes. We needed to have a new diamond made because the engines were heavier, but the BSPA agreed to pay for all the ancillary costs and they footed the bill for that to be done.

The five challenge matches took place at Hull, Sheffield, Reading, Newport and Peterborough. They were run over the normal Premier League format with the only difference being that the riders were on petrol-engined bikes. We took the bikes to each track and all the riders had to bring were their leathers and their sprockets. They all received the same flat fee to ride, no matter who they were.

The first scheduled match at Exeter was rained off so the Honda-engined bikes made their competitive debuts at Hull, where I was in my first season as team manager. As we had only nine bikes, we gave four to the Hull team and four to Peterborough, who were the visitors, and kept the remaining one as a spare – a system we used in all the other matches too. The only problem of note we encountered all night was electrical and nothing at all to do with Honda. Luckily the Honda representative who was with us had his computer with him and used it to re-progamme the mapping on the ignition system in between races. As a result of the electrical problems, two of the Peterborough bikes actually raced in every one of the first nine races! The oil was so hot it was boiling . . . but the engines kept running. There is no way a Jawa or a GM would have managed that.

Lap times throughout the series were about four seconds down on the times usually recorded by conventional speedway bikes which isn't a lot – probably barely noticeable in fact. Even though the engines were a big lump, they were stood upright so the riders could get round the inside all right, and that's the shortest way.

The engines had a six-speed gearbox in them but we only ran them in third. We took the pedal off but some smart alecs thought they could do better so they used mole grips to change it into a different gear before they went out to race. That didn't work because the engines had a rev limiter on so, when it got to 8,800 RPM, it automatically started missing. Obviously if we had gone ahead with the deal, Honda would have built engines without a gearbox to suit our needs.

We had an electric starter to fire the bikes up like they do in road racing. We lined all four bikes up before each meeting, adjusted a little cable on the carburettor to make them tick over faster, then walked away and left them running all by themselves. We then asked each team to select their four bikes for the night.

In the last of the five meetings, Hull were at Peterborough where Peter Oakes was the promoter. Each side chose their bikes and halfway through the meeting Peter came over to say that one or two of his lads were convinced that Paul Thorp had the best bike because he was really flying. I knew that couldn't be the case because we'd taken all nine to a dyno test and there was less than 2 BHP between the lot, so I told Peter to take Thorpy's bike and we would use one of theirs. Thorpy was more than happy to ride one of the Peterborough bikes while Mick Poole ended up taking his.

> "If it had gone ahead it would have been a massive change for speedway and some people just don't like change...It was a change for the better"

By a stroke of coincidence, they were up against each other in their next race – and Thorpy went out and won it. The Peterborough team didn't ask to swap bikes again after that.

After the five test meetings we staged, the BSPA told us they wanted more testing and more time before committing themselves to a deal. We reckoned that Honda had about £100,000 invested in the project but we had already kept them waiting longer than we had agreed and they, quite rightly, had made it clear they wanted a decision. Reluctantly we had to tell them that the BSPA wanted more time, so the whole thing was scuppered.

So, with no more time available the only thing Mick and I could do was put the engines back in their original bikes and hand them back to Honda.

The opportunity had been missed.

If it had gone ahead it wound have been a massive change for speedway and some people just don't like change. I likened it to the scenario of an office worker who is told by his boss that he has to move to a new office a few storeys up. He's dead against it to start with but, after he's been in his new surroundings for a while, he realises it's quieter and he can now see the park and the river from his new window. That's when he admits to himself that, despite his reservations, it was a change for the better after all.

We needed the backing of all the promoters and we were nowhere near getting it. I'm convinced it was politically motivated because the following year was when the Sky contract was due to start and they didn't want two types of engine in speedway. It wouldn't have mattered, though, because we could have introduced it just in the Premier League for a year or two and left the Elite League lads to carry on as they

were. Riders doubling up would have caused problems, but only a few, which would not have been insurmountable.

I was naturally very disappointed the idea wasn't followed up – but thank God it wasn't! I was working full-time at Hull during the 1998 season so I ended up at Mick's until 10.30 or 11 o'clock most nights preparing all nine bikes and it took over my life. I spent eight months on that project, running into a brick wall for most of that time, and a whole lot of blood, sweat and tears went into it. Can you imagine what a nightmare it would have been until it had become established? The moment anything went wrong with one of the bikes, I'd be the first person to get a phone call – every time.

So, with that project consigned to the dustbin, I could start to concentrate on my day job again.

㉓
ONE OF THOSE YEARS YOU DREAM ABOUT

HULL Vikings changed hands more times than a hot potato after they had been revived by Dave McCoy and Grenville Dicken in 1995. A list of promoters as long as your arm all gave it a go and all found that they couldn't make it pay. The crowds were terrific in the early days but, once they tailed off, nobody could find a way of bringing them back.

By the time I joined the set-up at Hull midway through the 1997 season, it was in the hands of Oceanic who had been the team sponsors. They were lovely people and very enthusiastic about their speedway but, although their heart was in the right place, they didn't have a clue about how to run a track.

A good example of that was when I arrived there early one Wednesday and asked them how much float they had at each turnstile before the gates were opened. There were blank looks all round because they didn't have a set amount and didn't seem bothered about it anyway. All the cash from programme sales and admission fees all went into the same pot so they had no idea whether gate money was up or down, or whether they were selling more or fewer programmes. It's keeping on top of things like that which can make a difference between losing a bit of money and losing a lot of money.

But at least they had a go. You have to take your cap off to them because, if they hadn't stepped in, Hull Speedway would have closed.

My role during Oceanic's reign was really just as team manager on a Wednesday night and as a consultant on the other end of a telephone for the rest of the week. When they announced they were pulling out at the end of the year it looked certain that, after just three seasons, Hull Vikings were finished. In fact it was announced that they wouldn't be running in 1998 when Tony Mole rode to the rescue. He bought Hull's licence and assets, then installed me as team manager and co-promoter.

Despite the uncertainty over the winter, the 1998 season proved to be much more successful than the previous one and the club, who finished bottom of the previous year's Premier League, ended fourth in the table.

It was Tony Mole who had kept the club alive and given me the chance to turn its fortunes around, of course, and the whole of speedway owes Tony a debt of thanks for his effort and investment in keeping a long list of tracks open when they looked doomed to closure. But, despite my admiration for what he has done, I must admit to being very, very disappointed at the way in which he told me I wouldn't be working for him in 1999.

Tony sold out at the end of 1998 to Allan Walker's H2O company – but he didn't tell me until the day before we flew out to Tenerife for the promoters' conference in early November. He phoned me up and explained he had sold out to a consortium of Hull businessmen and that my services would not be required by them because Graham Jones was going to be team manager. I was disappointed but no-one has a job for life and I was aware it would come to an end some time.

What I really wasn't happy about, however, was the way in which it had been done. It seemed clear to me that talks must have been going on for weeks, if not months, and I thought the least he could have done was to let me know that there were potential buyers. We'd had a good working relationship, both at Hull and Long Eaton, so I didn't see that it would have been a problem. All he needed to do was tell me the situation and warn me that, although he wanted to see me kept on by the new promoters, that might not be possible.

To me, the way he went about it gave the impression he didn't trust me or have much faith in my ability. He admitted he had handled it badly but, when he asked if I would accept his apologies, I said "No." I don't bear grudges against anyone but I couldn't accept his apology because I wouldn't have done it that way to him. When I decided to leave Long Eaton I could have waited until Christmas to break the news and gone on drawing my wages for another few months, but I didn't.

I've still got a lot of time for Tony because he is a true speedway supporter and there are a lot of tracks that wouldn't be here now if it weren't for him. But I expected more of him on this occasion and I felt let down

The treble with Halifax in 1966...and another treble, this time with Hull in 2004.
Left to right: Paul Hodder, Gary Stead, Emiliano Sanchez, Emil Cramer, Joel Parsons, Magnus Karlsson, myself and,
at the front, Paul Thorp.

Malcolm Wright was the overseer to the new consortium in the same way that I had been for Maurice Ducker at Sheffield some years earlier. The new owners decided to take the Vikings into the Elite League and signed Sam Ermolenko and Joe Screen to spearhead the side. But, as the season progressed, the consortium grew smaller to the point where it ended up being just Malcolm and Allan Walker left. If it hadn't been for Malcolm, it would have gone under by June because they lost a lot of money – and I mean a lot.

The crowds simply weren't big enough to sustain Elite League racing. They were getting around 1,100 people along every week and that simply wasn't enough, so Malcolm rang me one day to tell me he was planning to buy Allan out and wanted me to run the operation. It was around January time and my view was that, if he waited a bit, he wouldn't need to buy it because it was going under and he could have it for nothing.

But Malcolm always played fair and didn't want to see Allan lose any more money and, later that afternoon, he phoned back to say the deal was done. We entered the Premier League which was a very sensible option as we attracted the same crowds as the previous promotion had the year before, but our wage bill was a third of the size.

Despite all the comings and goings, New Craven Park was a lovely stadium to work in. It was owned by Hull Kingston Rovers rugby league club and there were quite a lot of changes to their management too. It was the first time I had ever been involved on the management side at a track which didn't stage stock car racing, so that was heaven! We could go into the stadium seven days a week if we wanted to and we never interfered with the rugby league or the greyhounds.

> "Maybe that's what's wrong with speedway – we are there to entertain the fans. You don't have to be a miserable arse to do your job"

I mentioned earlier in the book about my friendship with Ian Thomas, and we had a great laugh one evening during Malcolm's time in charge when I took the Vikings to Workington. Ian was the promoter at Derwent Park and, for a joke, he listed the visiting manager's name as Albert Boocock! Even in his programme notes he extended a special welcome to Albert Boocock because, unfortunately, his brother Eric was ill and couldn't attend.

What made it so funny was that everyone – the referee, the timekeeper, the staff, the riders – all went along with it. Every time I wanted to speak to the referee, I rang up to the box and said: "Hello, it's Albert Boocock here…" I was even jokingly threatened with paying £10 for a one-day licence! Even to this day when I go back to Workington we still have a laugh about it. Maybe that's what's wrong with speedway – we are there to entertain the fans, so what's wrong with having a laugh? You don't have to be a miserable arse to do your job.

The only major disagreement we had with the landlords came during Malcolm's time as promoter. Our agreement with the landlords had always been that we paid our weekly rent but it was the stadium owners' job to sheet up the greyhound track to keep the shale off it. We notified them of when our practice day was taking place but, when we arrived, we found that the dog track hadn't been sheeted up. It wasn't our responsibility so we left it and carried on – after all, it was a job which would have taken four men a morning to do.

It was a cold and frosty day and the track was as slick as a board so, after we had finished, the greyhound track was covered in a red dust.

The next morning there was hell on. The greyhound promoter was furious and called off his next scheduled meeting because he was worried the dogs would get hurt if the shale got into their feet. I told him it wasn't our problem, but he was quick to point out it was our bikes that had caused it. I felt sorry for him really because he was the one caught in the middle. We called an emergency meeting with the landlords and we agreed to get our grader onto the dog track to sort it out.

But we ended up with a bill of more than £2,000 to compensate for the cancelled dog meeting and an extra £100 a week on our rent to have the dog track sheeted up. We argued until we were blue in the face because it was something the rent money had always covered, but we got nowhere. There was no way I was going to take responsibility for sheeting up the dog track – the moment a greyhound got injured by some shale on the track, because it hadn't been sheeted up right, I would have been liable.

It wasn't the only run-in I had with the landlords that season. We used to lay all the track boards flat so that it didn't affect the view of the rugby pitch when there was a game on and we employed a lad to go in on a Tuesday night and stand them all up again. He rang me one day to say that he'd been to the track and discovered someone had taken a bulldozer to it and removed all the banking. Over the years we had managed to get a nice bit of banking built up and, when it rained, the water ran into the inside where we had put in some drains.

I raced over to the track and saw that, without even mentioning a word about it to us, the stadium owners had taken away so much shale that the track was sloping the other way! They claimed that the track level was building up on the outside and that spectators at the dog meetings couldn't see the greyhounds. What a load of rubbish. There would have been 250 people there at the most for a dog meeting and the only thing they would be interested in was who came first, second or third and how much money they had won or lost – it's not a spectator sport like speedway is.

All the angles had gone and there were Caterpillar tracks two inches deep all round the track – I was spewing mad. Luckily they had dumped all the shale on a concrete area around the back where the ambulance used to come in, so at least we could put it back on. In fact they had taken so much off that I didn't need to buy any shale that year – I just used what they had removed.

The 2003 season turned into something of a disaster for the Vikings but that was after I had made my first departure from New Craven Park. Malcolm Wright realised it was time to sell up and, when Nigel Wordsworth took over as promoter, he appointed John Bailey to succeed me as manager.

John had a reasonably good team at his disposal but, for some reason, he couldn't get them to perform to their potential. John was getting the blame for all manner of things which were out of his control and most definitely not his fault, which was very unfair. In the end he was sacked so, as usual, it was me who got the call to

Paul Thorp spearheaded the Hull Vikings to treble success in 2004.

come and rescue a team that was collapsing like a pack of cards.

I agreed to go back, but purely as team manager, because by then I was already involved with Somerset as team advisor. I didn't need to go back but, because I've always been passionate about speedway, I wanted to help out. If it meant I could play my part by preventing a track from shutting down, that was good enough for me and I had some happy memories of my previous stint at Hull.

Somerset was a long way to go for a day trip once a week but that's what I did for the best part of a season. Why? Because I'm stupid!

It started with a phone call from Andy Hewlett, the Rebels promoter, who wanted me to help out with the track and with managing the team on a race night. Andy was new to the game and needed a bit of help, so he asked if I'd be involved as an adviser. I made it clear I wasn't interested in being joint team manager – I've already described the problems it caused at Middlesbrough – but I agreed I'd be there to pass on any advice if I was asked.

Somerset was a hell of a place to get to from West Yorkshire, especially in the summer, and I used to set off at five o'clock on a Friday morning, pick up Graham Trollope at half-past and continue the long trip to the Oak Tree Arena. It was chaos getting across the M42 after about 8am because there were major roadworks being carried out and it was never easy getting around Bristol, but sometimes we would be making our regular visit to the supermarket café in Bridgewater and eating breakfast by quarter-to-nine.

Graham just came along as company, really, but he was great to have around. There were two tractors at the track so we would take one each, put some dirt on, do a bit of grading and then the track man would come along and do some work on it. Apart from answering a few questions my involvement with Somerset consisted of playing round with the track once a week. After the meeting we headed straight back home again and it could often be gone four o'clock before I got back home again, which made it almost a 24-hour day.

It was a long way to go for a day out and I don't suppose anyone else would do it except for a silly bugger like me!

There was some wonderful speedway at Somerset but Andy Hewlett wasn't always willing to take advice and that could make things difficult. The access road to the stadium was through a field and he fell out with the farmer who owned it, which left me as piggy in the middle all the time.

Towards the end of the season I had begun helping Hull out again, and that left me with a foot in each camp when the two teams met. It was an important fixture, too, because Hull and Somerset were the two teams battling to avoid the Premier League wooden spoon. The match was right at the end of the year and whoever lost was destined to finish bottom, so I made sure I kept out of the way. I didn't tell Hull anything and I didn't tell Somerset anything – it wouldn't have been fair if I had.

As it turned out, Hull finished bottom of the table, but it was still a happy place to be even though the team was doing badly. When I rejoined them they were going through a long losing streak and I wasn't able to stop it on my first night in charge. But, once we got off the mark, we went on a decent run. We were struggling at reserve and it seemed on some nights that whoever could ride a bike got the No.7 racejacket. We had a Swedish kid called Jimmy Jansson, nephew of the late Tommy Jansson, who John Bailey had signed and he was hopelessly out of his depth. Frankly, he was awful but he was on a nine point assessed average and the rest of the team had to carry him. Fortunately he resigned . . . after a bit of gentle persuasion!

At the end of the season Paul Hodder turned over a big wad of money to go in as co-promoter – but unfortunately he didn't know exactly how serious the financial situation was. In fact the situation was so serious that the BSPA annulled Nigel Wordsworth's promoting licence, which they were entitled to do if the debts were in excess of the bond that had been put down.

It's a shame I didn't know Paul was going to buy into the club before he parted with any cash – I could have warned him not to. Paul decided he wanted to keep the club afloat so he did a deal with the BSPA to buy back the assets, which became theirs once Nigel's licence had been taken away.

I went in with Paul Hodder as the overseer and team manager for 2004 – and what a year it turned out to be! We were the last team to complete our team-building but we went on to complete the Premier League, KO Cup and Young Shield treble. It wasn't the first silverware I'd brought to the club because we won the Premier Trophy in 2000 and the KO Cup a year later, but it was certainly the most successful season.

Paul was panicking a bit as the start of the season moved ever closer and as bids for Matej Zagar, Shane Parker and Paul Bentley all came to nothing. Other tracks got in ahead of us because they could offer more money and you can only have what you can afford.

But the team we put together did the trick and, having first managed a team almost 30 years earlier, I finally had a league title to celebrate. Mind you, I felt we should have won the league in 2001 when we finished runners-up to Newcastle, while the following year we led the way almost all year before being hit by injuries and finishing fifth.

David Walsh went into the back of Edinburgh rider Robert Eriksson on a wet night and that definitely cost us the 2001 title. It was a nasty crash – Eriksson stopped dead in front of him and Walshie just couldn't miss him. He actually never rode again after that because he damaged his spine, and the points we picked up from rider replacement in his absence that year were nowhere near what we could have expected him to get.

Although not as serious, we had injuries in 2002 as well. Paul Thorp and Ross Brady both had a spell on the sidelines and, after leading the way for much of the season, we ended up fifth. But, Danny Norton aside, all the lads stayed fit in 2004.

We deserved to win the treble because we were by far the best team in the league, although we had a slice of luck in that we went through the season with virtually the same side and that is so important in speedway. If you can get through a season with no major injuries, you get away without using guests or rider replacement. Once the lads start winning, it's a habit that comes naturally.

We started the year with Danny Norton at No.7 – on Paul Hodder's total insistence. I felt he wasn't ready and I was keen to have someone with more experience, although he was from Hull and it can be good to have a local rider in your side. In the event Danny crashed and hurt his shoulder and arm so I had to use a guest from the Conference League to replace him. I

> "It's not much fun opening the turnstiles knowing that it had just cost you another £1,000, because that's how much we were losing each week"

chose Joel Parsons, who I'd seen racing the previous year, and I was impressed with his attitude – he turned out to be a terrific choice. Joel just took off so we did a deal with Len Silver at Rye House to buy him. Len didn't really want him to go but he understood the situation. Having two reserves scoring points really made a difference. Whoever was going into the main body of the team had an average of around six, and whoever dropped down was only just behind.

It was one of those years you dream about and everything went so well – but I can't say I felt any great swell of personal satisfaction at the end. People say I'm an oddbod, but it wouldn't have mattered if I'd finished first or eighth – I would have genuinely given 100 percent to get the best out of myself and out of the riders I had available. That year it all worked well and, just as I saw my win in the British Final as the reward for 10 years' effort, this was my reward for all the years I'd been involved in speedway on the other side of the fence.

The riders did all the work – when the gate shut, they were on their own. It was a nice feeling to know we had won the treble, but I hadn't climbed Mount Everest three times or landed on the Moon three times! I was very proud of the lads, but all I had done was the job I'd been doing all my life.

We clinched the Premier League title when we took the bonus point at King's Lynn at the end of August – but there were still two months of the season left so I had to keep the lads going. I did that by telling them not to rest on their laurels and that now they had to do it all over again and win the KO Cup. They didn't let off, either, and we beat the Isle of Wight in the final, then Reading in the Young Shield

The treble was impressive but it could so easily have been a quadruple. That was because we missed out on qualifying for the knockout stages of the Premier Trophy in very contentious circumstances. Our scheduled tie at Glasgow was rained off and the only restaging date they could offer us was a Tuesday night which wasn't really ideal for them and totally unsuitable for us because that's when the Swedish League race and Magnus Karlsson was back home riding in it.

I always did my homework on fixtures and the Isle of Wight were the only team who rode on a Tuesday, so I made sure we went there in June when the Swedish League shut down for a month. But the Glasgow promotion insisted that's when they wanted to stage it but told me that, in the circumstances of a re-arranged fixture, teams were allowed a facility to cover for a rider if he had a racing commitment back in his home country. I'd never heard of that before but apparently two other teams had used it so I rang Graham Reeve at the SCB and he confirmed that, if the precedent had been set, I could go to Glasgow and use rider replacement.

The Glasgow promoters assured me they wouldn't object to me using rider replacement but, when we arrived at Saracen Park, we were given something of a shock. Ian Steel, the Glasgow team manager, was adamant we couldn't use rider replacement to cover for Magnus – and that was even after I pointed out it was his own promotion who had put me on to rule in the first place. Steel went to state his case to the referee who sided with him, saying there was nothing in the rulebook to say we could use R/R.

Looking at it from our point of view, there was nothing to say we couldn't either but, no matter how much I argued, I was getting nowhere. There was no way I would have been at Glasgow that night if I thought I couldn't use rider replacement and, as far I was concerned, I was there under false pretences. I'd been stitched up.

I wasn't going to put £200 down to ride under protest for two reasons. The first was that I didn't have £200 on me and the other was that I'd done nothing wrong. My mistake was that I didn't get anything in writing from Graham Reeve to say that we could use the facility, and we weren't able to get hold of him on the night by phone.

We had to borrow a junior rider, Gary Beaton, to use in place of Magnus and he failed to score a point as we lost 49-41. Magnus was going well at the time and I'm sure he would have scored at least the five points that would have made the difference between defeat and victory.

The keenest man in the team that season was Emiliano Sanchez. He approached every meeting like a World Final and was always geeing up the rest of the lads and telling them we could beat anyone and that whoever we were racing against, we could roll them over.

It's a shame the people of Hull weren't as keen because throughout that season the track was superb and we had some great meetings, but what was disappointing for me was that it didn't make a scrap of difference to the attendance on race right. We had some absolutely terrific racing but the crowds never moved. We had, without a doubt, the best press coverage of any speedway track in the country because the Hull Daily Mail were absolutely outstanding. Cathy Wigham took over from Dick Tingle as speedway correspondent and she used to ring up three or four times a week. The coverage she gave us throughout the week was out of this world, so it's not as if the people of Hull didn't know about speedway – it was in their face and they couldn't miss it.

We were the most successful speedway team in the country in 2004 but our average gate was just over 1,000, which was about 250 shy of being viable. It's not much fun opening the turnstiles every Wednesday knowing that it had just cost you another £1,000, because that's how much we were losing each week.

At the end of the season we were given a civic reception by Hull City Council, which was a little ironic given that the agreement we had with them to operate included a lot of constraints. For a start, air horns were banned – what difference would it have made for two hours a week on the dockside of Hull? The agreement also stated that we could run one meeting a week maximum apart from if we had a rain-off and needed to restage it, but even then we had to give them notice.

There was a 10 o'clock curfew because an old lady who lived over the back of the stadium had complained. She said that she went to bed early to read and, when the bikes started up it made her dog bark and kept her awake! I know that's true because I saw her letter.

Another restriction in place was that we weren't allowed to let any fireworks off. When Malcolm was in charge we thought it would be something a little different to set off a firework when the winner of the final heat crossed the line – but after about three weeks we were told to stop it because someone had complained. It annoyed me that the council could ignore the fact we were giving a lot of enjoyment to more than 1,000 people – mums, dads, kids, grandmas, the lot – every Wednesday, yet the council took more notice of one person complaining than they did of all the people in the stadium.

I had a meeting with one of the council officials and told him how frustrated I was. He wouldn't let me see the letters of complaint he had on file but he had to leave the room, so I picked up the file and had a look. There were about six letters in there . . . and they were all from the same woman!

Because of the council's restrictions we had to be a bit crafty when we staged the Premier Trophy final in 2000, too. The meeting, against Exeter, was scheduled to take place in October and we were running out of dates. In fact the only date we could find that suited us both was a Sunday – and we were expressly prevented from running on a Sunday except with the permission of the council. If we had sought permission, there was always the chance it would be refused – so we decided to conveniently forget about that particular restriction.

It was a fantastic occasion – for once it was warm in Hull - and the crowd was around 1,800, which was easily the biggest I ever saw at Hull during my involvement there and it made for a great atmosphere. We won the Trophy to bring silverware to Hull for the first time since speedway returned there and the meeting was so good that both teams went out for the victory parade.

Of course, it wasn't long before we received a letter from the council reminding us that we couldn't race on a Sunday without permission, but I wrote a polite letter back apologising for our oversight...

So, as you can see, I had a few bust-ups with various people during my time at Hull, but that had nothing to do with my reasons for leaving at the end of that treble-winning 2004 season. I called it a day because it seemed fairly clear to me that financial constraints were really biting into Paul Hodder and that, unless a major backer came in with some big money, he couldn't afford to run speedway at Hull in 2005.

We had just completed a clean sweep so the only was way down, even if we had finished second the following season – which meant there was no guarantee the crowds would even hold up at the same level.

I felt I'd had a reasonably good name as a speedway administrator for a lot of years and I didn't want to be involved in the sort of situation I saw brewing. I'd seen the financial side of the club with my own eyes and it was clear that the club could not be viable for another year. There were bills outstanding and, although they were settled before Christmas as I expected – probably using the following year's season ticket money – the fact they had gone unpaid initially was cause for concern to me.

I'm sure Paul Hodder thought he could talk me into staying but I'd made my mind up before the end of the season that I wouldn't be back in 2005. I tendered by resignation and, sure enough, the Vikings failed to fulfil their fixtures and Hull is now without a speedway team again. Maybe there is hope on the horizon – I'd like to think so.

㉔
WHEN SPEEDWAY'S IN YOUR BLOOD

HAVING left Hull, I was out of a job, but certainly not out of speedway. I've read Speedway Star every week since the year dot, I've always kept up to date with what's happening on Teletext and even today a lot of riders still ring me up for a bit of help with their various problems. When speedway's in your blood, you don't lose it.

These days I'm helping Josh Auty, who I genuinely believe could have a bright future in the sport. He lives in Mirfield, which is about seven miles from me, and the association came about after I was invited for a drink with his dad, Simon, and grandad, Bill. I'd known Simon for a while because he was British sand racing champion and used to be a customer at the shop I ran with Diane.

I wasn't sure what they wanted to talk to me about, but it transpired that they wanted some advice because Josh was coming to the age where he was about to start speedway. I'd seen Josh have a blast round after the meetings at Hull and I was impressed by the fact that he always came over to say "thank you." I'd watched him get better and better and he was a young British lad looking to make his mark in speedway, so I was happy to help.

It was obvious he had a bit of talent and it wasn't going to cost me anything to help him chop a few corners off and from then on it's almost been a full-time job! English speedway is short of a bit of talent and all the promoters should be pushing the few talented youngsters we've got. A lot has to be said for the chances Peter Oakes has given English youngsters, and it's thanks to the lowering of the age limit that Josh was able to start riding for Scunthorpe in the Conference League at 15.

I spent six or seven full-day sessions with Josh at Scunthorpe over the winter and a one-to-one can be really beneficial to a young rider trying to make the grade. I can't guarantee he will make it – nobody can – but I want to try and stop him making the mistakes that I did. You can chop years of your development time if you get it right from the word go because you don't get into any bad habits and then waste time getting out of them.

I'm still keeping my hand in on the management side too and during the first half of 2006 I've filled in for Reading and Workington when their regular team managers weren't available to go on a northern tour. That's me – always willing to help someone out and usually for very little pay but more often for nothing at all!

I was also chairman of the Sean Wilson testimonial committee so, not for the first time, I found myself immersed in unpaid work to make sure a big meeting at Sheffield went ahead. The previous occasion was when Owlterton was chosen to stage the 2002 World Cup semi-final – a meeting which almost didn't go ahead at all.

I got involved not because I was asked but because, once again, I was a mug! It had been chucking it down with rain all week and, three days before the meeting, Graham Trollope phoned and, during the conversation, told me that the Sheffield track was flooded. Graham prepared the track there and he was very worried that the meeting would be rained off.

I'd been planning to go to a steam engine rally with a mate of mine but, when we found out it had been cancelled because of the weather, we decided to go over to Sheffield and have a look at the track. When I got there, I couldn't believe it. Almost the entire track was under water, and the water went over the kickboards on the back straight, and they are a minimum of 12 inches high! There were advertising A frames floating like rafts.

Sheffield has proper sludge gulleys all the way around the track and the way the drainage system worked was that water ran to the second bend. When the water level reached a certain height it would trigger a pump to pump the water in the street. The pump was working but by that evening we had three pumps working on it because I managed to fix the one owned by the greyhound people which had a big bolt stuck in it, and my mate managed to borrow one from someone he knew.

We went home late that night but agreed to go back the next morning. I'd stuck a lollipop stick in the shale when we left and, when we got back, the water level had dropped by the grand total of an inch! Neil Machin, the Sheffield promoter, came over too and I told him straight – unless he did something drastic, the meeting was going to be off. Neil was convinced the local fire brigade wouldn't be able to help, but I talked him into phoning them and they agreed to come over and get their pumps working on it for a while.

By this time the salvage operation was really running at full pelt and my brother Nigel's son, Darren, arranged for someone he knew to come over with a massive sludge gulper to clean out the gulleys. Neil wasn't sure about spending any money, but it was a BSPA shared event after all – and the biggest meeting Sheffield had ever been asked to stage.

We had to stop work while a greyhound meeting took place there on Saturday evening, but we were back as soon as it had finished and we worked right through the night. By the time the birds started chirping the following morning my mobile phone had disappeared down one of the gulleys and we were covered from head to foot in red shale, but at least we were making progress.

It was overcast and there was no wind so even though the track was no longer under water, we couldn't dry it out. We had to take load after load of shale off and then lay down some new dry shale which we had ordered – much to Neil's dismay because that was another extra cost.

Graham phoned Tony Swales, who was coming over to help on the track anyway, and he laid a top dressing on it. We were making good progress until Ole Olsen, who is in charge of World Cup meetings, announced that the riders wanted a practice. They are perfectly entitled to have one, of course, but we could have done without it and, after they had finished, we had to start on preparing the track all over again.

We'd put some granite down to try and get a base for them to ride on instead of the slippery silt that was there, but the riders didn't like it so we couldn't put any more down. If we'd not lost an hour-and-a-half to the practice, and if we'd been able to put some more granite down, we would have been able to lay a reasonable track, but we soldiered on.

We got the meeting on, although the heavens opened near the end and Mark Loram was injured in a crash because he couldn't see where he was going. I'd virtually lived at the track for three days, and that was all because I'd popped in to have a look at the state of the surface.

But I did it because I love the sport and without all the effort that went into it, the meeting – televised live by Sky – wouldn't have taken place.

At the end of the day, the stadium did provide Diane and I with a lovely meal that evening – and Neil Machin gave me a 'decent drink', as we say in Yorkshire.

I'm having a sabbatical from full-time work at the moment because I'm overseeing some major building work at home, and at least that allows me to indulge in my passion for trials riding at a weekend. As I mentioned earlier in the book, I've been a

> "All in all, I think I've been the luckiest person alive, because I've had a paid hobby since the day I left school. I'd do it all again"

keen trials rider for a number of years and I'm still enjoying it as much as ever. I compete in the pre-65 class because I'm not good enough to ride a modern bike and my reactions are not quick enough! I ride a BSA C15T which is highly modified, which it has to be if you want to be competitive. It won't surprise anyone to learn that it's always immaculate looking when I arrive at every event, just as my bike was when I rode speedway.

It's a wonderful hobby and the people are so down to earth – there are

Trials riding is a wonderful hobby.

Above left: My daughter Sallie, who is enjoying life in Turkey, pictured in 1998.
Above right: Father and daughter enjoying a quiet meal in Dalyan, September 2004.
Below: Having dinner with some of our large family. Opposite me is my youngest sister Elaine, with her husband Jack alongside her and our daughter Sallie in the foreground. That's my wife, Diane, next to me.

no stars in their own bathrooms and some of the old boys are a mine of information. To me, it's an extension of what I've done all my life. I'm still cleaning and preparing a bike during the week and competing somewhere or the other most weekends if I'm not at a speedway meeting with Josh Auty.

All in all, I think I've been the luckiest person alive because I've had a paid hobby since the day I left school. Looking back now, I wouldn't do it any differently, except for putting my family a lot higher up the list than I ever did. Speedway has taken me to the most exotic places all over the world, places that a lot of people can only dream about, and I'd do it all again.

I've got some amazing memories of my career but, apart from photographs and a few programmes and magazines, that's about all I still have. I've never been

It's a pleasure helping a bright kid like Josh Auty, who has the potential to go to the very top...

particularly bothered about trophies – what's the point in keeping some Mickey Mouse pot from a meeting you probably forgot all about after a year or so? We've moved 13 times since we've been married and we had tea chests that were never opened from one move to the next – they were just stuck in the attic or out of the way somewhere. Inside them were trophies in green baize bags and I was sick of moving them, so one day I took them all to the tip and got rid of them. Some of the nicer ones I gave to the Yorkshire Classic Trials Club, but the rest were dumped. I got a lot of pleasure out of winning them, but we were always on the move so I never had a nice cabinet to put them in.

I got rid of all my racejackets too, although I gave away more than I binned. What good would they be to me now? It's not as if I'm ever going to wear them again! Knowing that they were going to someone who would appreciate them gave me as much pleasure as wearing them.

And what of the rest of the Boocock family? I told you much earlier how my father just lived for his mill – and that's where he was, working as hard as ever at the age of 77, the day he passed away in 1983. He'd mentioned a chest infection earlier in the day and the doctor came out to see him, but he insisted on "doing a little job" at the mill. He died in his sleep later that night.

My mother lived to the ripe, old age of 92, and I can tell you she wasn't quite fit enough to climb ladders to berate a referee by the time she passed away in a nursing home on Our Nigel's birthday – September 17, 2003.

Nigel sold up in Sydney years ago and now lives on the lovely Queensland Gold

Me outside the old mill which was managed by my father and where he worked so hard all his life.

Coast. He visited England last year and stayed with our youngest sister, Elaine, who lives with her second husband Jack Dickinson just two miles from Diane and me, in the village of Overton. Elaine had originally married Mick Dews, the brother of John, my old school mate and the former Sheffield rider and promoter. They have a son, Adrian, who acted as mechanic for Shawn Wilson when he rode for Sheffield, so you can see how much speedway blood there is in our family. Elaine and Jack, who are both retired, have two daughters, Sharon and Alison.

My eldest sister, Nina, who is three years older than Nigel, emigrated to Tazmania when I was 16 but, after getting a divorce, she then moved on to Manley, near Sydney, before settling in a suburb of Johannesburg, where she has lived since the early 70s.

I tell you, the Boococks are scattered far and wide! Our daughter, Sallie, gave up nursing to live and work in Dalyan, a beautiful part of southern Turkey, where she is employed by a company called Simply Turkey, selling and leasing luxury villas and apartments. She's been there for 10 years now and loves it.

Son Richie and his partner, Diane, live only half-a-mile up the road from us in Ossett, so we see plenty of them. Diane is expecting in September, so me and my Diane are really looking forward to our first grandchild.

I'm reluctant to say I'm retired at the age of 61 but, if anyone in speedway ever tried to tempt me back into a job, I'd have to think about it. Speedway's been my life for 45 years so I can't just turn my back on in – I've tried that before and it didn't work!

Perhaps I'd consider it if the job was just as team manager, which would mean I wouldn't be involved in track preparation, paperwork, booking slips or trekking 48,000 miles up and down in seven months, like I did in 2004 with Hull. The sport's on a bit of a downer at the moment, with money tight for the promoters, so I can't see that happening, but you never know . . .

After all, I've spent all my life going around in circles, so would it hurt if I did one last lap?

ERIC BOOCOCK

Riding Career Statistics & Year-by-Year At A Glance

BRITISH LEAGUE & INTERNATIONAL RECORD

Year	Club	Matches	Total Pts	CMA
1965	Halifax	33	328	9.33
1966	Halifax	34	367	10.41
1967	Halifax	35	397	10.38
1968	Halifax	30	324	10.20
1969	Halifax	36	416	11.02
1970	Halifax	34	384	10.59
1971	Halifax	34	399	10.17
1972	Halifax	32	379	10.46
1973	Halifax	18	213	10.52
1974	Halifax	23	253	10.02

Note: The above figures relate to British League matches only.

Year	Series	M	TP	CMA
1966	GB v Poland	2	18	7.20
	England v USSR	3	42	9.33
1967	GB v Sweden	4	54	9.82
	GB v Poland	5	60	8.28
	England v Sweden	1	16	10.67
1968	World League	3	22	8.00
	GB v Sweden	3	22	5.87
	England v USSR	3	46	10.22
	England v Poland	2	16	6.40
1969	GB v Sweden	4	36	7.20
	England v Australia	2	24	9.60
	England v NZ	1	3	3.00
1970	GB v Sweden	3	21	6.00
	England v NZ	1	14	9.33
	England v Australia	1	15	10.00
1971	GB v Poland	3	30	7.06
	England v Sweden	2	30	10.00
	England v USSR	2	18	6.55
1972	Internations Tourn.	4	27	6.75
1973	Internations Tourn.	7	40	6.67
Totals		**56**	**554**	**7.94**

Leading Sweden's Anders Michanek in the 1971 Test match at Wimbledon.

BOOEY
DOWN THE YEARS...

1945
Born February 2 in Dewsbury, West Yorkshire. Attended Netherton Primary and Ossett Grammar schools.

1961
Aged 16, has his first practice rides at Sheffield, Belle Vue, Coventry and Stoke. Leave school to join his father, Carl, working in the local Coxley Mill.
May 4 – Booey has his first second half ride at Middlesbrough, who are newcomers to the Provincial League. Scores 66 points from 12 PL matches and 38pts from nine Northern League matches.

1962
Booey jumps to fourth in Boro's PL averages with 216pts from 34 matches.

1963
May 16 – wins the Silver Sash for the first time by beating Stoke's Colin Pratt at Cleveland Park. He's the only teenager to reach the PLRC at Belle Vue. Eric leads the way for Boro with 289 pts, plus 15 bonus, from 34 matches.
On a sad note, Eric was guesting for Edinburgh the night Peter Craven was killed at Old Meadowbank.

1964
Despite lack of progress, Booey retains heat leader status for Middlesbrough, who close at the end of a dismal year for speedway. The new amalgamated British League beckons...

1965
April 17 – Newcomers Halifax open at The Shay in the newly-formed BL and Eric top-scores for the Dukes with 12+2 in a 36-41 defeat by Long Eaton.

July 3 – His first big individual success with victory at The Shay in the Whitaker Brewery Trophy, after a run-off with best mate Dave Younghusband.
July 31 – after scoring a maximum against Wolves, Booey becomes the first Dukes rider to win the Silver Sash, by defeating Bob Andrews. He defended it six times before losing out to Oxford's Jimmy Gooch. Finishes his first season as the Halifax No.1, pipping Younghusband to top spot.

1966
June 22 – Makes his England debut, scoring 13+4 in the 78-30 thrashing of Scotland at The Shay. Ken McKinlay denied him a paid max. Goes on to top-score in two of the first three Tests v the USSR. Eric is the only Brit to beat Igor Plechanov in the first Test at Newcastle. But a thumb injury costs Eric the chance to make the GB's World Team Cup squad for Poland.
October 8 – Booey scores a paid max v Belle Vue as Dukes clinch the BL championship for the first and only time in their history. The KO Cup and Northern Trophy are soon added to complete a tremendous treble.
Eric rounds off the year with his first visit to Australia.

1967
April 3 – Eric marries Diane Miller at St. Luke's Church, Middlestown.
Eric signals his intent to oust brother Nigel from the England No.1 spot by finishing top Englishman in the Internationale. In fact, Eric is the highest placed Brit in the Wembley World Final – his first big night appearance.
Booey scores five points on his World Team Cup Final debut in Malmo, where the Swedes are again dominant.

Booey is the only Brit to score an 18-max v Poland. At the end of the season, only Barry Briggs, Charlie Monk and brother Nigel are higher than Eric in the final BL averages.
Booey rides for British Lions in Australia – the first official Test series between the countries in seven years.

1968
Major blow for Booey who is taken ill before the European Final of the World Championship and is ruled out.
Despite beating Barry Briggs in heat 16, Booey is beaten by the Kiwi in a run-off to decide the BLRC. This time, Eric is fifth in the final BL averages – behind Ivan Mauger, Briggo, Martin Ashby and brother Nigel.

1969
Eric takes over the Halifax captaincy following the retirement of Eric Boothroyd – and is set for his best-ever season at club level.
July 5 – Eric beats Nigel four times in one night at the Shay, including the Silver Sash match-race! He records his highest-ever BL average (11.02) and scores 23 full or paid maximums in league and cup matches for Dukes. Including cup matches, his final figures would have read 11.08. Only Mauger (11.74),

Briggs (11.09) finished higher than Eric, while this time Nigel (10.84) was pushed into fourth place. Booey again toured Australia, this time as Lions' skipper.

1970
May 6 – Eric makes his World Pairs debut at Belle Vue, where he and Nigel finish third behind New Zealand and Scotland in the semi-final round. The Kiwis and Sweden are the only pairs to out-score the Booey brothers – Eric 13, Nigel 6 – in the final at Malmo.
July 25 – another slice of Halifax history as Eric brings the new Golden Helmet match-race title to The Shay for the first time, after beating King's Lynn's Howard Cole.
After winning the Dews Trophy at Halifax, Eric adds the Northern Riders' Championship to his collection at Sheffield.
Eric scores five points for Great Britain in the World Team Cup Final at Wembley, where Sweden are still the masters.

1971
April 10 – Eric knocks a second off the Shay track record in beating Sheffield's Jim Airey – and took more than that off it again when beating Wolves' Ole Olsen on May 1.

Eric was the first Halifax rider to win the Golden Helmet.

In his second World Final appearance – at Gothenburg – Eric beats Nigel but could only score four points.

The season ends on a high with victory in the £100 Autumn Classic at The Shay – two points clear of new England No.1 Ray Wilson.

1972

Eric withdraws another winter transfer request to lead the Dukes again. Qualifies for his third, and last, individual World Final and scores a disappointing two points at Wembley.

But on the domestic front, Booey remained up their with the best – only Mauger, Olsen and Michanek bettered him and Terry Betts in the final BL averages.

1973

August 1 – Booey causes uproar when he is excluded in the British-Nordic Final at Coventry and parks his bike across the track in protest.

August 10 – Disaster as Eric suffers a badly broken right arm in a crash at Newport. At the time, Eric is the top English rider in the

BL averages again – only Mauger, Olsen and Anders Michanek were doing better. When Eric beat Mauger in August, it was the first point the mighty Kiwi had dropped in a league match all season. His appearance for England in the final of the Daily Mirror International Tournament against Sweden at Wembley turns out to be his 56th, and last, cap for his country.

1974

June – The individual highlight of Eric's career as he is crowned British Champion at Coventry.

July 14 – he's honoured at Halifax with a richly deserved testimonial to mark his 10 years' service to the club – the first British rider to ever be awarded one.

At 29, Eric announces that his racing career has finished . . . and that he's going into management at Belle Vue.

1983

At 38, Eric makes a reluctant comeback for Halifax in the British League, but retires before the season is out and decides that, this time, he's definitely hanging up his leathers for good!

Index

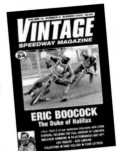

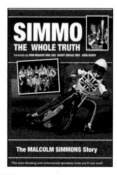